STRONG SEAMS
The Catalogue to Design Durable Clothing

Strong Seams
The Catalogue to Design Durable Clothing.

Copyright © 2024 by ABC Seams® Pty. Ltd.

All rights reserved. No parts of this book may be reproduced, stored in a retrieval system or transmitted, in any format or by any means, electronic, mechanical, photocopying, recording or otherwise, without the written permission of the author.

ABC Seams® is a Trade Mark
P.O. Box 30 (4886), QLD, Australia

Email: *hello@abcseams.com*

ISBN: 978-1-7635770-0-8

Discover more at *www.abcseams.com*

ABC Seams® Team

To those skilled women and men who help bring our design visions to life—the **sewers**.

Thank you for transforming sketches and ideas into reality. We are forever grateful for your artistry and dedication to this essential role.

CONTENTS

Contents 006
Seams contents 008
Preface 010
Introduction 012
How to use this book 014
Abbreviations 020
Icons 021

Part One:
INTRODUCTION

Introduction to quality and durability 025
Quality and the Apparel Industry 025
    Good Quality vs. High Quality 026
Durability 027
    How to make durable clothing 028
    Durability and Seams Selection 028

Part Two
SEAMS CATALOGUE

Constructions 033
    My notes 062
    My samples 063
Finishes 065
    My notes 108
    My samples 109
Details 111
    My notes 126
    My samples 127
Overview 128

Part Three
REFERENCE MATERIAL

Pictures	135
What affects the strength of a Seam	144
Materials and Processes	144
Garment Assembly	147
Reinforcements and Sewing Techniques	152
Seam Allowance Finishing	152
Securing and Stabilizing Seams	155
Stressed Areas	160
Stress Levels	160
Checking Seams and Quality Control	162
Types of evaluations	162
Quality Manual	164
Seams and common defects	170
Seam Inspection Checklist	172
Book Conventions & Technical Vocabulary	174
Stitches	174
Topstitches	178
Trimmings	180
Sewing Thread	184
Index	186
Seam Codes (Index)	188

CREDITS

Bibliography & Sources Consulted	189
Acknowledgments	197
About ABC Seams	198

SEAMS CONTENT

CONSTRUCTIONS

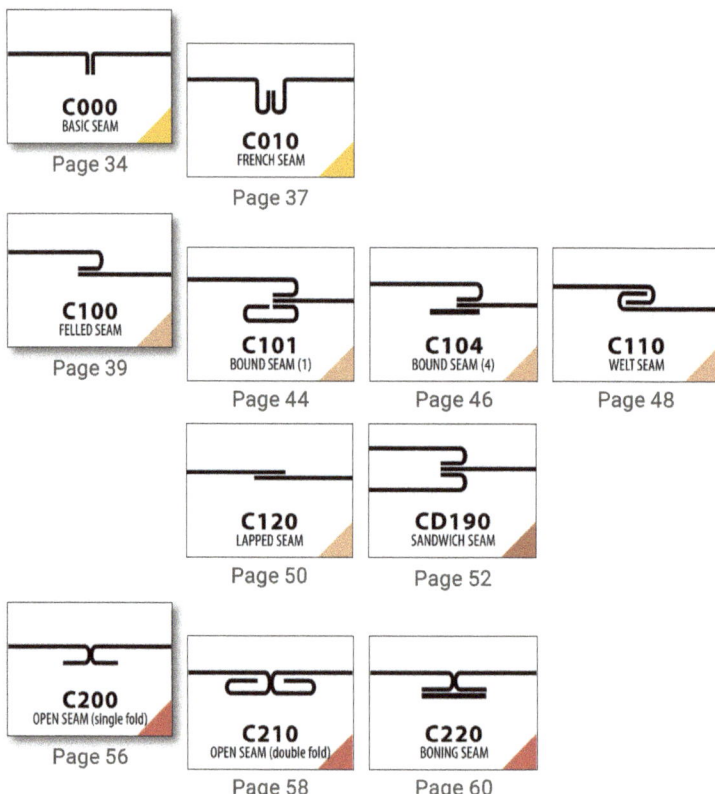

FINISHES

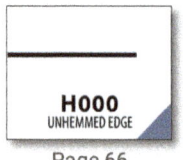

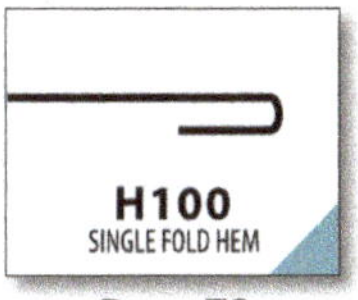

Strong Seams

H100 SINGLE FOLD HEM
Page 70

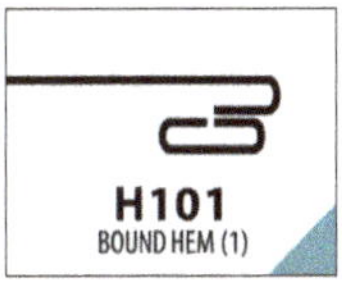

H101 BOUND HEM (1)
Page 72

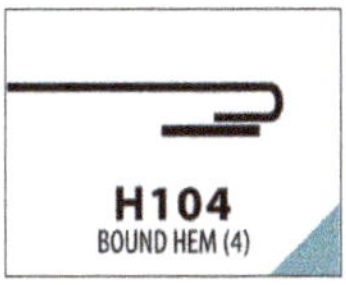

H104 BOUND HEM (4)
Page 74

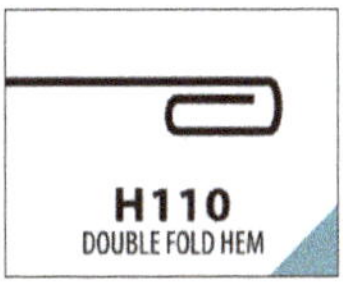

H110 DOUBLE FOLD HEM
Page 76

HD190 SANDWICH HEM
Page 78

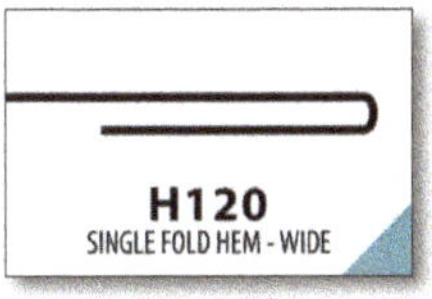

H120 SINGLE FOLD HEM - WIDE
Page 82

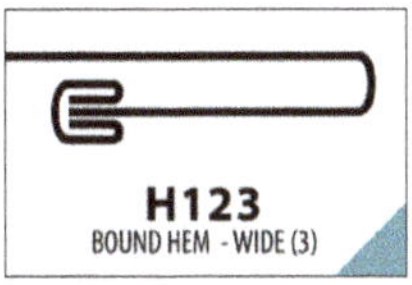

H123 BOUND HEM - WIDE (3)
Page 84

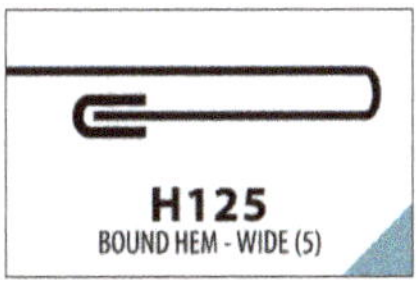

H125 BOUND HEM - WIDE (5)
Page 86

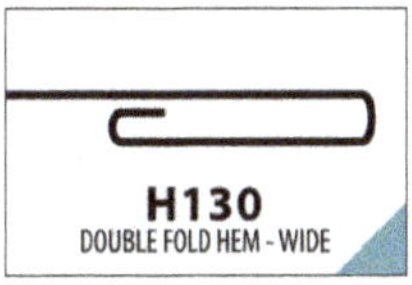

H130 DOUBLE FOLD HEM - WIDE
Page 88

H150 FACED HEM / SELF POLISHED
Page 90

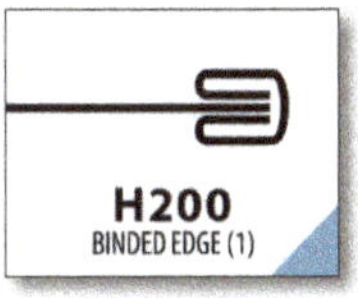

H200 BINDED EDGE (1)
Page 94

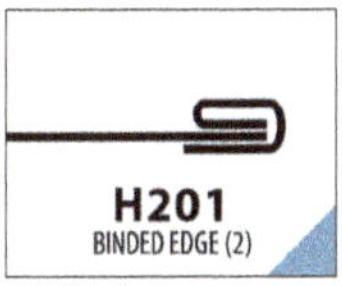

H201 BINDED EDGE (2)
Page 96

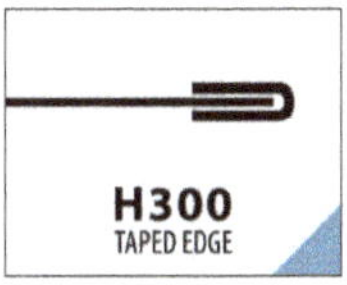

H300 TAPED EDGE
Page 98

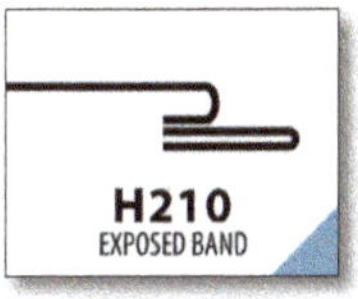

H210 EXPOSED BAND
Page 100

H211 EXPOSED BAND / BOUND (1)
Page 104

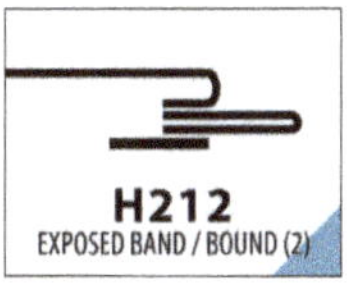

H212 EXPOSED BAND / BOUND (2)
Page 106

DETAILS

D110 PLEAT
Page 112

D112 INVERTED BOX PLEAT
Page 114

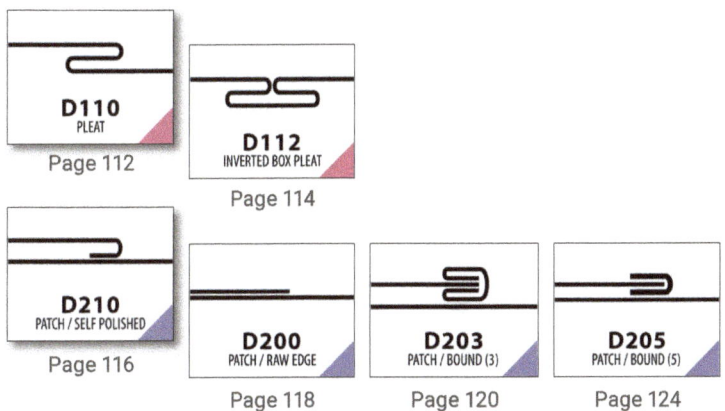

D210 PATCH / SELF POLISHED
Page 116

D200 PATCH / RAW EDGE
Page 118

D203 PATCH / BOUND (3)
Page 120

D205 PATCH / BOUND (5)
Page 124

PREFACE

Indeed, the big (and not-so-big) brands that stand out today, those that we admire and follow, are not simply the result of chance. They have a set of tricks, a "something", a Midas touch that brings success to everything they do.

What are those tricks?... There are many. Some are tactics that solidify fellowship, skills that make real connections, and magic that makes people fall in love with them. They also have traits that keep their people coming back, and strategists that keep customers loyal. Many brands know a few of those tricks, some more than others. Those that use the most effective tricks are the big winners in the market. "Strong Seams" is a tool that helps you to apply some of the tricks used by winners, so you can play the game too, and **ensure that your clients come back, over and over.**

The Tricks... and The Challenge

The fashion industry is facing a challenge. Recent research shows that more and more people are choosing quality over quantity. Experts talk about responsible consumerism, a society that is more aware of the environment. And the apparel industry has no choice but to adjust its business model for more demanding clients – clients that seek clothing to wear for many years. We live in a time when fashion brands need to create not only attractive clothing, but also garments that are well-made, garments that last.

A fashion brand's reputation is crucial to succeed in such a competitive market, and it depends on reliability. For people to love your brand and keep returning, **your products must be as reliable as the brand itself**. That is where this book steps in, helping you to create garments beyond the surface, **ensuring durability, strength against wear and wash**, and ultimately, building a brand that stands the test of time.

The **purpose** of this book is simple: to be a guiding light for fashion brands keen to create a legacy of quality and trust. The goal is to **give you a practical tool to deal with the challenge of making durable clothing**. And do it professionally, with confidence.

This book is not just a guide about stitching fabrics; it's about stitching a brand's reputation. It's a technical book focused on creating not only stylish clothing, but **strong garment construction to produce reliable products that customers will treasure, repeatedly choosing your brand over others**.

INTRODUCTION

"We only use high-quality materials!" The seller repeatedly emphasized this during the purchase, and he was right! I loved their design and comfort, and expected them to be my companions for years. However, just a few months after bringing them home, I noticed the frames had started to weaken, leading to sagging cushions and instability. After less than a year, my stylish new dining chairs became unusable. That incident left me so disappointed that it broke my trust in both the shop and its products. Have you ever felt that way?

My experience describes a common issue in any market: **Inconsistency in quality and durability leads to customer dissatisfaction, eroding trust in the brand and discouraging clients from buying again**.

This problem happens with all products, whether we buy a car, a mobile phone, or a book. Clothing is not an exception. Garments can fail for many reasons. Low-quality materials are the number one factor, followed by **weak seams, poor finishing, and improper construction**. Those problems can severely damage any brand's reputation, and repairing them requires a significant amount of time and money.

From this perspective, fashion brands must produce quality products –clothing that people cherish for years. **As designers and product developers, it is our job to ensure the clothing we produce is comfortable and correctly made**. Avoiding and filtering out any seams that may fail prematurely is our duty. By producing durable clothing, we not only meet our clients' expectations, but we also reduce the environmental impact of fashion.

Welcome to *Strong Seams*, a catalogue of sewing seams focused on creating garments that stand the test of time, ensuring reliability, durability, and a lasting bond between the brand and clients. This book delves into the technical side of durability, focusing on the structural components, assembly techniques, construction methods, and finishes that boost garment longevity.

The **first part** of the book is an *Introduction to Quality and Durability*, and provides a deep insight into this topic, focused on the apparel industry perspective. What do quality and durability mean in this business? How to make durable clothing? These are some of the questions analyzed in this chapter.

The *Seams Catalogue* is the **second and central part of the book**. It is your **source for selecting seams, explaining your designs, and writing the assembly sheet of your tech packs**. It presents traditional and contemporary seams for woven and knit fabrics, and we provide detailed explanations on how to use the catalogue in the pages that follow.

The **third part** gathers *Reference Material* related to the *Seams Catalogue*. It covers aspects such as the elements that affect the strength of seams, techniques to reinforce them, how to check and set standards to guarantee quality, and some tests to ensure clothing durability.

Note: We could only include some of the information analyzed during the research for this book. However, you can find more data at this link: *www.abcseams.com/ products/book-strong-seams/research*.

HOW TO USE THIS BOOK

This book is a seam catalogue that focuses on strong seams. It will be helpful **to specify the assembly of your designs** to your manufacturer and colleagues. You can also refer to this catalogue **to clear any doubts about seams**, either to find stitch and topstitch types or to learn about their properties and general uses. You can **discover new constructions, finishes, and details** in the *Related Seams* section. For example, if you have used the same hem for most of your designs, you can find another structure to add a special touch to the garments and make them more unique.

Seams Catalogue

The *Seams Catalogue* organizes all seams into **three categories** based on their primary function: construction, finish, and detail. Each of these categories is **further divided into groups of seams based on their different structures**: welt seams, flat seams, open seams, etc. Then, you will find a selection of **stitches and topstitching options for each structure type**.

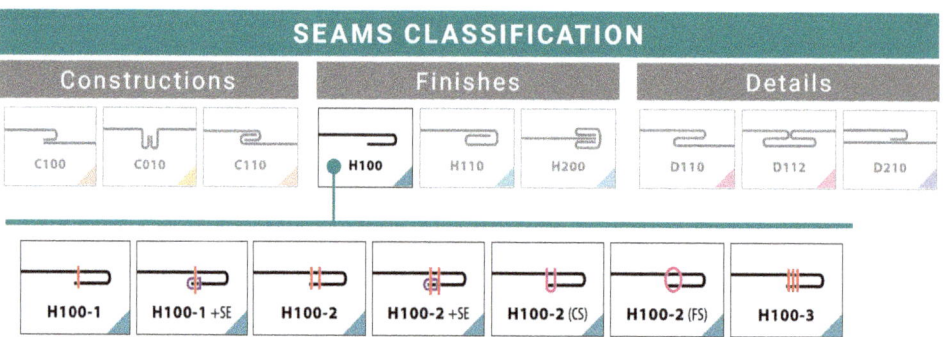

Figure 0.1: Seams classification

Note: for more information about the seam classifications, visit our website at www.abcseams.com/blog-and-resources/ or refer to our book, *101 Sewing Seams*.

Each group of seams include:

1. A page with general information.

Common properties and uses, related seam groups that suggest similar constructions to vary and new techniques to try, and a 3D structure sketch for improved comprehension.

2. The seams catalogue

All seams within the group share the same structure, but the stitch and topstitch types vary, making every seam unique. Seams are represented by a sketch and a code.

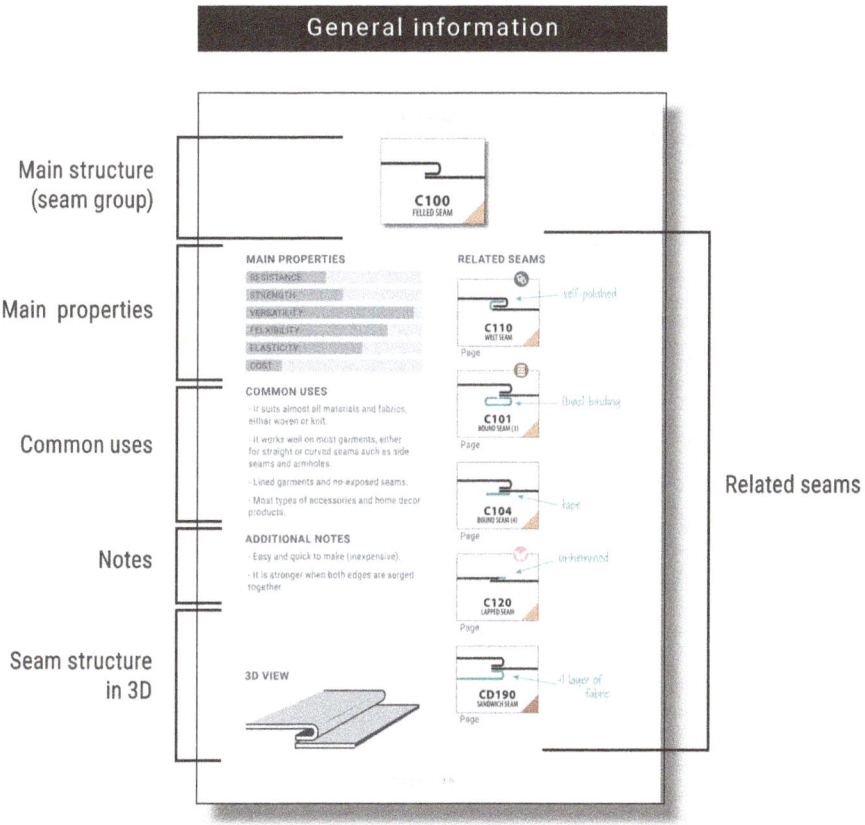

Figure 0.2 - Page whit general information of the seam group

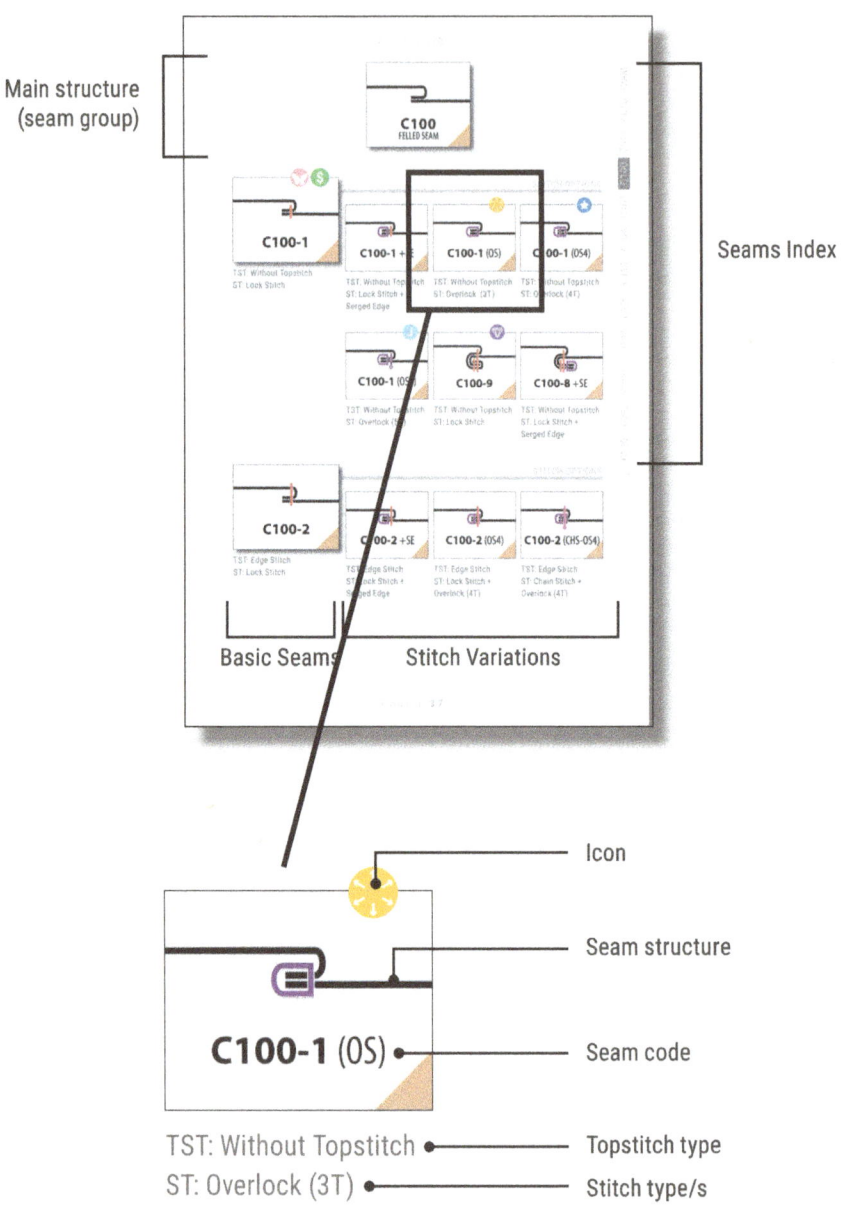

Figure 0.3- Page with seams options.

You'll also find icons over some seams. These icons highlight properties such as strength, elasticity and low cost. Sometimes, the icon will help you decide which seam is best suited for your design. For instance, the icon may mark the strongest or most elasticated seam within the group.
Note: The icons are referenced on page 21.

Overview Chart

The Overview Chart (see pages 128 to 131) provides a complete view of all the seams included in the book. It will help you to refer to, select and compare seams quickly.

Note: A large poster-size chart is available for download and printing at *www.abcseams.com/products/book-strong-seams-resources*.

Figure 0.4 - Overview chart with all the seams included in this book (pages 128 to 131)

Selecting Seams: The 3 Steps Method

Based on the location of the seam, refer to constructions (pp. 33), finishes (pp. 65) or detail seams (pp. 111). For example, shoulders and side seams are "constructions."

Then, follow these 3-steps method to select the best seam option:

Step 1: Select the seam **structure**. To view all the seam structures in the book, refer to pages 8 and 9. Once you find the appropriate structure, go to the page mentioned to find the stitch and topstitch options.

Step 2: Select the top**stitch** type. After selecting the seam structure, choose one of the topstitching options inside the seam group.

Step 3: Select the type of **stitch**. Finally, choose the stitch that best suits the fabric and seam structure. For more details, see Stitch Types and Characteristics on page 174.

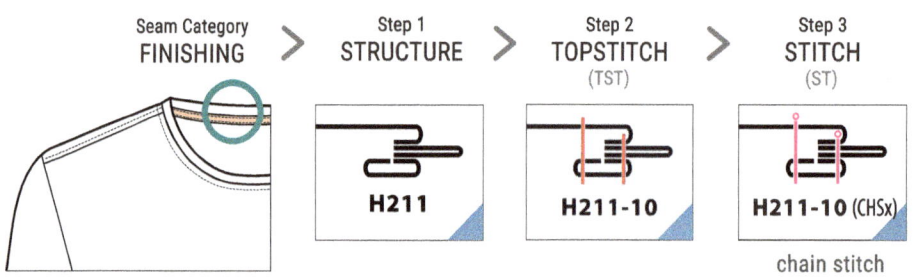

Figure 0.5: 3-Steps Method for selecting seams

For more detailed information on each step of this method, please refer to page 148 of the *Reference Material* (Part 3).

Other Considerations:

- **Brand standards**: This includes quality requirements and expectations. For example, some brands require exposed back necklines of T-shirts reinforced with a (bias) binding or tape (see *Figure 0.5*). Knowing the product's price range and production budget will also affect the type of seam we choose. High-quality brands use the finest finishes and more complex details, with a higher production budget than lower-quality brands.

- **Design**: This includes the garment's intended use, look and requirements to ensure the correct performance. For example, tight-fitting garments with seams in contact with the skin must be chafe-free for comfort. And robust clothes, such as workwear, require double topstitch in most seamlines to accentuate the strong appearance. The seam allowance finish technique might also vary depending on whether the garment is lined or unlined.

- **Fabric type**: Evaluate the type of fiber and fabric properties, such as weight, shrinkage and wave structure (see *Fabric Characteristics* on pages 144 and 145). Ensure the seam structure and stitch type meet the fabric requirements (see *Stitch and Topstitch Types* on pages 174 and 178)

- **Seam location and needs**: Consider the amount of stress the seam needs to withstand (see *Stressed Areas* on page 160) and whether it requires any reinforcement (see *Reinforcements and Sewing Techniques* on page 152).

Note: Find examples of **Seams Implementation** at *www.abcseams.com/strong-seams-implementation*

ABBREVIATIONS

1N, 2N, 3N: Number of needles used in the sewing machine

3T, 4T, 5T: Number of threads used in the sewing machine

AATCC: American Association of Textile Chemists and Colorists

AQ: Acceptable Quality

AQL: Acceptable Quality Level

ASTM: American Society for Testing and Materials

ASCS: ABC Seams Codification System

GSM: Grams per Square Meter (fabric weight)

ISO: International Organization for Standardization

PLM: Product Lifecycle Management

QA: Quality Assurance

QC: Quality Control

QMS: Quality Management System

RSL: Restricted Substances List

SA: Seam Allowance

SPC: stitches per centimeter

SPI: stitches per inch

ST: Stitch

TST: Topstitch

Stitches:

BS: Blind Stitch

CS: Cover Stitch

FS: Flatlock Stitch

OS: Overlock Stitch

RS: Roll Stitch

SA: Seam Allowance

SE: Serged Edge

ZZ: Zig-zag

General:

BOM: Bill of Materials

BS: Back Side (or WR: Wrong Side)

CAD: Computer-Aided Design

CB: Center Back

CF: Center Front

CMT: Cut, Make, Trim

FOB: Free on Board (shipping terms)

MOQ: Minimum Order Quantity

PP: Prototype

RS: Right Side

ICONS

 The Most Used
These are the seams we most commonly find in the apparel industry.

 The Most Resistant
Seams that withstand stress, such as tearing, pulling, and washing. They are typically made using one or more reinforcement techniques, such as serging the seam allowance and adding topstitching or inner tape.

 The Most Delicate
These seams lack reinforcements like topstitching or seam allowance polishing, making them too weak to support stress and repeated washings.

 High-end
These seams are commonly polished on both sides, usually by decorative trims like bands, tapes or bias bindings. Their complexity makes them require more steps, increasing their time and cost.

 The Cheapest
These simple seams require fewer steps in the assembly, making them less time-consuming and inexpensive.

 The Most Flexible
Seams whose stitch type and structure allow them to have a higher stretchability.

 The Thickest
These are the seams whose structure has multiple fabric layers, making the seam thicker than other structure types.

 Favourite
Creative fine seams that add a touch of uniqueness to the style.

 Knit Fabrics
Stretchable seams commonly used on garments made of knit or stretchable fabrics.

 Denim (and heavy-weight fabrics)
Seams that work well on denim and products made of heavy-weight fabrics.

 Sports & Activewear
These seams provide significant support against stress, are stretchable enough to add comfort, and possess a high elongation recovery.

 Picture
Seams whose photo is featured in Part 3 of the book: Reference Material (pages 135 to 143).

Note: Download a printable version of the **Seams Properties Icons** at *www.abcseams.com/strong-seams-icons*

Part One

INTRODUCTION

INTRODUCTION TO QUALITY & DURABILITY

Quality and the Apparel Industry

In the fashion industry, the term "quality" refers to the **perceived value level of a product or brand**, which can be **subjective or objective** to each individual. Some may consider quality as luxury, elegance or popularity in the market (*subjective value*). For some, a handbag from a renowned fashion house like Louis Vuitton or Chanel means "quality".

Others may associate it with functionality, durability and sustainability over luxury (*objective value*). They value products made of durable materials, reinforced seams, and produced with ethical and environmentally responsible practices. For them, quality extends beyond aesthetics to include fit, comfort and the long-term impact of their clothing choices.

QUALITY TYPES	
Subjective	Objective
- Aesthetic	- Construction
- Luxury	- Fabric composition
- Elegance	- Dimensional stability
- Popularity	- Colorfastness
- Comfort	- Environmental impact

Figure 1.1: Subjective and objective quality values

Whether perceived subjectively or objectively, **quality is always associated with long-lasting products**. Durability, for example, is an objective measure of lifespan, but how long someone considers an item durable can be subjective.

Good Quality vs. High Quality

The terms "good" and "high" quality are closely related but have distinct meanings. Although they can complement each other, they also differ in certain aspects. **"Good" quality refers to high-standard performance and materials selection** compared to regular products. However, it does not necessarily prioritize refined constructions and finishes. Not every brand that produces good quality products is interested in sophisticated seams or stylish details. For example, most sportswear brands prioritize comfort and performance over elegance.

On the other hand, achieving **"high" quality usually requires complex sewing techniques and additional pieces or elements** such as tape and binding. These require more skilled operators and more sewing steps. As a result, their assembly is **more elaborate, time-consuming and therefore, more expensive**.

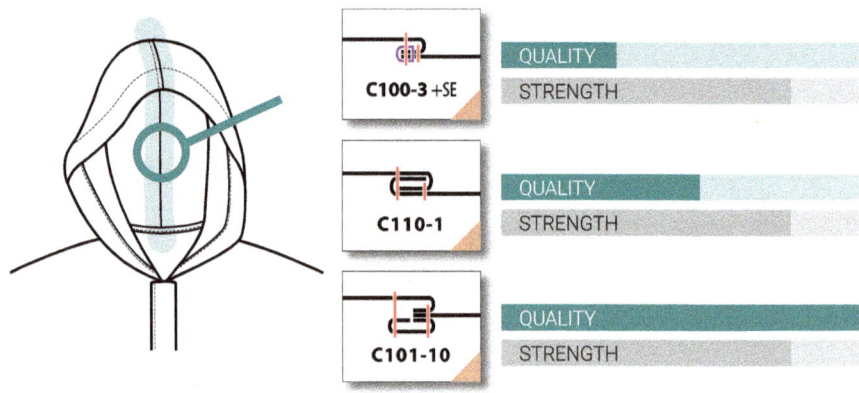

Figure 1.2: Quality levels and seam strength

Durability

Definition and Types

We commonly associate durability with **clothing that withstands continual use and washing**. These are well-made garments that maintain their shape and appeal for months and even years. However, this only addresses the *physical* aspect of durability. Durability in the apparel industry extends beyond mere longevity.

While well-made garments endure continual use and washing, *emotional durability* fosters a deeper connection between consumers and their clothing. Why do people prefer to keep wearing some garments over others? Beyond price and social exchange, **emotional durability increases attachment to some pieces of clothing**. Attributes like comfort, flattering style, and freshness contribute to this emotional bond, influencing consumers' desire to wear and care for their garments over time.

DURABILITY TYPES	
Physical	Emotional
- Fiber strength	- Timeless design
- Seam strength	- Versatility
- Colorfastness	- Ethical production
- Pilling resistance	- Uniqueness

Figure 1.3: Physical and emotional durability

The primary emphasis of this book is on the *physical* aspects of durability. However, we acknowledge the importance of *emotional* durability in shaping consumer perceptions and preferences. As fashion designers and product developers, our ultimate goal in producing durable garments is to create clothing that not only lasts for years, but also resonates with consumers emotionally, prompting continued use and preference.

How to make durable clothing

Physical Properties & Characteristics

From a broad perspective of durability, we must ensure our products' physical strength and emotional resonance. Developing durable garments that maintain quality throughout their lifespan requires a **holistic approach from different aspects**.

Setting the garment construction starts with the design process. Designers and product developers explain the new styles to the manufacturer, especially those details that make the style unique. **Specifying the construction helps ensure the seams' quality from the beginning, saving time on adjustments during the development process**.

Note: You can find more information about the production process in our previous book, *Sewing Seams for Tech Packs*.

Durability and Seams Selection

To select the most suitable seams, we will consider two crucial factors. First, we will examine general aspects of the brand. Second, we will delve into particular aspects of the product.

1. General aspects related to the brand

We must thoroughly understand the **brand's quality standards and values**, such as **product longevity expectations, commitment to sustainability, and pricing range**.

To maintain clarity and consistency, the brand will outline its quality standards within its Quality Manual, detailing the requirements for approving or rejecting materials and finished products. This manual will cover everything from methods and techniques to measurements and testing, tolerances, procedures and any other relevant information necessary to specify and check each style. For example, if we work as a swimwear designer and the minimum value for colorfastness to chlorine is 3, we will only consider fabrics that have a value note of 5 to 3. And we will reject any fabric below note 3.

Designers must know what is critical to the brand before starting the design process. That information is essential to selecting the correct materials and designing the product.

2. Specific aspects related to each product

This includes **selecting the correct materials, developing satisfactory performance, and requiring accurate assembly**.

While some durability attributes are common to most types of clothing (e.g., pilling resistance, colorfastness and resistance to tearing), we also need to consider some particular requirements for specific clothing types. For example, when designing swimwear, the materials' colors and sewing threads should resist chlorinated water and seawater, and seams must be elastic enough to resist stretching and be chafe-free to ensure comfort.

You will find more information on this topic in the 3rd part of this book (*Reference Material*). We especially suggest you keep reading the note **"What Makes a Seam Strong"** on page 144.

DURABILITY & SEAM SELECTION			
General aspects	Specific aspects		
Quality standards & values	Materials	Performance	Assembly
- Required tests & methods - Control criteria & AQL - Longevity expectations - Eco-friendly approach - End-of-life considerations - Cost analysis	- Fabric - Trimmings (incl. thread type) - Processes More info: P.144	- Intended use and requirements - Fit and comfort	- Seam selection (incl. stitch type) - Reinforcements - Machine settings - Operator skill More info: P.147

Figure 1.4: Considerations for making durable clothing

Part Two

SEAMS CATALOGUE

CONSTRUCTIONS

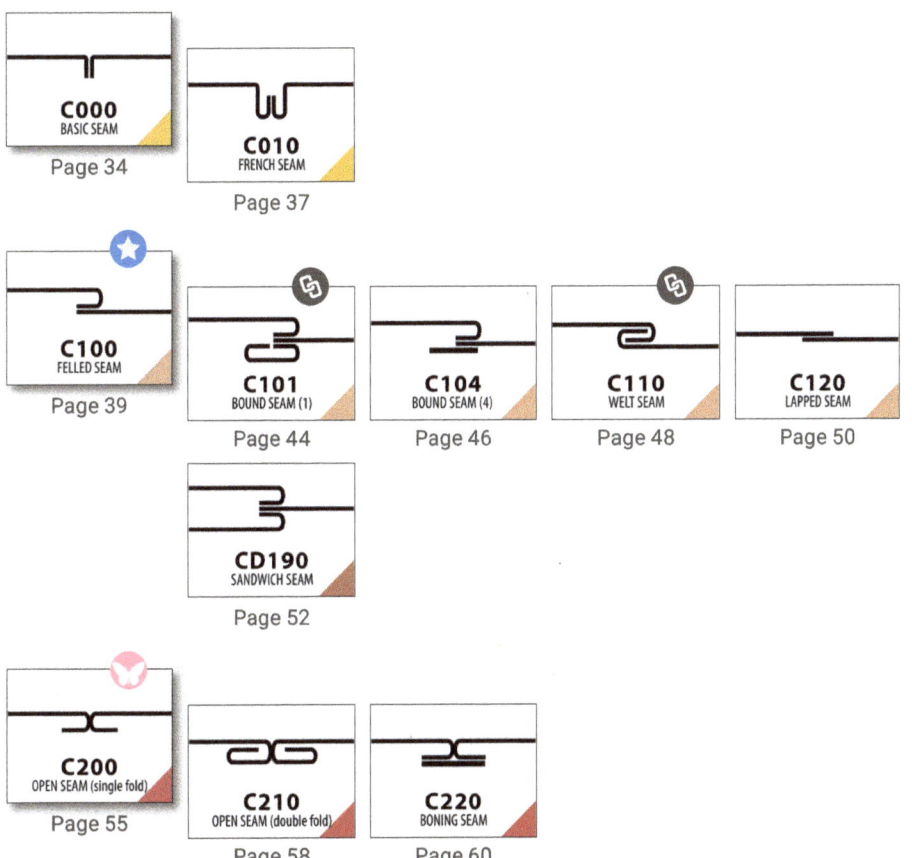

ABC Seams®

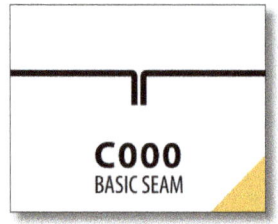

C000
BASIC SEAM

MAIN PROPERTIES

RESISTANCE
STRENGTH
VERSATILITY
FLEXIBILITY
ELASTICITY
COST

COMMON USES

- It suits a wide range of materials and fabrics, either woven or knit.
- Curved seams such as armholes.
- Side seams (including sleeves) of casual clothing, especially for knit fabrics.
- Crotch seam of leggings, underwear, and sweatpants.
- Centre seams of hoods.
- Bags and accessories such as soft pouches.

ADDITIONAL NOTES

- Easy and quick to make (inexpensive).
- It is stronger when both edges are serged together.

3D VIEW

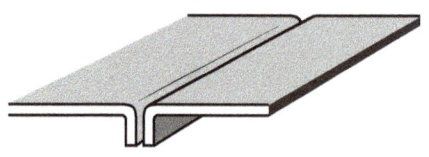

RELATED SEAMS

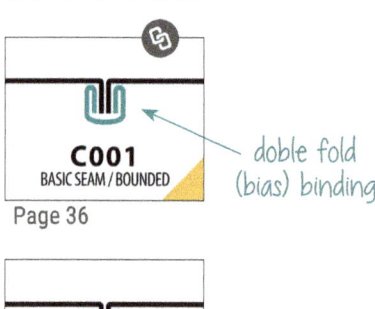

C001 BASIC SEAM / BOUNDED ← doble fold (bias) binding
Page 36

C002 BASIC SEAM / BOUNDED ← folded tape
Page 36

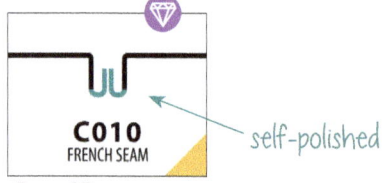

C010 FRENCH SEAM ← self-polished
Page 37

C011 HAIRLINE SEAM ← self-polished (one side)
Page 36

Strong Seams

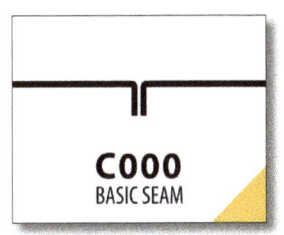

C000 — BASIC SEAM

STITCH OPTIONS

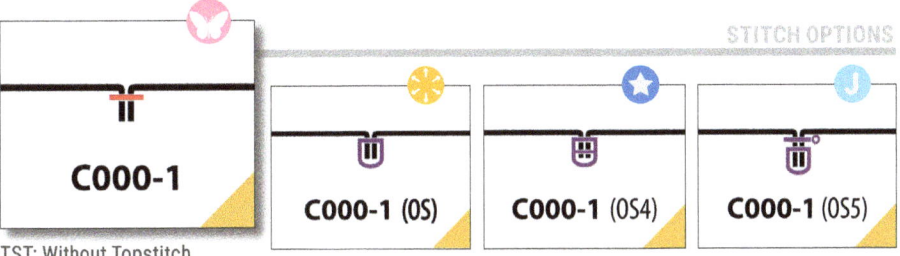

C000-1
TST: Without Topstitch
ST: Lock Stitch

C000-1 (OS)
TST: Without Topstitch
ST: Overlock (3T)

C000-1 (OS4)
TST: Without Topstitch
ST: Overlock (4T)

C000-1 (OS5)
TST: Without Topstitch
ST: Overlock (5T)

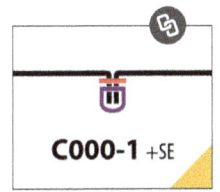

C000-1 +SE
TST: Without Topstitch
ST: Lock Stitch +
Serged Edge

INSPIRATION

C000B   C000T   C000C

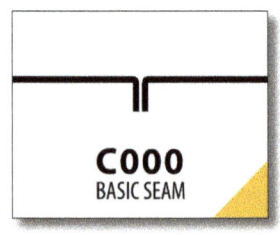

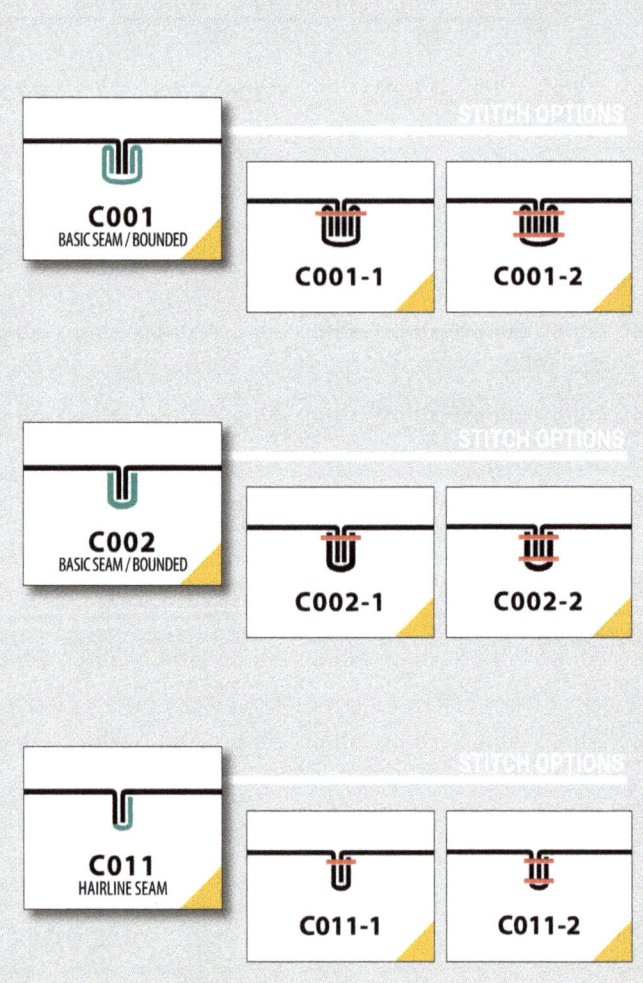

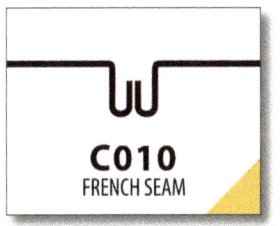

C010
FRENCH SEAM

MAIN PROPERTIES

- RESISTANCE
- STRENGTH
- VERSATILITY
- FLEXIBILITY
- ELASTICITY
- COST

COMMON USES

- Woven fabrics such as sheer, lace, and most lightweight fabrics.
- Women's clothing.
- High-quality garments.
- Side seams and sleeve seams of blouses and shirts.

ADDITIONAL NOTES

- Neat finishing on the inside.
- It could be too bulky and stiff if using heavy-weight fabrics. In that case, check group C011 (Hairline Seam).
- It works better on straight or slightly curved seams.

3D VIEW

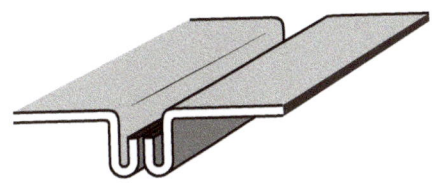

RELATED SEAMS

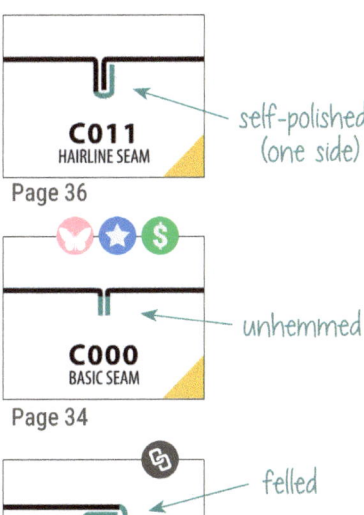

C011 HAIRLINE SEAM — self-polished (one side)
Page 36

C000 BASIC SEAM — unhemmed
Page 34

C110 WELT SEAM — felled
Page 48

ABC Seams®

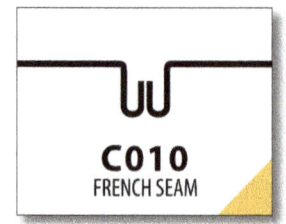

C010
FRENCH SEAM

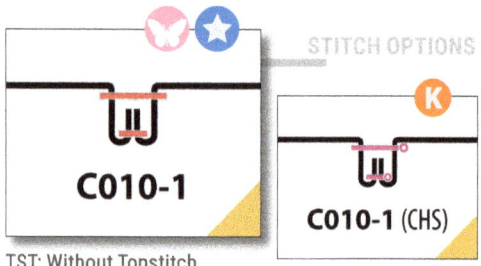

C010-1
TST: Without Topstitch
ST: Lock Stitch

C010-1 (CHS)
TST: Without Topstitch
ST: Chain Stitch

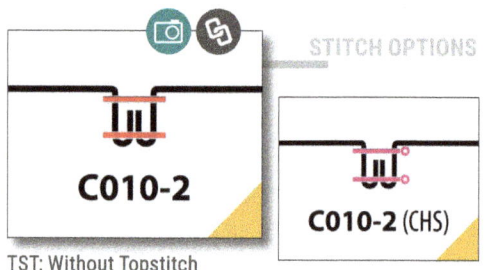

C010-2
TST: Without Topstitch
ST: Lock Stitch

C010-2 (CHS)
TST: Without Topstitch
ST: Chain Stitch

Strong Seams

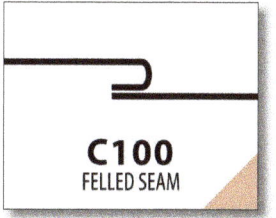

MAIN PROPERTIES

- RESISTANCE
- STRENGTH
- VERSATILITY
- FLEXIBILITY
- ELASTICITY
- COST

COMMON USES

- It suits almost all materials and fabrics, either woven or knit.

- It works well on most garments, either for straight or curved seams such as side seams and armholes.

- Lined garments and no-exposed seams.

- Most types of accessories and home decor products.

ADDITIONAL NOTES

- Easy and quick to make (inexpensive).

- It is stronger when both edges are serged together.

3D VIEW

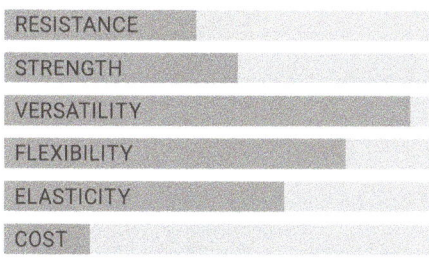

RELATED SEAMS

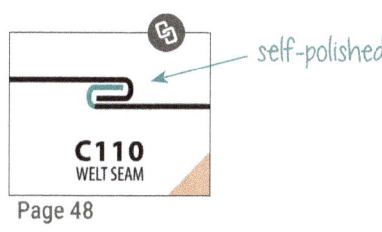
self-polished
Page 48

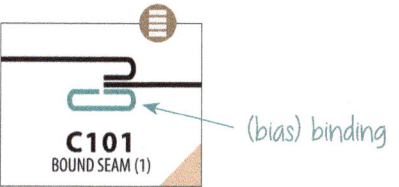
(bias) binding
Page 44

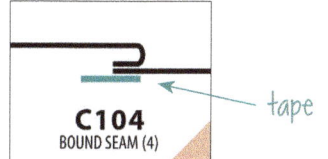
tape
Page 46

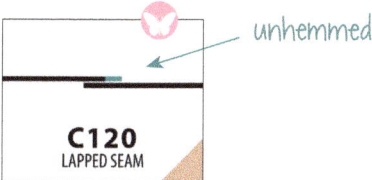
unhemmed
Page 50

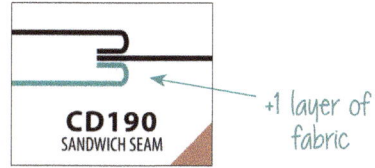
+1 layer of fabric
Page 52

ABC Seams®

C100 FELLED SEAM

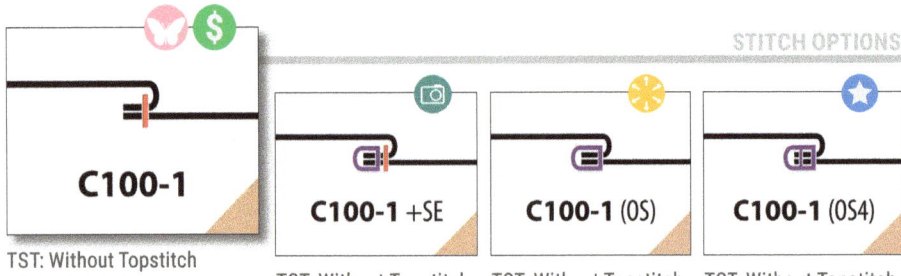

C100-1
TST: Without Topstitch
ST: Lock Stitch

C100-1 +SE
TST: Without Topstitch
ST: Lock Stitch +
Serged Edge

C100-1 (OS)
TST: Without Topstitch
ST: Overlock (3T)

C100-1 (OS4)
TST: Without Topstitch
ST: Overlock (4T)

STITCH OPTIONS

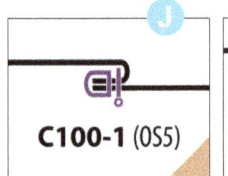

C100-1 (OS5)
TST: Without Topstitch
ST: Overlock (5T)

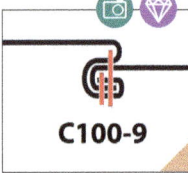

C100-9
TST: Without Topstitch
ST: Lock Stitch

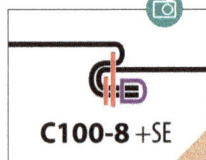

C100-8 +SE
TST: Without Topstitch
ST: Lock Stitch +
Serged Edge

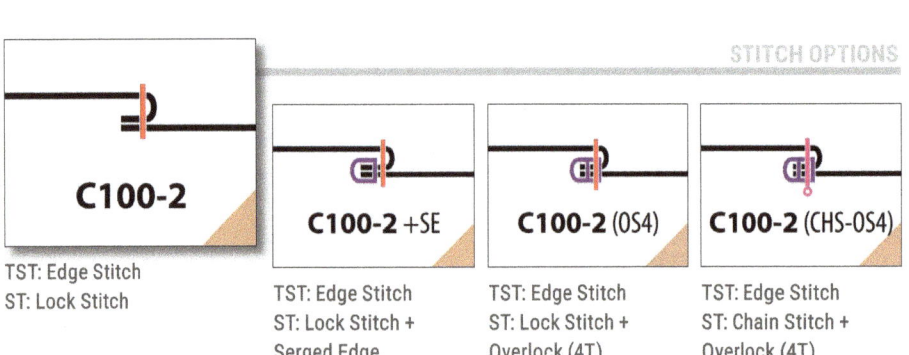

C100-2
TST: Edge Stitch
ST: Lock Stitch

C100-2 +SE
TST: Edge Stitch
ST: Lock Stitch +
Serged Edge

C100-2 (OS4)
TST: Edge Stitch
ST: Lock Stitch +
Overlock (4T)

C100-2 (CHS-OS4)
TST: Edge Stitch
ST: Chain Stitch +
Overlock (4T)

STITCH OPTIONS

Strong Seams

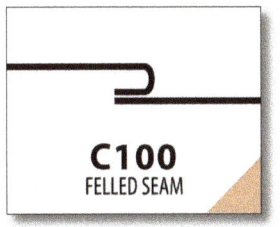

C100 FELLED SEAM

STITCH OPTIONS

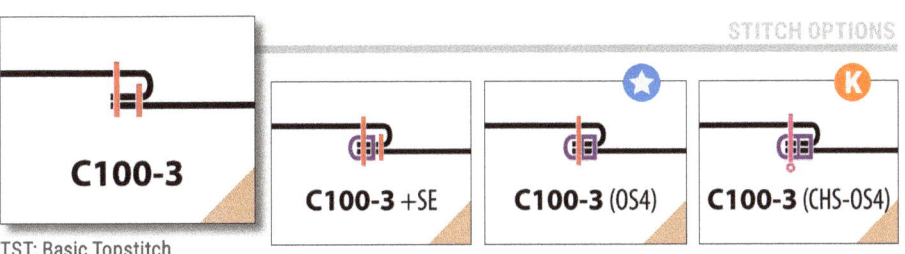

C100-3
TST: Basic Topstitch
ST: Lock Stitch

C100-3 +SE
TST: Basic Topstitch
ST: Lock Stitch + Serged Edge

C100-3 (OS4)
TST: Basic Topstitch
ST: Lock Stitch + Overlock (4T)

C100-3 (CHS-OS4)
TST: Basic Topstitch
ST: Chain Stitch + Overlock (4T)

STITCH OPTIONS

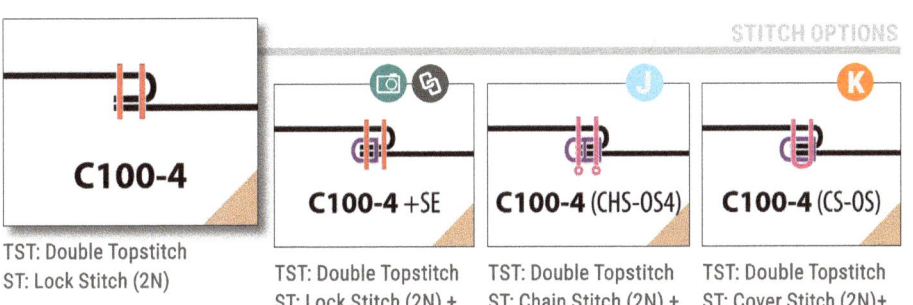

C100-4
TST: Double Topstitch
ST: Lock Stitch (2N)

C100-4 +SE
TST: Double Topstitch
ST: Lock Stitch (2N) + Serged Edge

C100-4 (CHS-OS4)
TST: Double Topstitch
ST: Chain Stitch (2N) + Overlock (4T)

C100-4 (CS-OS)
TST: Double Topstitch
ST: Cover Stitch (2N) + Overlock

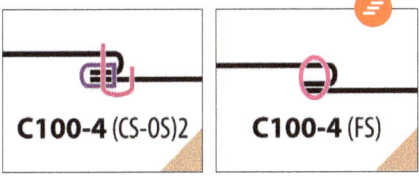

C100-4 (CS-OS)2
TST: Double Topstitch
ST: Cover Stitch (2N) + Overlock

C100-4 (FS)
TST: Cover Basic Topstitch
ST: Flatlock Stitch (2N)

ABC Seams®

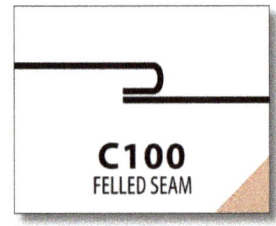

C100 FELLED SEAM

STITCH OPTIONS

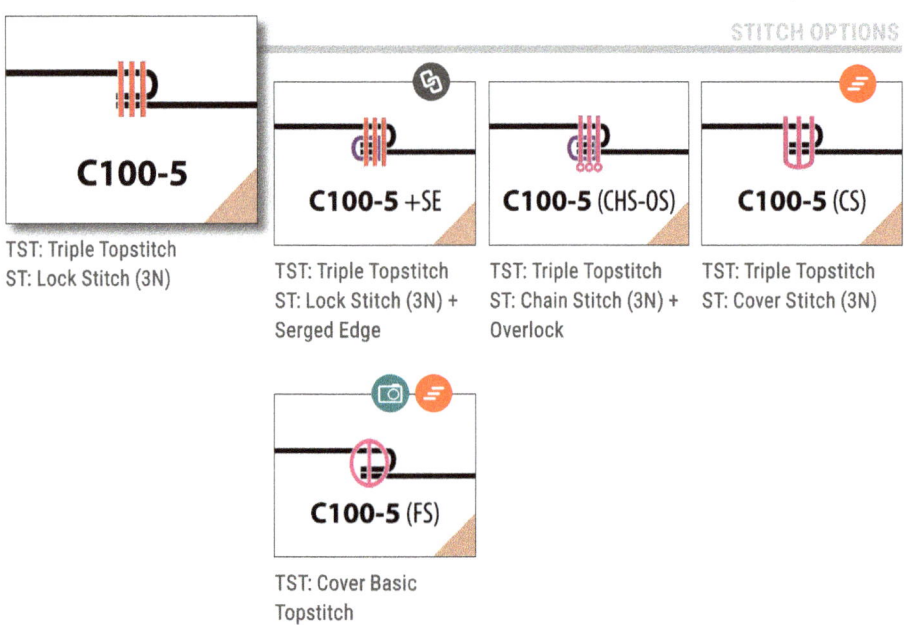

C100-5
TST: Triple Topstitch
ST: Lock Stitch (3N)

C100-5 +SE
TST: Triple Topstitch
ST: Lock Stitch (3N) + Serged Edge

C100-5 (CHS-OS)
TST: Triple Topstitch
ST: Chain Stitch (3N) + Overlock

C100-5 (CS)
TST: Triple Topstitch
ST: Cover Stitch (3N)

C100-5 (FS)
TST: Cover Basic Topstitch
ST: Flatlock Stitch (3N)

INSPIRATION

C100B   C100T   C100C

C100-4 (CS-OS)2

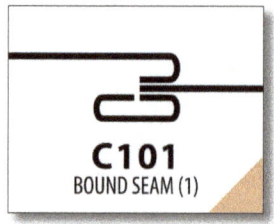

MAIN PROPERTIES

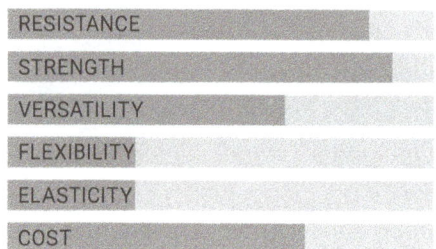

COMMON USES

- High-quality garments.
- Unlined clothing such as outerwear.
- Neckline seam of polo shirts.
- Shoulder seams of t-shirts.
- Side seams.
- Seams with decorative trimming.

ADDITIONAL NOTES

- Reversible Seam (exposed): The backside can be used as the right side.
- When sewing curved seams, it works better to use a bias-cut binding.
- Regular Binding Width: 1.2 cm (or 1/2").

3D VIEW

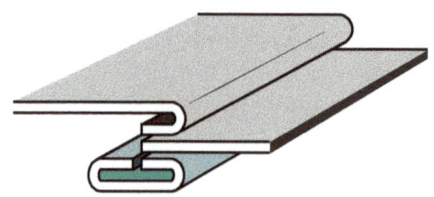

RELATED SEAMS

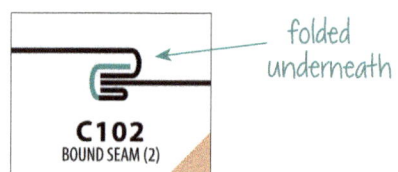
folded underneath

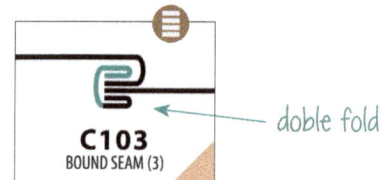
doble fold

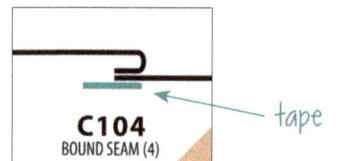
tape

Page 46

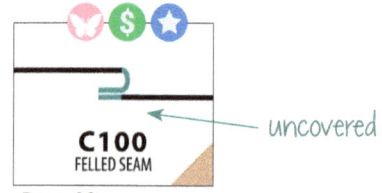
uncovered

Page 39

Strong Seams

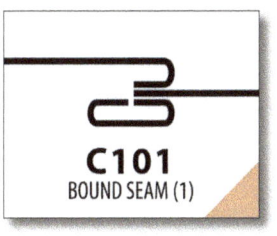

C101
BOUND SEAM (1)

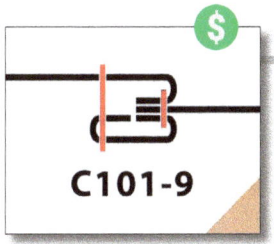

STITCH OPTIONS

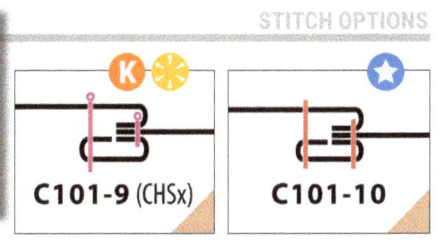

C101-9
TST: Basic Topstitch
ST: Lock Stitch

C101-9 (CHSx)
TST: Basic Topstitch
ST: Exposed Chain Stitch

C101-10
TST: Basic Topstitch + Understitch
ST: Lock Stitch

STITCH OPTIONS

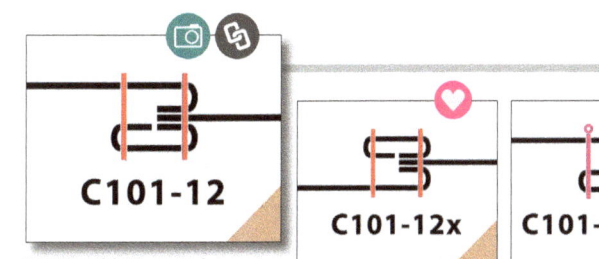

C101-12
TST: Double Topstitch
ST: Lock Stitch

C101-12x
TST: Double Topstitch
ST: Lock Stitch

C101-12 (CHSx)
TST: Double Topstitch
ST: Exposed Chain Stitch

C101-13 (CHSx)
TST: Double Topstitch (centered)
ST: Exposed Chain Stitch

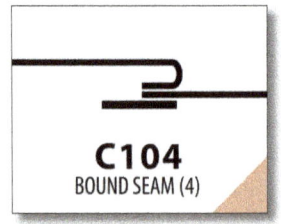

C104
BOUND SEAM (4)

MAIN PROPERTIES

RESISTANCE
STRENGTH
VERSATILITY
FLEXIBILITY
ELASTICITY
COST

COMMON USES

- High-quality garments.
- Lingerie, swimwear, and sportswear.
- Unlined clothing such as outerwear.
- Neckline seam of polo shirts.
- Seams with decorative trimming.

ADDITIONAL NOTES

- Reversible Seam (exposed): The backside can be used as the right side.
- It works better on straight or slightly curved seams.
- The tape can be stretchable.
- Regular Tape Width: 1.2 cm (or 1/2").

3D VIEW

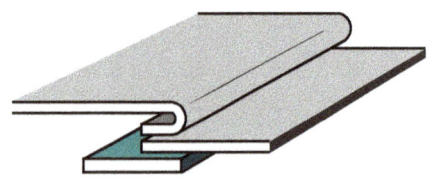

RELATED SEAMS

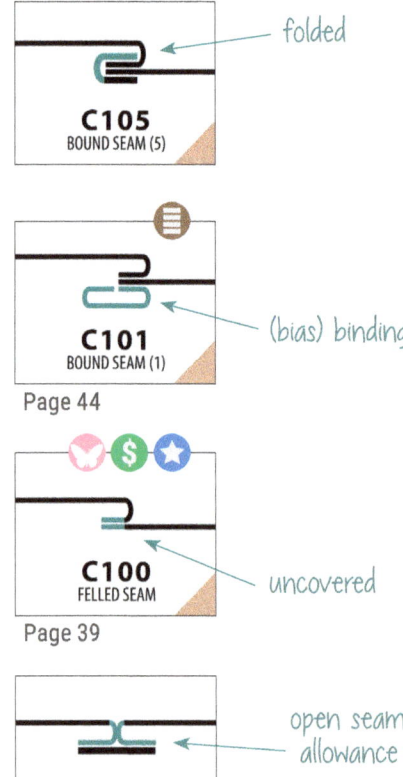

C105 BOUND SEAM (5) — folded

C101 BOUND SEAM (1) — (bias) binding
Page 44

C100 FELLED SEAM — uncovered
Page 39

C220 BONING SEAM — open seam allowance
Page 60

Strong Seams

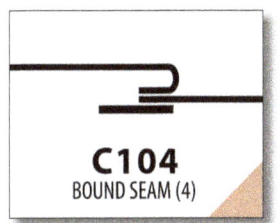

C104
BOUND SEAM (4)

STITCH OPTIONS

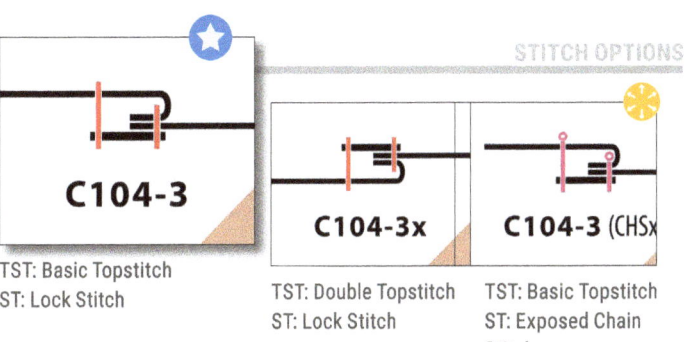

C104-3
TST: Basic Topstitch
ST: Lock Stitch

C104-3x
TST: Double Topstitch
ST: Lock Stitch

C104-3 (CHSx)
TST: Basic Topstitch
ST: Exposed Chain Stitch

STITCH OPTIONS

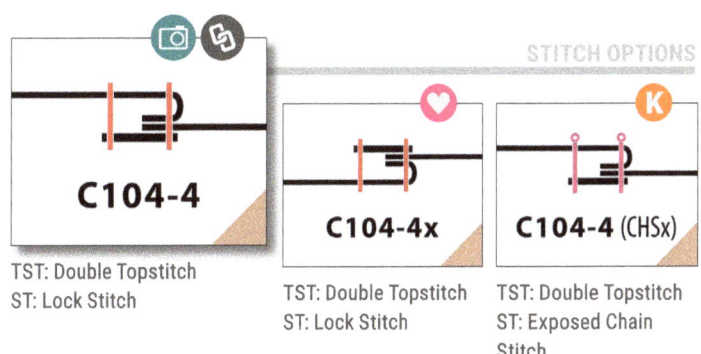

C104-4
TST: Double Topstitch
ST: Lock Stitch

C104-4x
TST: Double Topstitch
ST: Lock Stitch

C104-4 (CHSx)
TST: Double Topstitch
ST: Exposed Chain Stitch

ABC Seams®

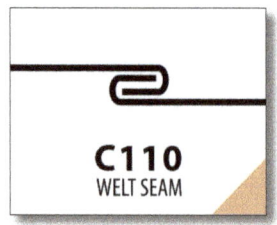

MAIN PROPERTIES

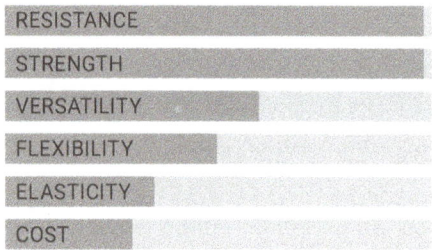

COMMON USES

- It works better on medium to heavy-weight fabrics such as denim.

- Mostly used on woven garments.

- Widely used on men's clothing, especially shirts and work garments.

- Shoulders, armholes, and yoke seams.

- Crotch, yoke, side seams, and inseams of pants.

- Unlined jackets and coats.

ADDITIONAL NOTES

- Stretch resistance.

- Neat finishing on the inside.

- It works better on straight or slightly curved seams.

- Regular Seam Width: 1.2 cm (1/2").

3D VIEW

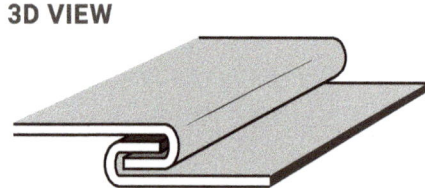

RELATED SEAMS

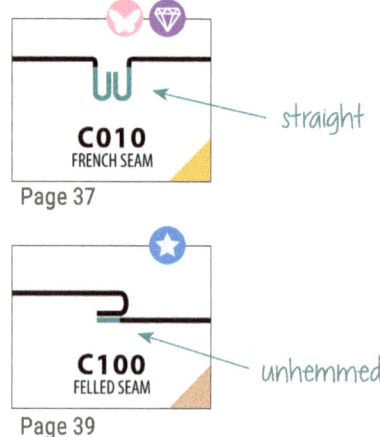

Strong Seams

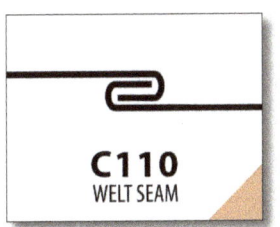

C110 WELT SEAM

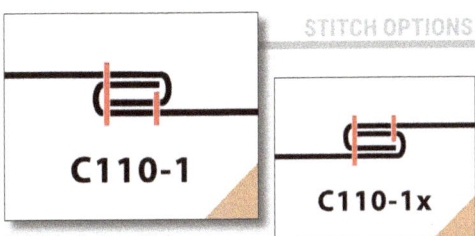

STITCH OPTIONS

C110-1
TST: Basic Topstitch
ST: Lock Stitch

C110-1x
TST: Double Topstitch
ST: Lock Stitch

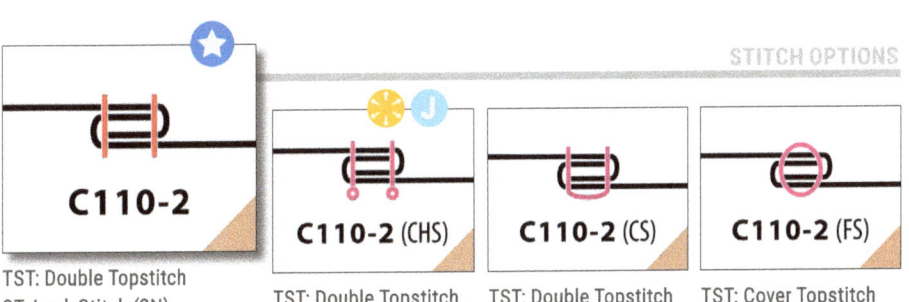

STITCH OPTIONS

C110-2
TST: Double Topstitch
ST: Lock Stitch (2N)

C110-2 (CHS)
TST: Double Topstitch
ST: Chain Stitch (2N)

C110-2 (CS)
TST: Double Topstitch
ST: Cover Stitch (2N)

C110-2 (FS)
TST: Cover Topstitch
ST: Flatlock Stitch (2N)

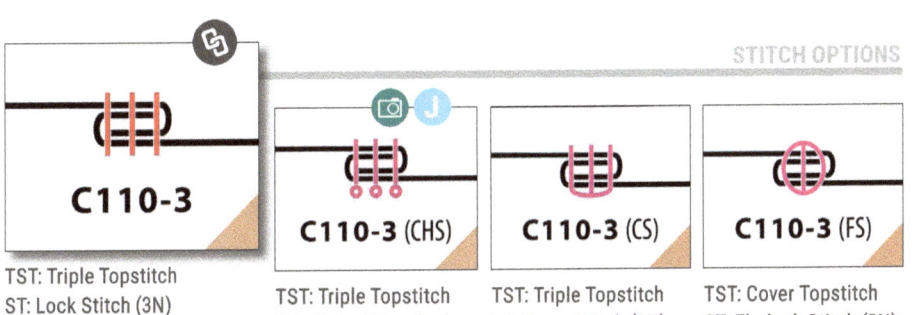

STITCH OPTIONS

C110-3
TST: Triple Topstitch
ST: Lock Stitch (3N)

C110-3 (CHS)
TST: Triple Topstitch
ST: Chain Stitch (3N)

C110-3 (CS)
TST: Triple Topstitch
ST: Cover Stitch (3N)

C110-3 (FS)
TST: Cover Topstitch
ST: Flatlock Stitch (3N)

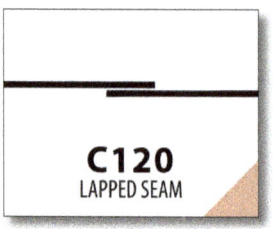

MAIN PROPERTIES

RESISTANCE
STRENGTH
VERSATILITY
FLEXIBILITY
ELASTICITY
COST

COMMON USES

- Fabrics/materials that do not fray, such as leather, PU, suede, vinyl, and laces.

- Irregular-shaped and curved seams.

- Lingerie.

- Bags, footwear, and other accessories.

- Upholstery.

ADDITIONAL NOTES

- Easy and quick to make (inexpensive).

- Good option to avoid thickness when using heavy-weight fabrics.

3D VIEW

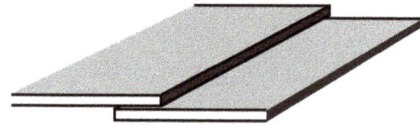

RELATED SEAMS

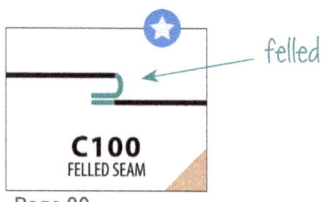

Page 39

Strong Seams

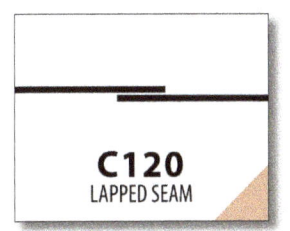

C120 LAPPED SEAM

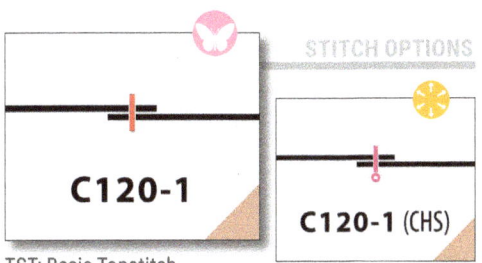

C120-1
TST: Basic Topstitch
ST: Lock Stitch

C120-1 (CHS)
TST: Basic Topstitch
ST: Chain Stitch

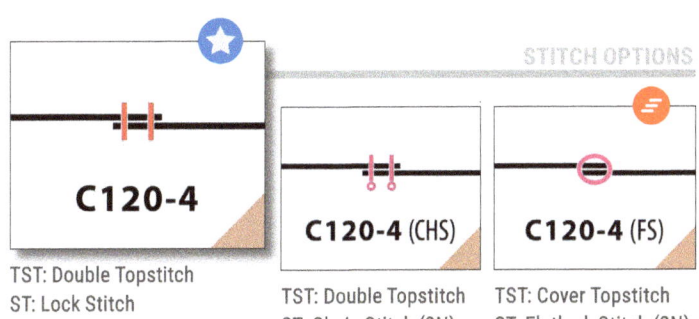

C120-4
TST: Double Topstitch
ST: Lock Stitch

C120-4 (CHS)
TST: Double Topstitch
ST: Chain Stitch (2N)

C120-4 (FS)
TST: Cover Topstitch
ST: Flatlock Stitch (2N)

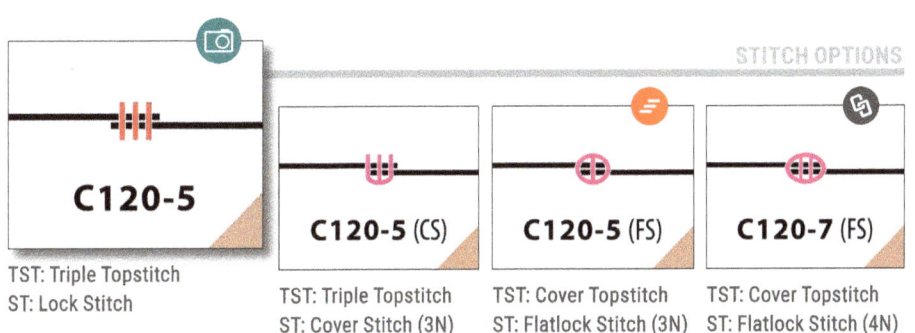

C120-5
TST: Triple Topstitch
ST: Lock Stitch

C120-5 (CS)
TST: Triple Topstitch
ST: Cover Stitch (3N)

C120-5 (FS)
TST: Cover Topstitch
ST: Flatlock Stitch (3N)

C120-7 (FS)
TST: Cover Topstitch
ST: Flatlock Stitch (4N)

MAIN PROPERTIES

RESISTANCE
STRENGTH
VERSATILITY
FLEXIBILITY
ELASTICITY
COST

COMMON USES

- Mostly used on woven garments.
- Lined garments.
- Yoke of shirts and blouses.
- Shoulders of tops with back yoke.
- Neckline seam of jackets with collar (or hood).
- Cuffs.
- Waistband seam of skirts and pants.
- Plackets.

ADDITIONAL NOTES

- Neat finishing on the inside.
- A piece of interfacing might be needed to get the best result.

3D VIEW

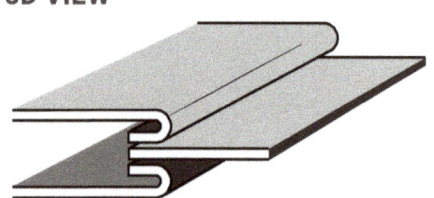

RELATED SEAMS

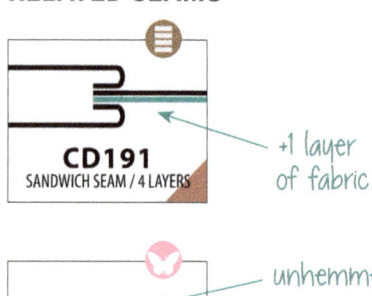

+1 layer of fabric

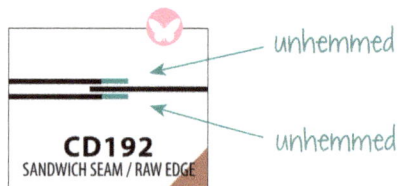

unhemmed

unhemmed

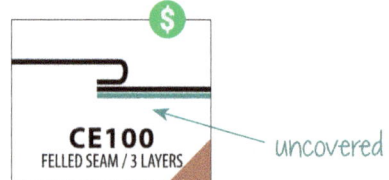

uncovered

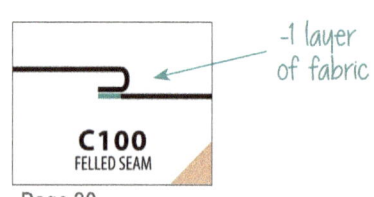

-1 layer of fabric

Page 39

Strong Seams

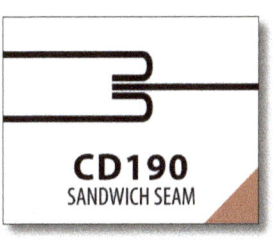

CD190
SANDWICH SEAM

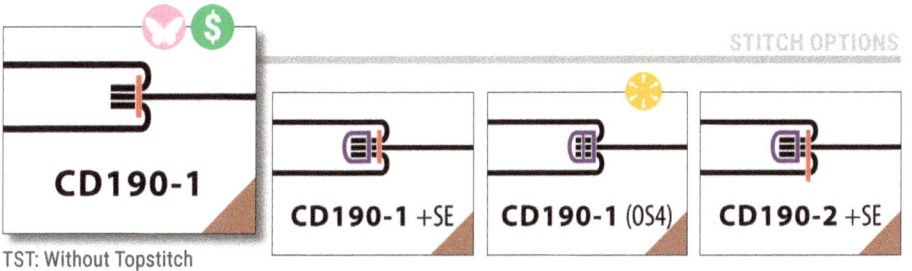

STITCH OPTIONS

CD190-1
TST: Without Topstitch
ST: Lock Stitch

CD190-1 +SE
TST: Without Topstitch
ST: Lock Stitch + Serged Edge

CD190-1 (OS4)
TST: Without Topstitch
ST: Overlock (4T)

CD190-2 +SE
TST: Understitch
ST: Lock Stitch + Serged Edge

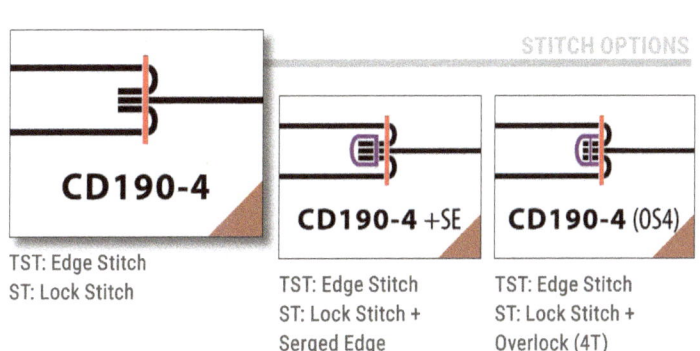

STITCH OPTIONS

CD190-4
TST: Edge Stitch
ST: Lock Stitch

CD190-4 +SE
TST: Edge Stitch
ST: Lock Stitch + Serged Edge

CD190-4 (OS4)
TST: Edge Stitch
ST: Lock Stitch + Overlock (4T)

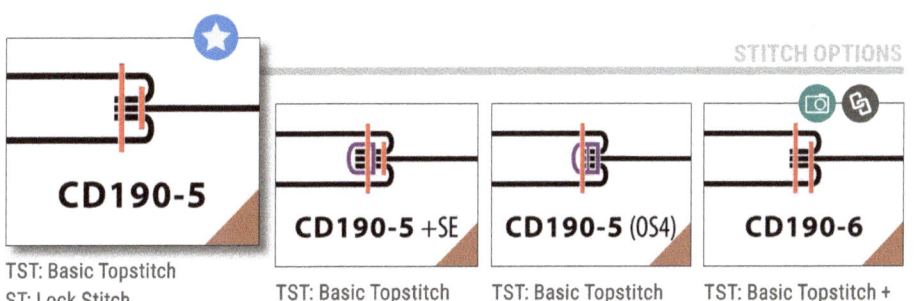

STITCH OPTIONS

CD190-5
TST: Basic Topstitch
ST: Lock Stitch

CD190-5 +SE
TST: Basic Topstitch
ST: Lock Stitch + Serged Edge

CD190-5 (OS4)
TST: Basic Topstitch
ST: Lock Stitch + Overlock (4T)

CD190-6
TST: Basic Topstitch + Understitch
ST: Lock Stitch

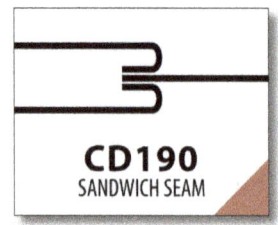

CD190 SANDWICH SEAM

STITCH OPTIONS

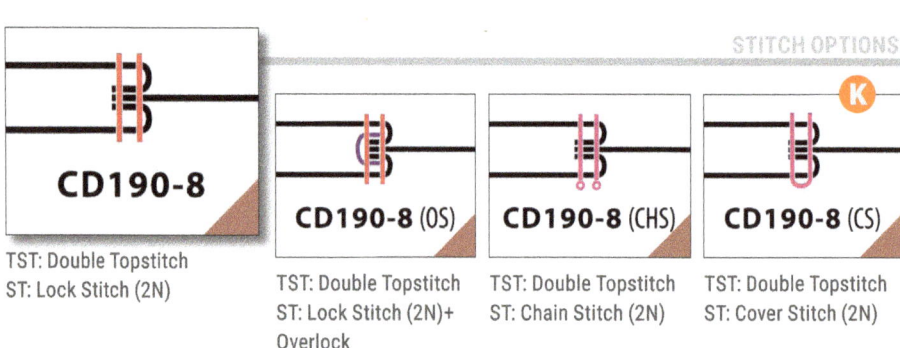

CD190-8
TST: Double Topstitch
ST: Lock Stitch (2N)

CD190-8 (OS)
TST: Double Topstitch
ST: Lock Stitch (2N)+ Overlock

CD190-8 (CHS)
TST: Double Topstitch
ST: Chain Stitch (2N)

CD190-8 (CS)
TST: Double Topstitch
ST: Cover Stitch (2N)

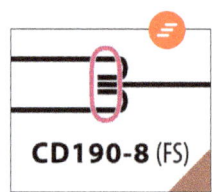

CD190-8 (FS)
TST: Cover Basic Topstitch
ST: Flatlock Stitch (2N)

STITCH OPTIONS

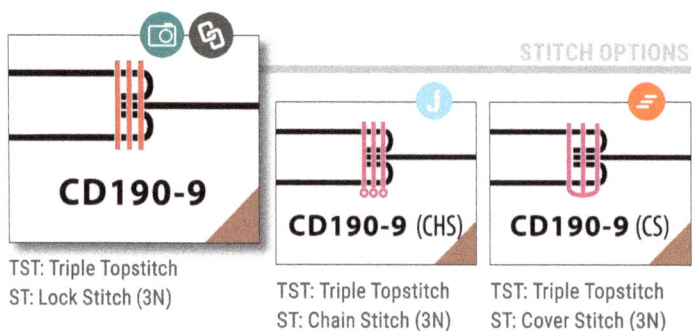

CD190-9
TST: Triple Topstitch
ST: Lock Stitch (3N)

CD190-9 (CHS)
TST: Triple Topstitch
ST: Chain Stitch (3N)

CD190-9 (CS)
TST: Triple Topstitch
ST: Cover Stitch (3N)

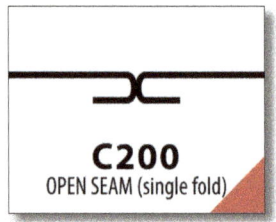

C200
OPEN SEAM (single fold)

MAIN PROPERTIES

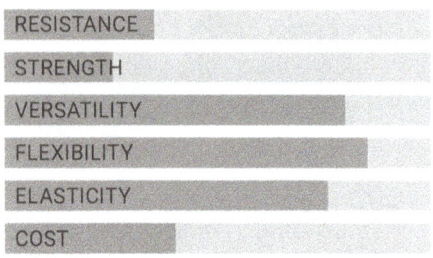

RESISTANCE
STRENGTH
VERSATILITY
FLEXIBILITY
ELASTICITY
COST

COMMON USES

- Mainly used on woven garments made of medium to heavy-weight fabrics.
- Lined garments.
- Side seams of formal trousers, dresses, and skirts.
- Collar band seam.
- Bags and footwear.
- Upholstery.

ADDITIONAL NOTES

- Not suitable for tight-fitting garments.
- It becomes stronger when a shorter stitch joins the fabrics.
- Good option to avoid thickness when using heavy-weight fabrics.

3D VIEW

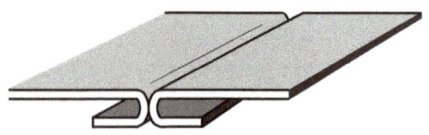

RELATED SEAMS

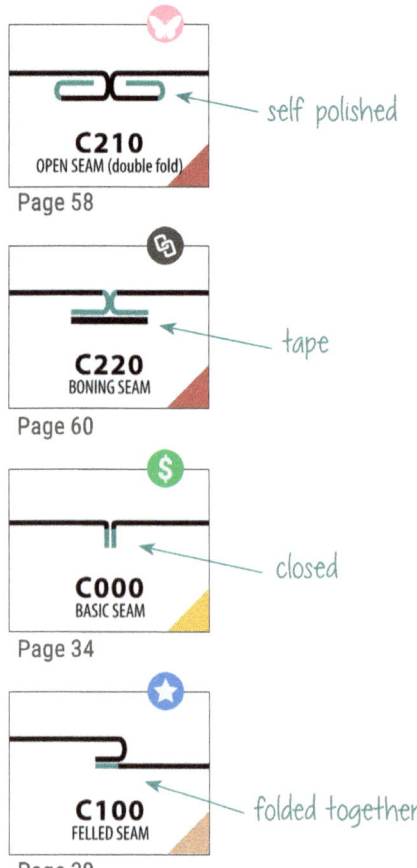

C210 — OPEN SEAM (double fold) — Page 58 — *self polished*

C220 — BONING SEAM — Page 60 — *tape*

C000 — BASIC SEAM — Page 34 — *closed*

C100 — FELLED SEAM — Page 39 — *folded together*

Strong Seams

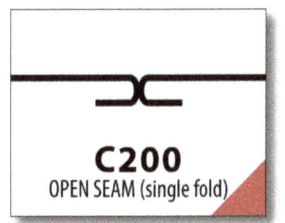

C200
OPEN SEAM (single fold)

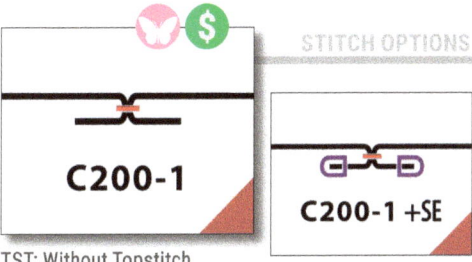

C200-1
TST: Without Topstitch
ST: Lock Stitch

C200-1 +SE
TST: Without Topstitch
ST: Lock Stitch +
Serged Edge

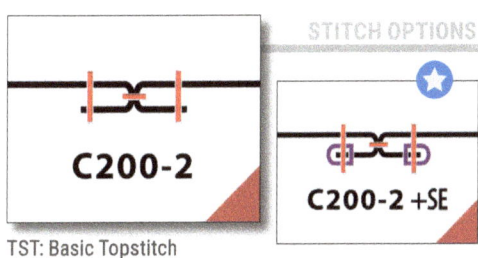

C200-2
TST: Basic Topstitch
ST: Lock Stitch

C200-2 +SE
TST: Basic Topstitch
ST: Lock Stitch +
Serged Edge

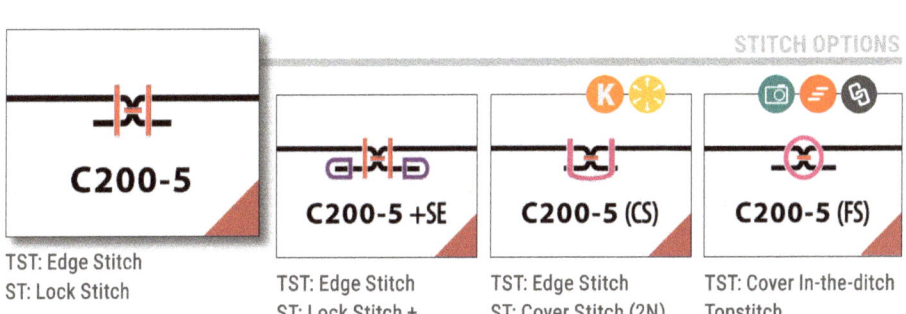

C200-5
TST: Edge Stitch
ST: Lock Stitch

C200-5 +SE
TST: Edge Stitch
ST: Lock Stitch +
Serged Edge

C200-5 (CS)
TST: Edge Stitch
ST: Cover Stitch (2N)

C200-5 (FS)
TST: Cover In-the-ditch Topstitch
ST: Flatlock Stitch (2N)

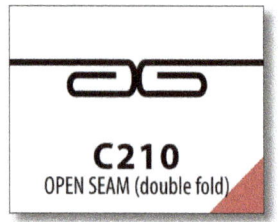

C210
OPEN SEAM (double fold)

MAIN PROPERTIES

RESISTANCE
STRENGTH
VERSATILITY
FLEXIBILITY
ELASTICITY
COST

COMMON USES

- Used mainly on woven fabrics of light to medium weight.
- Formal clothing.
- Delicate garments.
- Unlined jackets and coats.
- Exposed seams such as the centre back of jackets.

ADDITIONAL NOTES

- Clean finishing on the inside.
- It strengthens when using a shorter stitch length to join the fabrics.
- It works better on straight or slightly curved seams.
- Regular Hem Width (each side): 1 cm (or 3/8").

3D VIEW

RELATED SEAMS

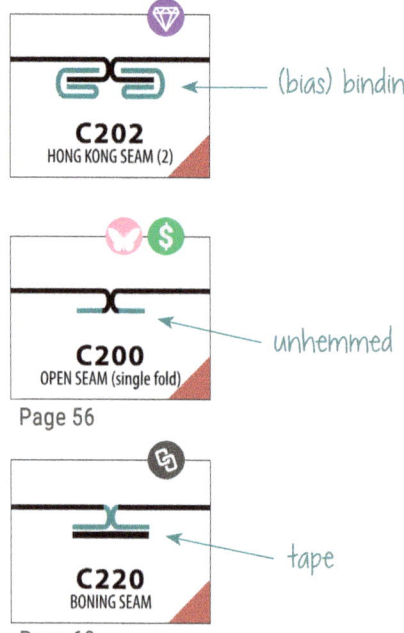

C202 HONG KONG SEAM (2) ← (bias) binding

C200 OPEN SEAM (single fold) ← unhemmed
Page 56

C220 BONING SEAM ← tape
Page 60

Strong Seams

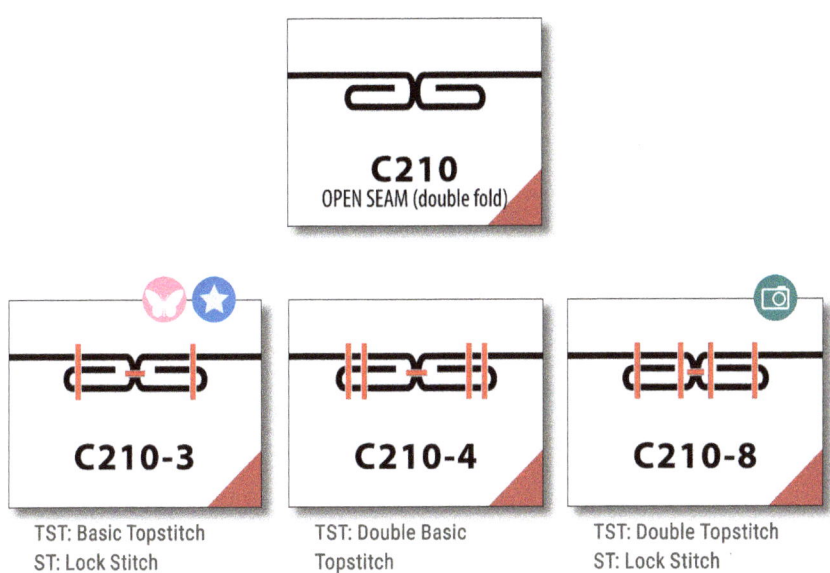

C210
OPEN SEAM (double fold)

C210-3
TST: Basic Topstitch
ST: Lock Stitch

C210-4
TST: Double Basic Topstitch
ST: Lock Stitch

C210-8
TST: Double Topstitch
ST: Lock Stitch

INSPIRATION

C203
HONG KONG SEAM (3)

C202
HONG KONG SEAM (2)

C204
HONG KONG SEAM (4)

C220
BONING SEAM

MAIN PROPERTIES

- RESISTANCE
- STRENGTH
- VERSATILITY
- FLEXIBILITY
- ELASTICITY
- COST

COMMON USES

- Medium to heavy-weight fabrics.
- Lingerie and corsetry.
- Seams with decorative trimming.
- Bags, footwear, and other accessories.
- Upholstery.

ADDITIONAL NOTES

- Ideal for seams that need stability and stretching resistance.
- Decorative finishing on the inside.
- Good option to avoid thickness when using heavy-weight fabrics.
- Reversible Seam (exposed): The backside can be used as the right side.
- Regular Tape Width: 1.2 cm (or 1/2").

RELATED SEAMS

C204 — double tape
HONG KONG SEAM (4)

C200 — unhemmed
OPEN SEAM (single fold)
Page 56

C104 — folded together
BOUND SEAM (4)
Page 46

3D VIEW

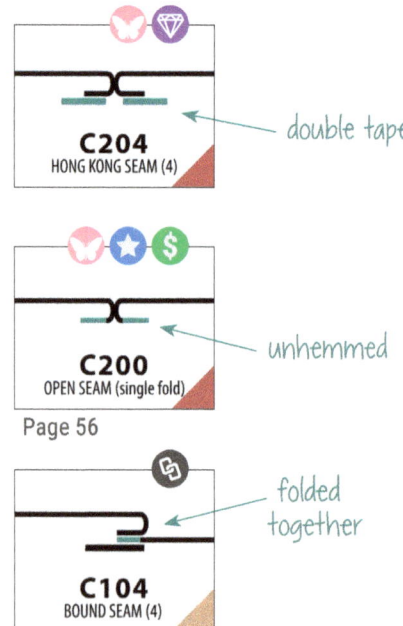

Strong Seams

C220
BONING SEAM

STITCH OPTIONS

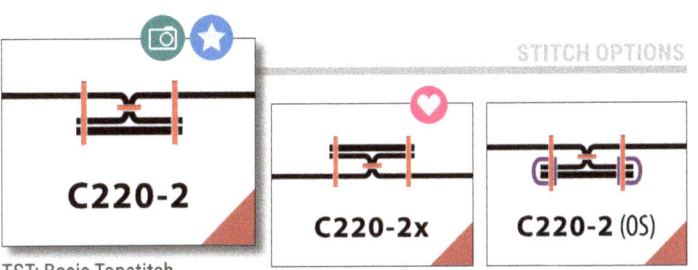

C220-2
TST: Basic Topstitch
ST: Lock Stitch

C220-2x
TST: Basic Topstitch
ST: Lock Stitch

C220-2 (OS)
TST: Basic Topstitch
ST: Lock Stitch + Overlock

STITCH OPTIONS

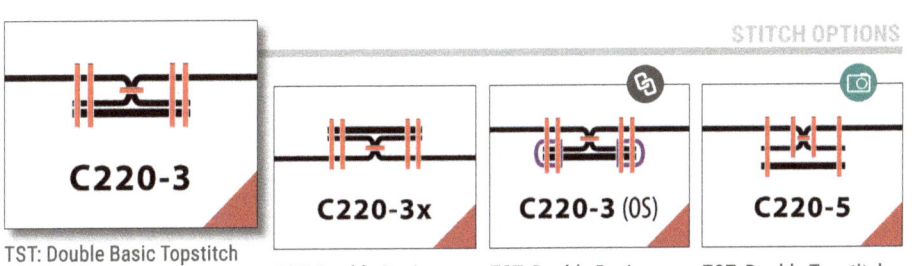

C220-3
TST: Double Basic Topstitch
ST: Lock Stitch

C220-3x
TST: Double Basic Topstitch
ST: Lock Stitch

C220-3 (OS)
TST: Double Basic Topstitch
ST: Lock Stitch + Overlock

C220-5
TST: Double Topstitch
ST: Lock Stitch

MY NOTES
CONSTRUCTIONS

Strong Seams

MY SAMPLES
CONSTRUCTIONS

GLUE	GLUE
GLUE	GLUE
GLUE	GLUE

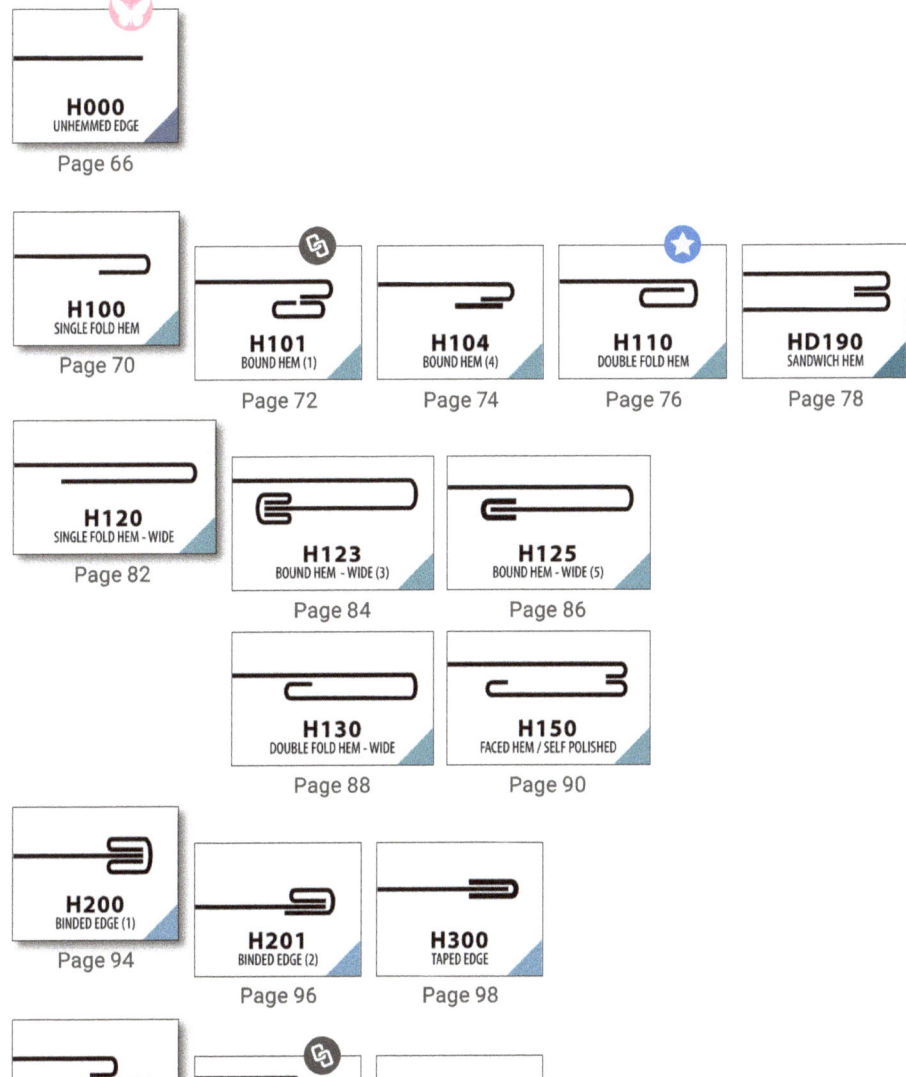

H000
UNHEMMED EDGE

MAIN PROPERTIES

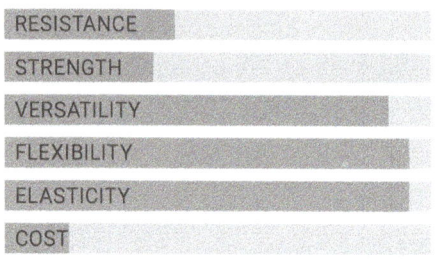

RESISTANCE
STRENGTH
VERSATILITY
FLEXIBILITY
ELASTICITY
COST

COMMON USES

- Widely used on products made of leather, PU, suede, vinyl, laces, and knit.

- Casual clothing.

- Unhemmed products.

- Lingerie.

- Irregular-shaped and curved edges.

- Draped and bias-cut edges.

- Bottom of full skirts made of lightweight fabrics.

- Ruffles and flounces.

- Accessories and upholstery products.

ADDITIONAL NOTES

- Good option to avoid thickness when using heavy-weight fabrics.

3D VIEW

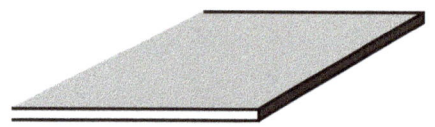

RELATED SEAMS

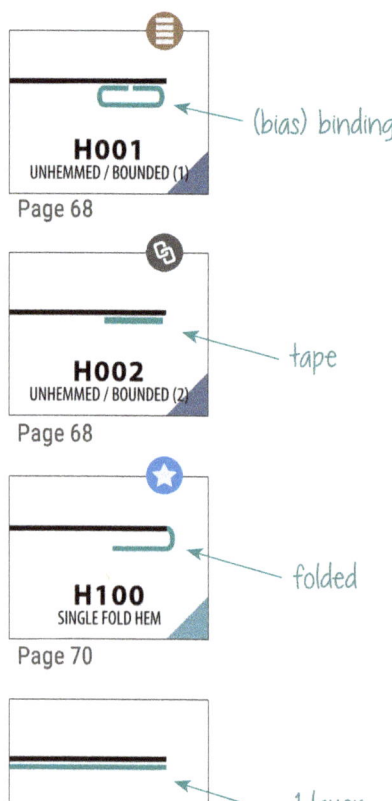

H001
UNHEMMED / BOUNDED (1)
Page 68
← (bias) binding

H002
UNHEMMED / BOUNDED (2)
Page 68
← tape

H100
SINGLE FOLD HEM
Page 70
← folded

HD000
UNHEMMED EDGE / 2 LAYERS
Page 68
← +1 layer of fabric

Strong Seams

STITCH OPTIONS

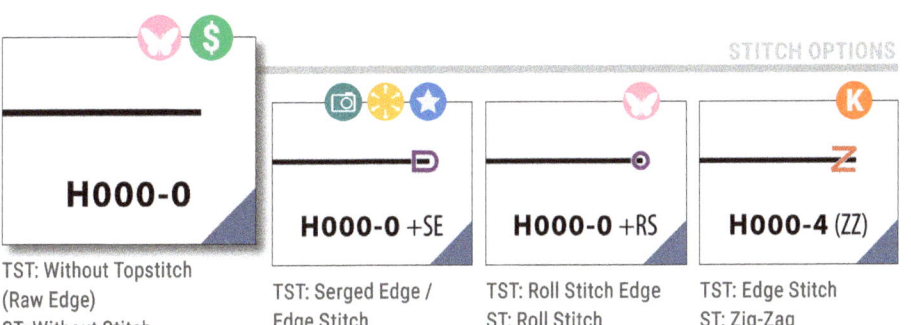

H000-0
TST: Without Topstitch (Raw Edge)
ST: Without Stitch

H000-0 +SE
TST: Serged Edge / Edge Stitch
ST: Overlock (3T)

H000-0 +RS
TST: Roll Stitch Edge
ST: Roll Stitch

H000-4 (ZZ)
TST: Edge Stitch
ST: Zig-Zag

STITCH OPTIONS

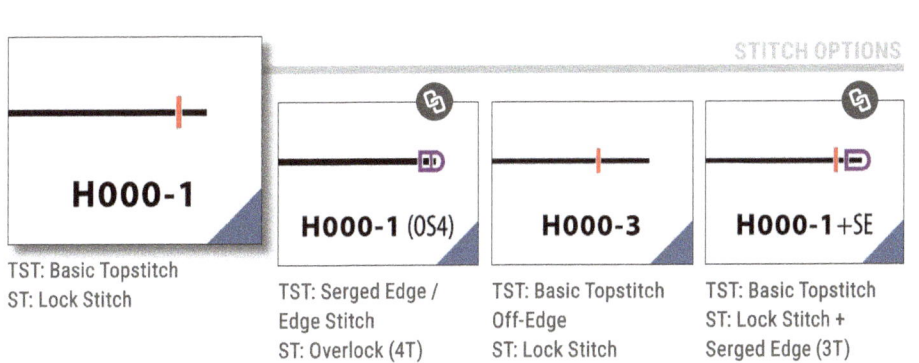

H000-1
TST: Basic Topstitch
ST: Lock Stitch

H000-1 (OS4)
TST: Serged Edge / Edge Stitch
ST: Overlock (4T)

H000-3
TST: Basic Topstitch Off-Edge
ST: Lock Stitch

H000-1 +SE
TST: Basic Topstitch
ST: Lock Stitch + Serged Edge (3T)

ABC Seams®

H000
UNHEMMED EDGE

BONUS

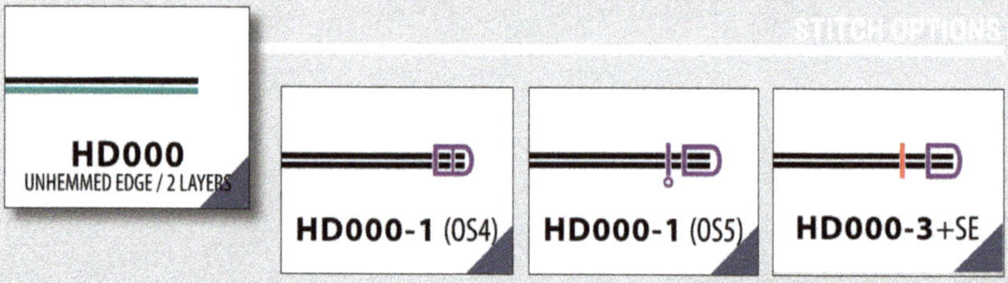

HD000
UNHEMMED EDGE / 2 LAYERS

STITCH OPTIONS

HD000-1 (OS4)   **HD000-1** (OS5)   **HD000-3**+SE

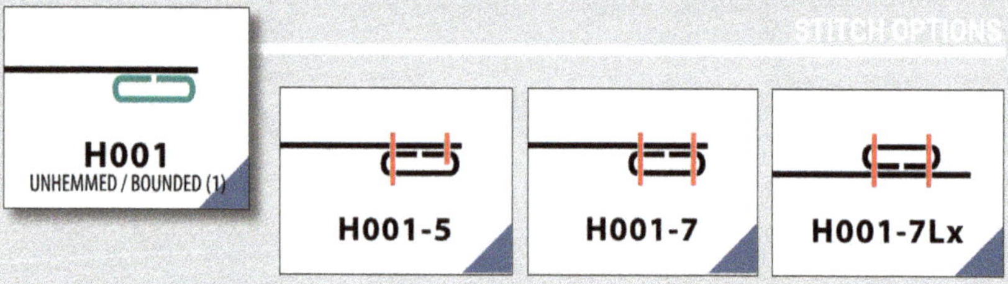

H001
UNHEMMED / BOUNDED (1)

STITCH OPTIONS

H001-5   **H001-7**   **H001-7Lx**

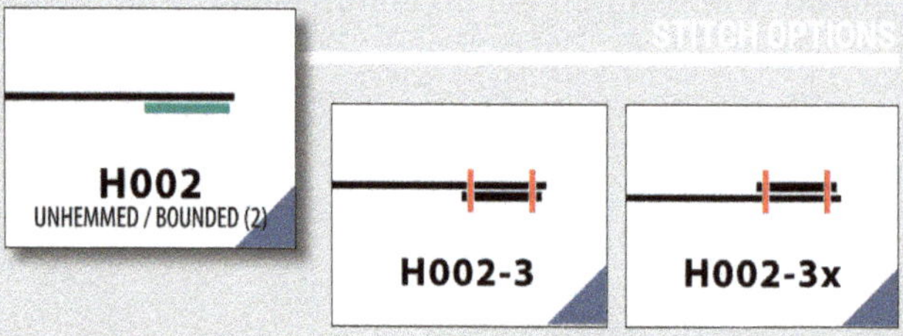

H002
UNHEMMED / BOUNDED (2)

STITCH OPTIONS

H002-3   **H002-3x**

Strong Seams

C110-2 (CHS)

ABC Seams®

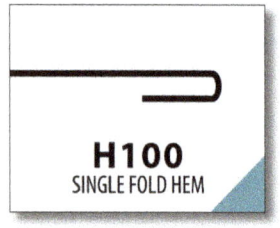

H100
SINGLE FOLD HEM

MAIN PROPERTIES

RESISTANCE
STRENGTH
VERSATILITY
FLEXIBILITY
ELASTICITY
COST

COMMON USES

- Widely used on garments made of knit fabrics.

- Materials/fabrics that do not fray, such as fleece, PU, velvet, vinyl, and lace.

- Casual clothing.

- Sleeve and bottom hem of t-shirts.

- Curved and bias-cut hems.

- Plackets and slits.

- Ruffles and flounces.

- Bags, footwear, and accessories in general.

- Upholstery.

ADDITIONAL NOTES

- Regular Hem Width: 1.2cm (or 1/2"). If a wider hem is required, check the group H120 (Single Fold Hem - WIDE).

3D VIEW

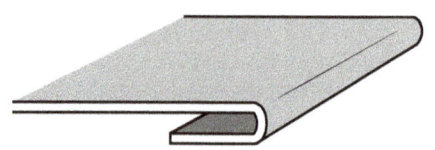

RELATED SEAMS

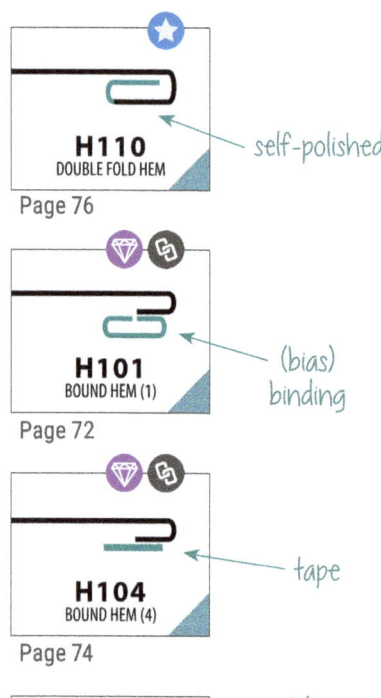

H110 DOUBLE FOLD HEM — self-polished
Page 76

H101 BOUND HEM (1) — (bias) binding
Page 72

H104 BOUND HEM (4) — tape
Page 74

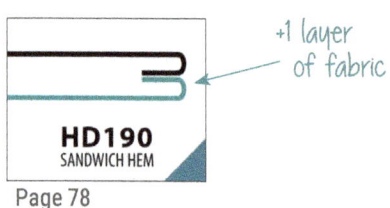

HD190 SANDWICH HEM — +1 layer of fabric
Page 78

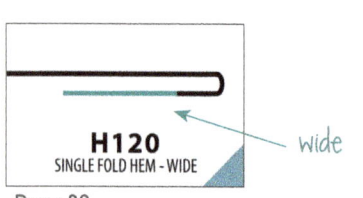

H120 SINGLE FOLD HEM - WIDE — wide
Page 82

Strong Seams

H100
SINGLE FOLD HEM

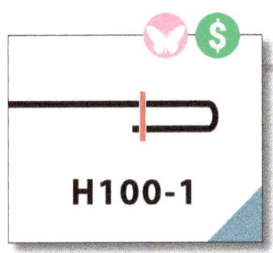

H100-1
TST: Basic Topstitch
ST: Lock Stitch

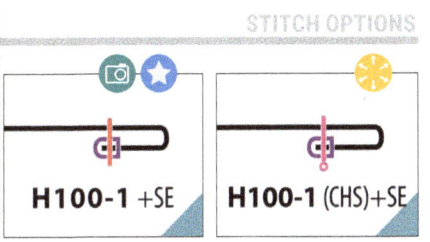

STITCH OPTIONS

H100-1 +SE
TST: Basic Topstitch
ST: Lock Stitch + Serged Edge

H100-1 (CHS)+SE
TST: Basic Topstitch
ST: Lock Stitch + Serged Edge

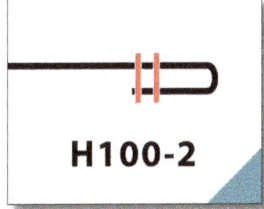

H100-2
TST: Double Basic Topstitch
ST: Lock Stitch (2N)

STITCH OPTIONS

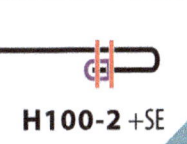

H100-2 +SE
TST: Double Basic Topstitch
ST: Lock Stitch (2N) + Serged Edge

H100-2 (CS)
TST: Double Basic Topstitch
ST: Cover Stitch (2N)

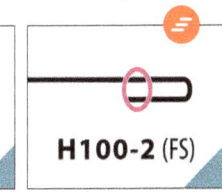

H100-2 (FS)
TST: Cover Basic Topstitch
ST: Flatlock Stitch (2N)

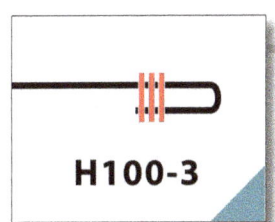

H100-3
TST: Triple Basic Topstitch
ST: Lock Stitch (3N)

STITCH OPTIONS

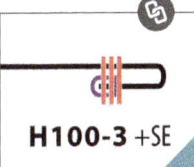

H100-3 +SE
TST: Triple Basic Topstitch
ST: Lock Stitch (3N) + Serged Edge

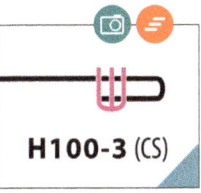

H100-3 (CS)
TST: Triple Basic Topstitch
ST: Cover Stitch (3N)

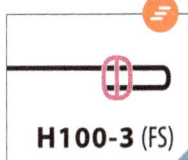

H100-3 (FS)
TST: Cover Basic Topstitch
ST: Flatlock Stitch (3N)

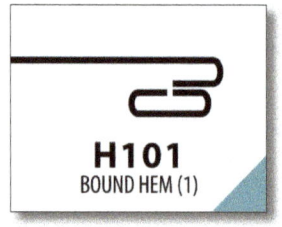

MAIN PROPERTIES

RESISTANCE
STRENGTH
VERSATILITY
FLEXIBILITY
ELASTICITY
COST

COMMON USES

- Curved edges such as necklines.
- Bottoms of bias-cut skirts.
- Narrow plackets.
- Slits on side seams.
- Edges with decorative trimming.
- Bags and accessories.

ADDITIONAL NOTES

- Stretch resistance.

- Decorative finishing on the inside.

- When sewing curved edges, it works better to use a bias-cut binding.

- Regular Binding Width: 1.2 cm (or 1/2"). Check the group H150 (Faced Hem) for similar but broader options.

3D VIEW

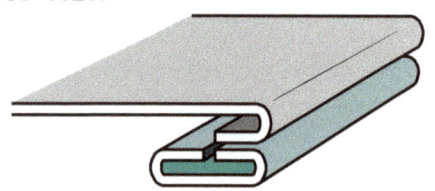

RELATED SEAMS

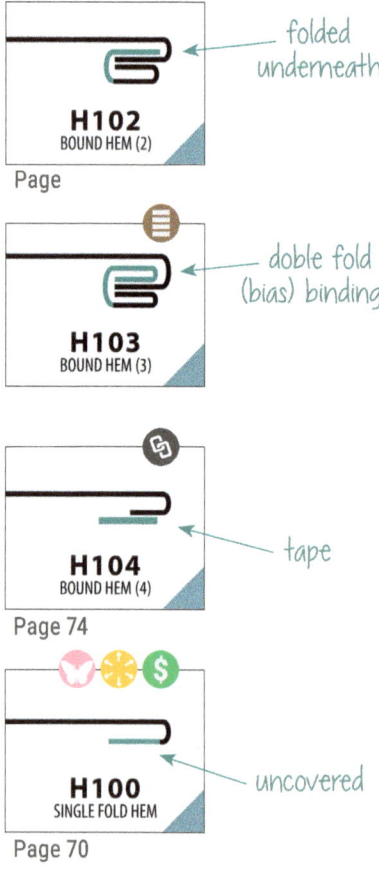

H102 BOUND HEM (2) — folded underneath
Page

H103 BOUND HEM (3) — doble fold (bias) binding

H104 BOUND HEM (4) — tape
Page 74

H100 SINGLE FOLD HEM — uncovered
Page 70

H150 FACED HEM / SELF POLISHED — wide + facing
Page 90

Strong Seams

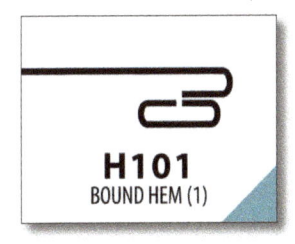

H101
BOUND HEM (1)

STITCH OPTIONS

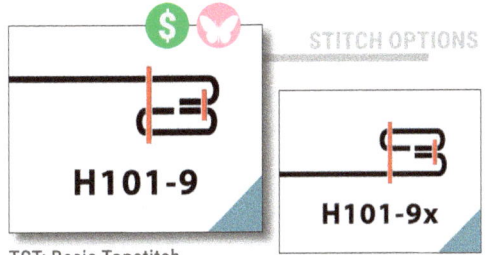

H101-9
TST: Basic Topstitch
ST: Lock Stitch

H101-9x
TST: Edge Stitch
ST: Lock Stitch

STITCH OPTIONS

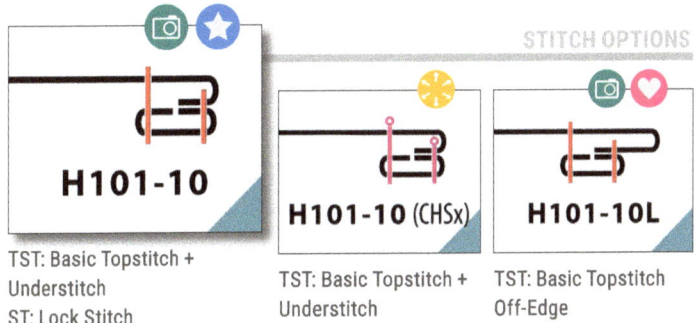

H101-10
TST: Basic Topstitch + Understitch
ST: Lock Stitch

H101-10 (CHSx)
TST: Basic Topstitch + Understitch
ST: Exposed Chain Stitch

H101-10L
TST: Basic Topstitch Off-Edge
ST: Lock Stitch

STITCH OPTIONS

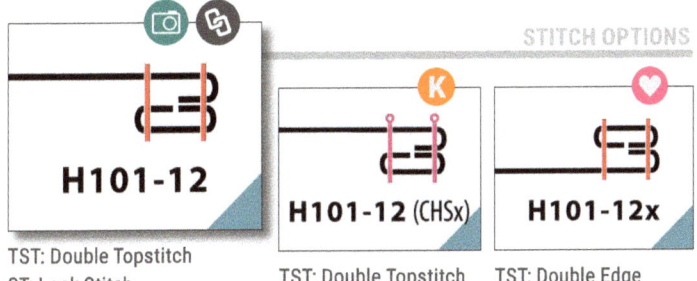

H101-12
TST: Double Topstitch
ST: Lock Stitch

H101-12 (CHSx)
TST: Double Topstitch
ST: Exposed Chain Stitch

H101-12x
TST: Double Edge Stitch
ST: Lock Stitch

ABC Seams®

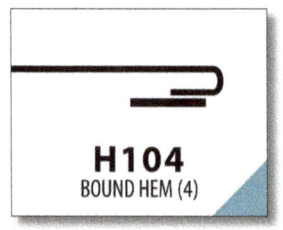

H104
BOUND HEM (4)

MAIN PROPERTIES

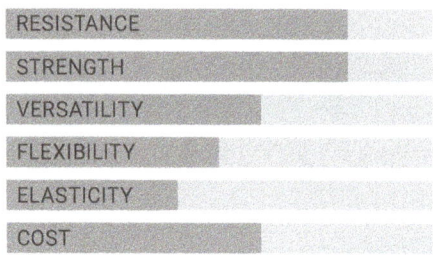

RESISTANCE
STRENGTH
VERSATILITY
FLEXIBILITY
ELASTICITY
COST

COMMON USES

- Widely used on knit garments and products made of heavy-weight fabrics.
- Lingerie, swimsuits, and sportswear.
- Narrow plackets.
- Slits on side seams.
- Edges with decorative trimming.
- Bags, footwear, and accessories.
- Upholstery.

ADDITIONAL NOTES

- The tape stabilizes the edge.
- Excellent stretching resistance.
- Reversible Seam (exposed): The backside can be used as the right side.
- Regular Tape Width: 1.2 cm (or 1/2").

3D VIEW

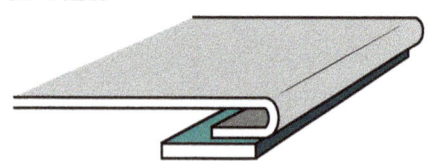

RELATED SEAMS

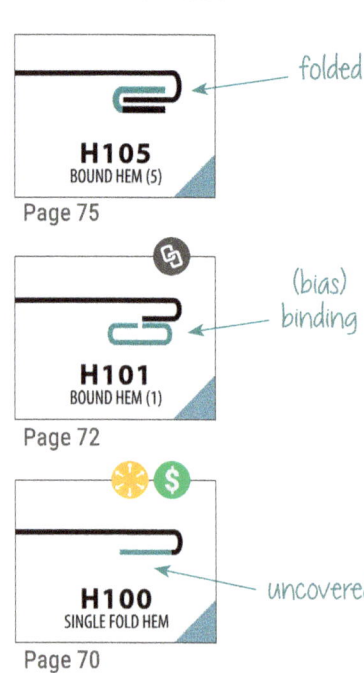

— folded
H105
BOUND HEM (5)
Page 75

(bias) binding
H101
BOUND HEM (1)
Page 72

— uncovered
H100
SINGLE FOLD HEM
Page 70

— unhemmed
H002
UNHEMMED / BOUNDED (2)
Page 68

Strong Seams

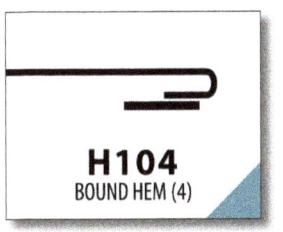

H104-3
TST: Basic Topstitch
ST: Lock Stitch

H104-3 (CHSx)
TST: Basic Topstitch
ST: Exposed Chain Stitch

H104-3L
TST: Basic Topstitch
ST: Lock Stitch

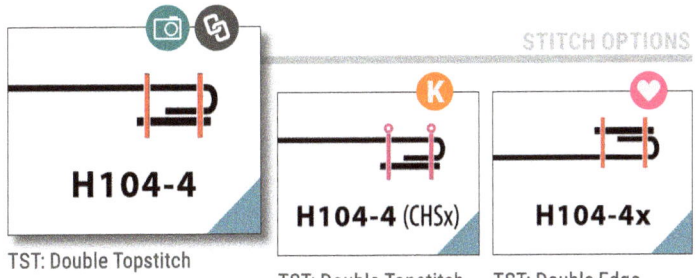

H104-4
TST: Double Topstitch
ST: Lock Stitch

H104-4 (CHSx)
TST: Double Topstitch
ST: Exposed Chain Stitch

H104-4x
TST: Double Edge Stitch
ST: Lock Stitch

BONUS

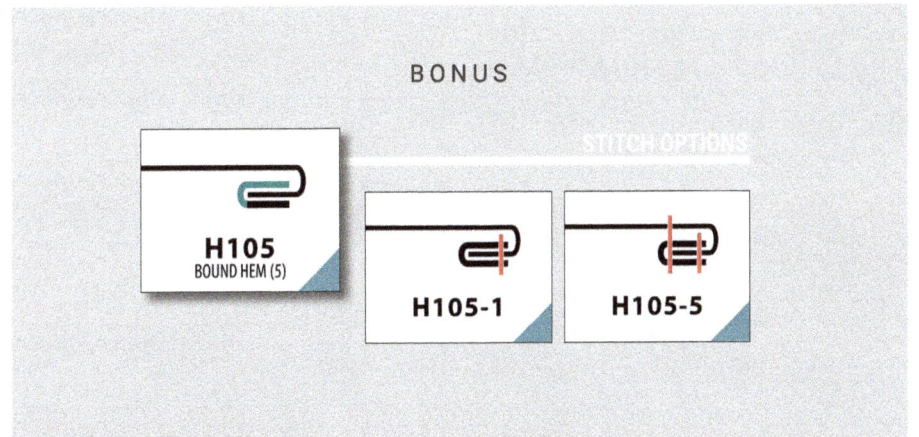

ABC Seams®

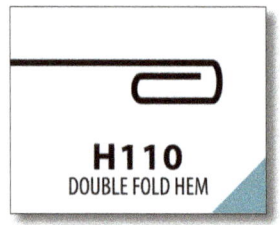

H110
DOUBLE FOLD HEM

MAIN PROPERTIES

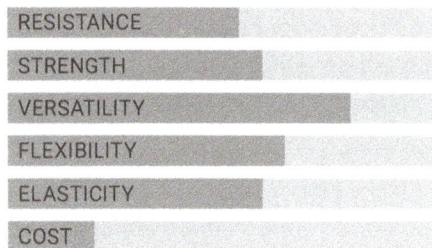

RESISTANCE
STRENGTH
VERSATILITY
FLEXIBILITY
ELASTICITY
COST

COMMON USES

- Mainly used on woven fabrics.
- Casual clothing.
- Bottoms of most types of woven products.
- Narrow plackets and slits.
- Pocket openings.
- Ruffles and flounces.
- Accessories and home decor products such as curtains.

ADDITIONAL NOTES

- Regular Hem Width: 1.2 cm (or 1/2"). If a wider hem is required, check group H130 (Double Fold Hem - WIDE).

3D VIEW

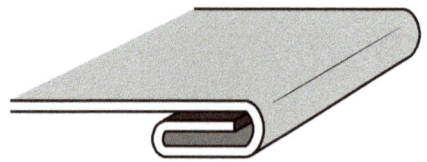

RELATED SEAMS

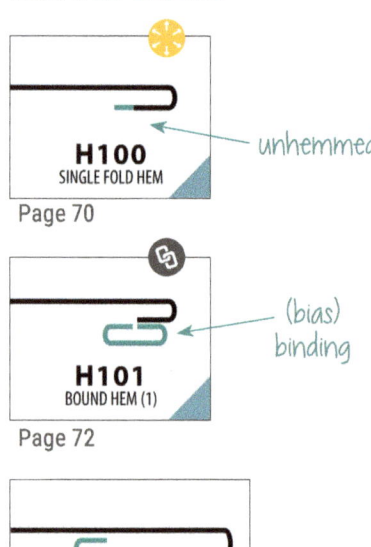

H100
SINGLE FOLD HEM — unhemmed
Page 70

H101
BOUND HEM (1) — (bias) binding
Page 72

H130
DOUBLE FOLD HEM - WIDE — wide
Page 88

Page | 76

Strong Seams

H110 DOUBLE FOLD HEM

STITCH OPTIONS

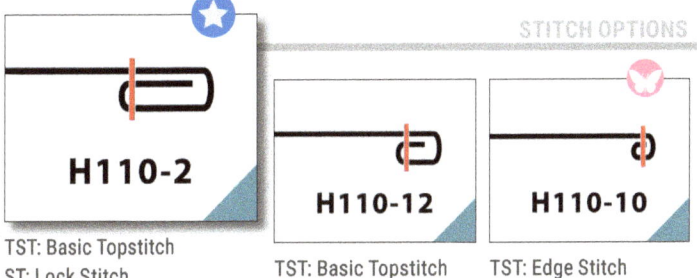

H110-2
TST: Basic Topstitch
ST: Lock Stitch

H110-12
TST: Basic Topstitch (narrow)
ST: Lock Stitch

H110-10
TST: Edge Stitch
ST: Lock Stitch

STITCH OPTIONS

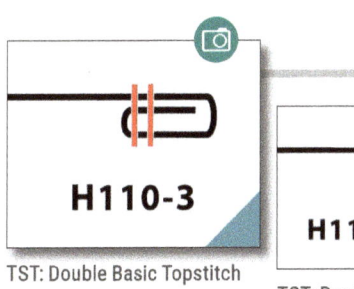

H110-3
TST: Double Basic Topstitch
ST: Lock Stitch

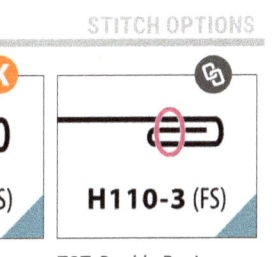

H110-3 (CS)
TST: Double Basic Topstitch
ST: Cover Stitch (2N)

H110-3 (FS)
TST: Double Basic Topstitch
ST: Flatlock Stitch (2N)

INSPIRATION

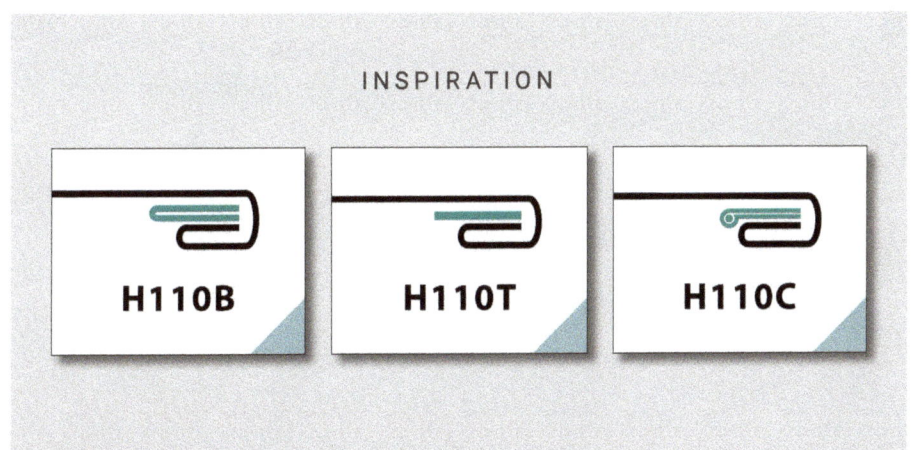

H110B

H110T

H110C

MAIN PROPERTIES

RESISTANCE
STRENGTH
VERSATILITY
FLEXIBILITY
ELASTICITY
COST

COMMON USES

- Lined garments.
- Reversible garments.
- Collar, lapel, and hood edges.
- Opening of side pockets and pocket bag edges.
- Keyhole cut-out edges.
- Bags, footwear, accessories, and home decor products.

ADDITIONAL NOTES

- A piece of interfacing might be needed to get the best result.

3D VIEW

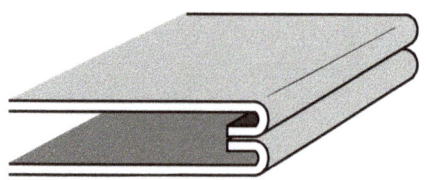

RELATED SEAMS

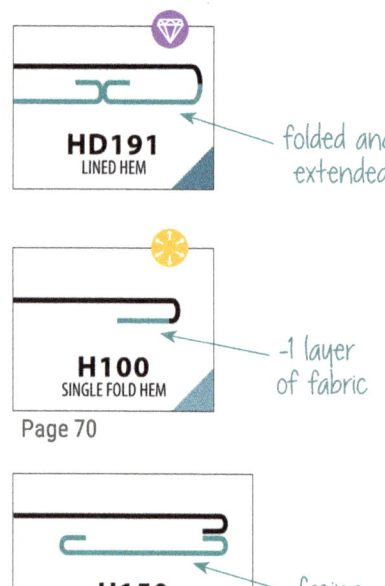

Page 70

Page 90

Strong Seams

HD190 — SANDWICH HEM

HD190-1
TST: Without Topstitch
ST: Lock Stitch

HD190-1 (OS)
TST: Without Topstitch
ST: Overlock

HD190-1 (OS4)
TST: Without Topstitch
ST: Overlock (4T)

HD190-2
TST: Without Topstitch + Understitch
ST: Lock Stitch

STITCH OPTIONS

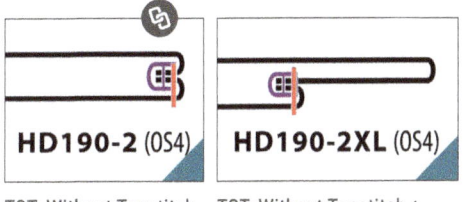

HD190-2 (OS4)
TST: Without Topstitch + Understitch
ST: Lock Stitch + Overlock (4T)

HD190-2XL (OS4)
TST: Without Topstitch + Understitch
ST: Lock Stitch + Overlock (4T)

STITCH OPTIONS

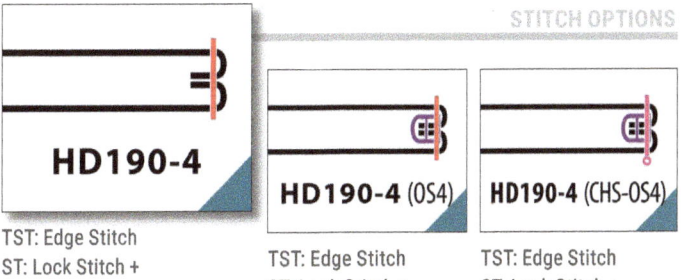

HD190-4
TST: Edge Stitch
ST: Lock Stitch +

HD190-4 (OS4)
TST: Edge Stitch
ST: Lock Stitch + Overlock (4T)

HD190-4 (CHS-OS4)
TST: Edge Stitch
ST: Lock Stitch + Overlock (4T)

Page | 79

ABC Seams®

HD190
SANDWICH HEM

STITCH OPTIONS

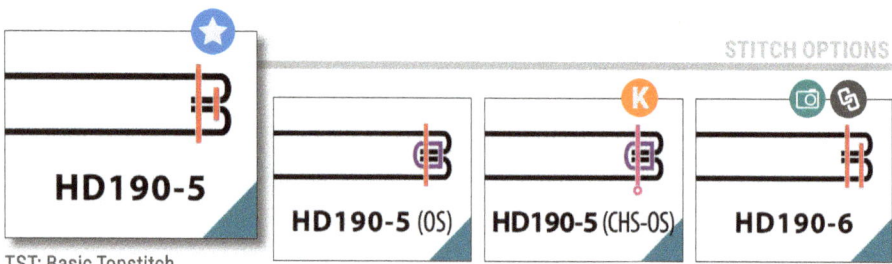

HD190-5
TST: Basic Topstitch
ST: Lock Stitch +

HD190-5 (OS)
TST: Basic Topstitch
ST: Lock Stitch +
Overlock

HD190-5 (CHS-OS)
TST: Basic Topstitch
ST: Chain Stitch +
Overlock

HD190-6
TST: Basic Topstitch +
Understitch
ST: Lock Stitch

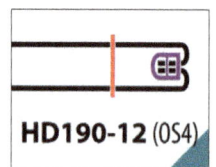

HD190-12 (OS4)
TST: Basic Topstitch
off Edge
ST: Lock Stitch +
Overlock (4T)

STITCH OPTIONS

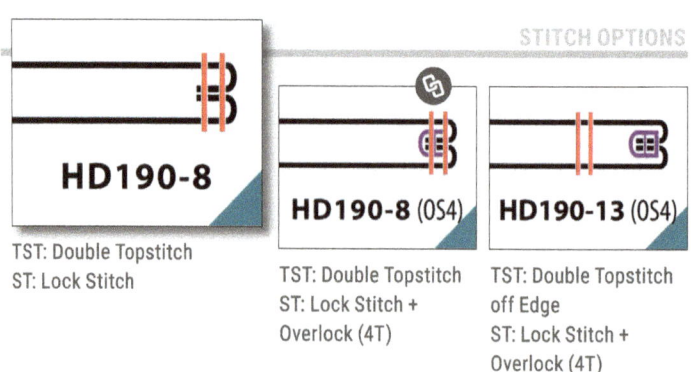

HD190-8
TST: Double Topstitch
ST: Lock Stitch

HD190-8 (OS4)
TST: Double Topstitch
ST: Lock Stitch +
Overlock (4T)

HD190-13 (OS4)
TST: Double Topstitch
off Edge
ST: Lock Stitch +
Overlock (4T)

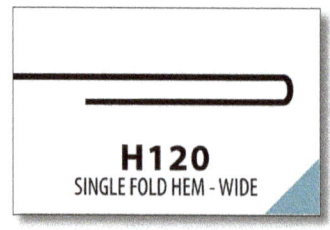

H120
SINGLE FOLD HEM - WIDE

MAIN PROPERTIES

RESISTANCE
STRENGTH
VERSATILITY
FLEXIBILITY
ELASTICITY
COST

COMMON USES

- Fabrics/materials that do not fray, such as fleece, velvet, vinyl, and leather.

- Casual clothing.

- Bottoms of skirts, pants, dresses, blouses, and outerwear.

- Bottom sleeves and plackets.

- Patch pocket openings.

- Bag openings, footwear such as boots, and home decor products.

- Upholstery.

ADDITIONAL NOTES

- Good option to avoid thickness when using heavy-weight fabrics.

- A piece of interfacing might be needed to get the best result.

3D VIEW

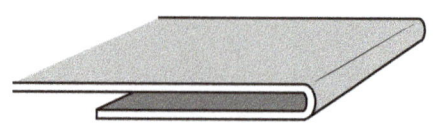

RELATED SEAMS

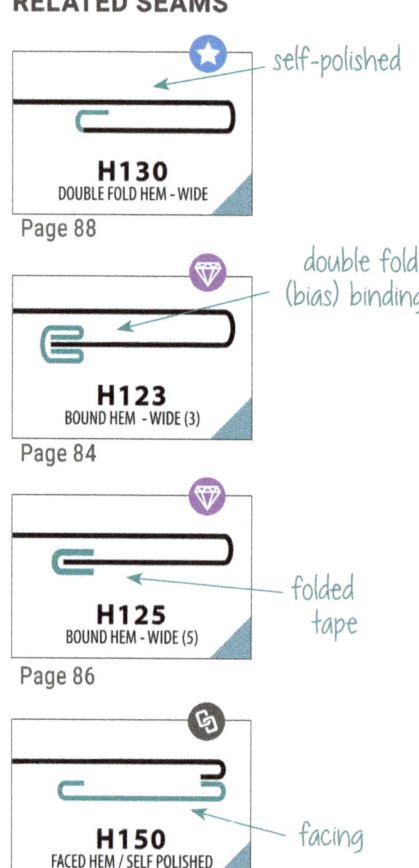

H130 — DOUBLE FOLD HEM - WIDE — Page 88 — *self-polished*

H123 — BOUND HEM - WIDE (3) — Page 84 — *double fold (bias) binding*

H125 — BOUND HEM - WIDE (5) — Page 86 — *folded tape*

H150 — FACED HEM / SELF POLISHED — Page 90 — *facing*

H100 — SINGLE FOLD HEM — Page 70 — *narrower*

Strong Seams

H120
SINGLE FOLD HEM - WIDE

STITCH OPTIONS

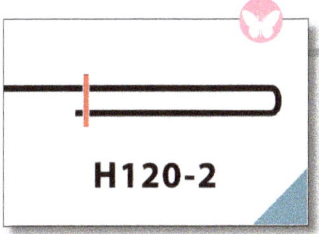

H120-2
TST: Basic Topstitch Off-edge
ST: Lock Stitch

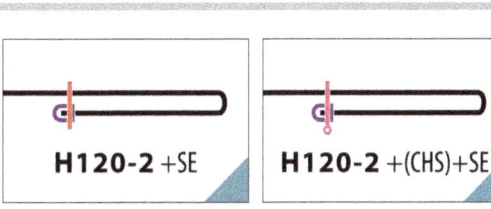

H120-2 +SE
TST: Basic Topstitch Off-edge
ST: Lock Stitch + Serged Edge

H120-2 +(CHS)+SE
TST: Basic Topstitch Off-edge
ST: Chain Stitch + Serged Edge

STITCH OPTIONS

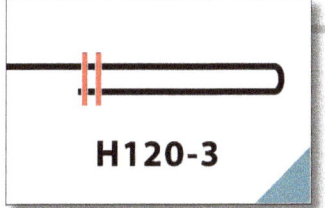

H120-3
TST: Double Topstitch Off-seam
ST: Lock Stitch (2N) + Serged Edge

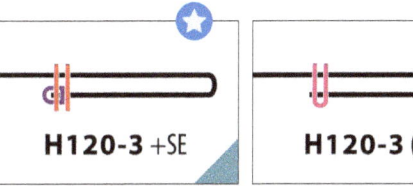

H120-3 +SE
TST: Double Topstitch Off-seam
ST: Lock Stitch (2N) + Serged Edge

H120-3 (CS)
TST: Double Topstitch Off-seam
ST: Cover Stitch (2N)

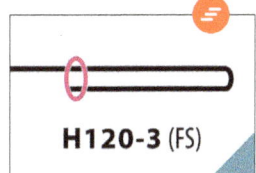

H120-3 (FS)
TST: Cover Topstitch Off-edge
ST: Flatlock Stitch (2N)

H120-7 +SE
TST: Double Topstitch Off-seam + Edge Stitch
ST: Lock Stitch + Serged Edge

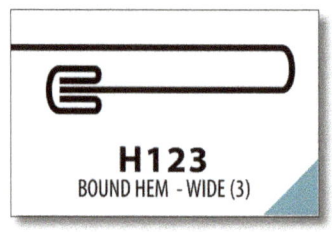

MAIN PROPERTIES

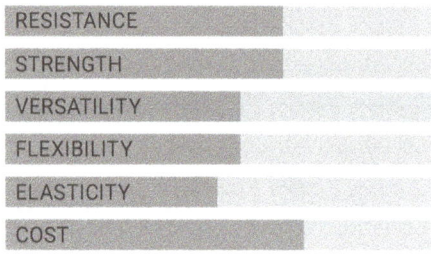

COMMON USES

- High-end quality garments.
- Mainly used on garments made of woven fabrics.
- Unlined garments.
- Hems of formal clothing such as blouses, dresses, skirts.
- Bottom sleeves of jackets.
- Plackets.

ADDITIONAL NOTES

- Good choice to add weight to the hem.
- Decorative finishing on the inside.
- A piece of interfacing might be needed to get the best result.
- Regular Binding Width (finished): 0.6 cm (or 1/4").

3D VIEW

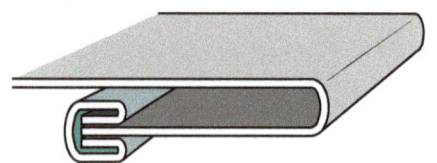

RELATED SEAMS

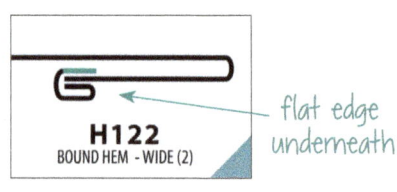
flat edge underneath

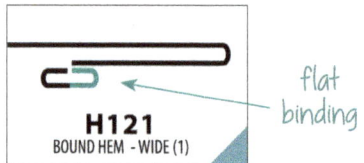
flat binding

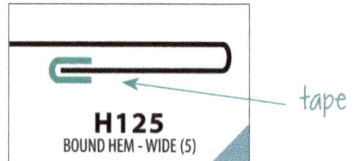
tape

Page 86

uncovered

Page 82

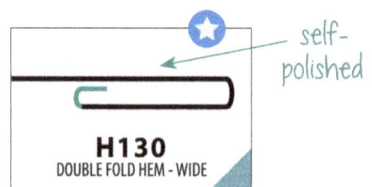
self-polished

Page 88

Strong Seams

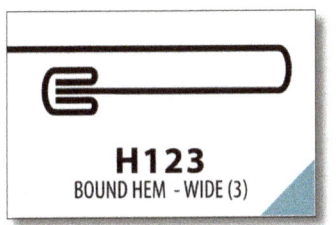

STITCH OPTIONS

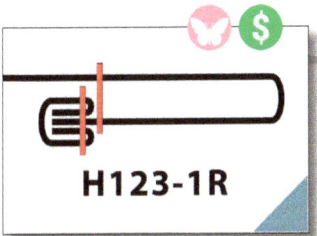

TST: Basic Topstitch Off-edge
ST: Lock Stitch

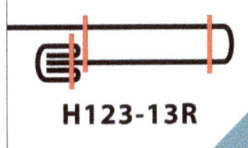

TST: Basic Topstitch
Off-edge + Basic Topstitch
ST: Lock Stitch

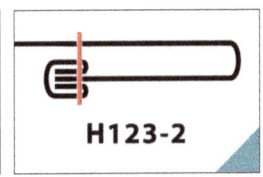

TST: Basic Topstitch
Off-edge
ST: Lock Stitch

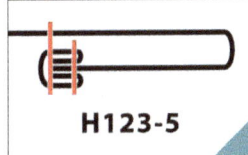

TST: Basic Topstitch
Off-edge
ST: Lock Stitch

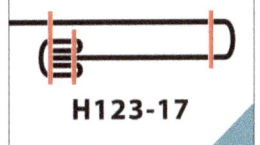

TST: Basic Topstitch
Off-edge + Basic Topstitch
ST: Lock Stitch

STITCH OPTIONS

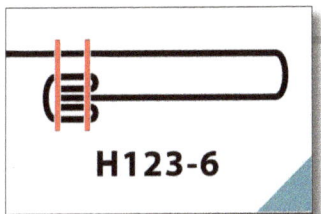

TST: Double Topstitch Off-edge
ST: Lock Stitch

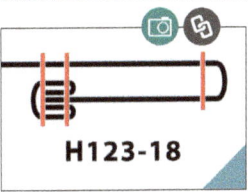

TST: Double Topstitch
Off-edge + Basic Topstitch
ST: Lock Stitch

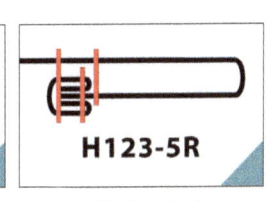

TST: Double Topstitch
Off-edge
ST: Lock Stitch

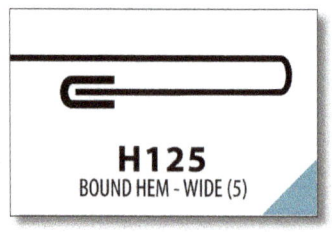

H125
BOUND HEM - WIDE (5)

MAIN PROPERTIES

- RESISTANCE
- STRENGTH
- VERSATILITY
- FLEXIBILITY
- ELASTICITY
- COST

COMMON USES

- Medium to heavy-weight fabrics.
- High-end quality garments.
- Unlined garments.
- Hems of formal clothing such as skirts.
- Bottom sleeves of jackets.
- Plackets.
- Bags, accessories, and home decor products.
- Upholstery.

ADDITIONAL NOTES

- Decorative finishing on the inside.
- A piece of interfacing might be needed to get the best result.
- Regular Tape Width (finished): 0.6 cm (or 1/4").

3D VIEW

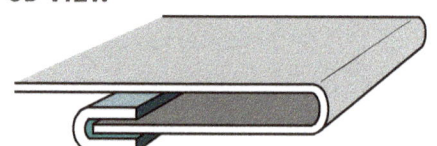

RELATED SEAMS

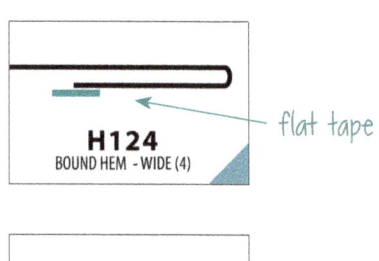

H124 — BOUND HEM - WIDE (4) — flat tape

H123 — BOUND HEM - WIDE (3) — (bias) binding
Page 84

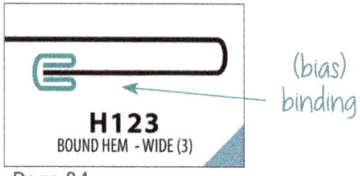

H120 — SINGLE FOLD HEM - WIDE — uncovered
Page 82

H130 — DOUBLE FOLD HEM - WIDE — self-polished
Page 88

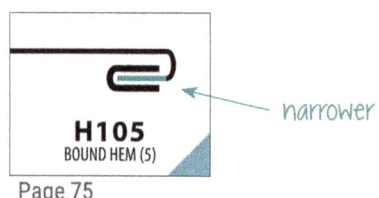

H105 — BOUND HEM (5) — narrower
Page 75

Strong Seams

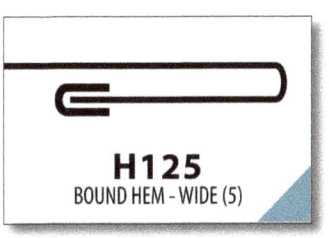

STITCH OPTIONS

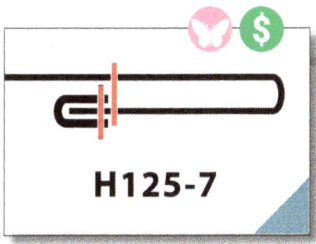

TST: Basic Topstitch Off-edge
ST: Lock Stitch

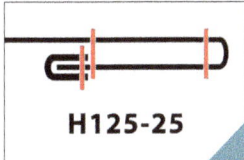

TST: Basic Topstitch Off-edge + Basic Topstitch
ST: Lock Stitch

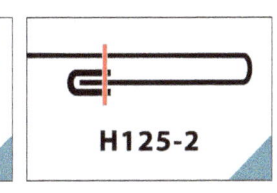

TST: Basic Topstitch Off-edge
ST: Lock Stitch

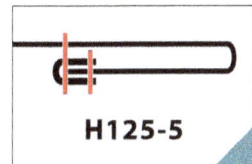

TST: Basic Topstitch Off-edge
ST: Lock Stitch

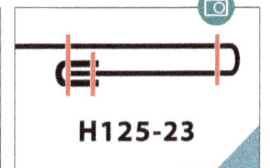

TST: Basic Topstitch Off-edge + Basic Topstitch
ST: Lock Stitch

STITCH OPTIONS

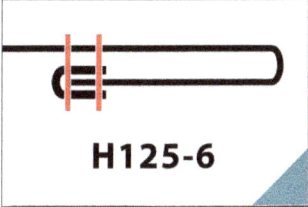

TST: Double Topstitch Off-edge
ST: Lock Stitch

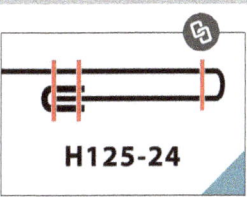

TST: Double Topstitch Off-edge + Basic Topstitch
ST: Lock Stitch

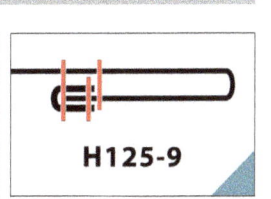

TST: Double Topstitch Off-edge
ST: Lock Stitch

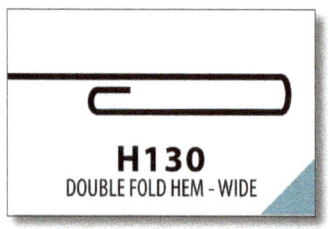

H130
DOUBLE FOLD HEM - WIDE

MAIN PROPERTIES

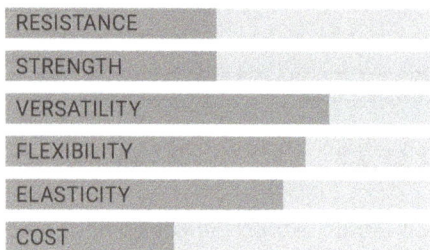

RESISTANCE
STRENGTH
VERSATILITY
FLEXIBILITY
ELASTICITY
COST

COMMON USES

- Mainly used on garments made of woven fabrics.

- Bottoms of pants, blouses, dresses, and outerwear.

- Sleeve hems of unlined jackets.

- Plackets of shirts and outerwear.

- Slits and back vents of blazers.

- Pocket openings.

- Home décor products such as curtains and bedsheets.

ADDITIONAL NOTES

- It works better on straight or slightly curved edges.

- A piece of interfacing might be needed to get the best result.

3D VIEW

RELATED SEAMS

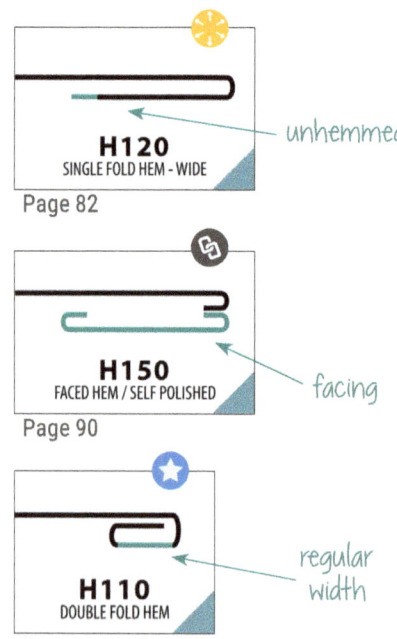

H120 SINGLE FOLD HEM - WIDE — unhemmed
Page 82

H150 FACED HEM / SELF POLISHED — facing
Page 90

H110 DOUBLE FOLD HEM — regular width
Page 76

Strong Seams

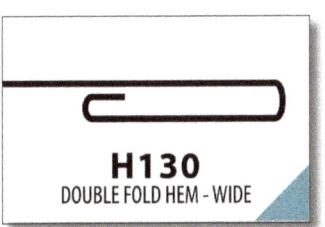

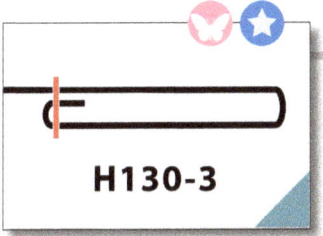

TST: Basic Topstitch Off-edge
ST: Lock Stitch

STITCH OPTIONS

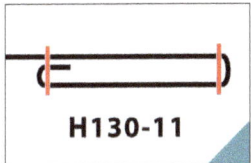

TST: Basic Topstitch
Off-edge + Edge Stitch
ST: Lock Stitch

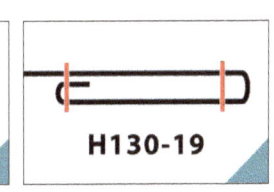

TST: Basic Topstitch
Off-edge + Basic Topstitch
ST: Lock Stitch

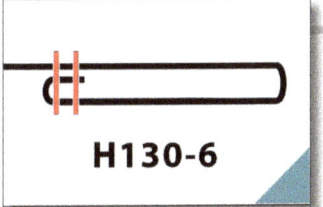

TST: Double Topstitch Off-edge
ST: Lock Stitch

STITCH OPTIONS

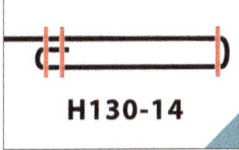

TST: Double Topstitch
Off-edge + Edge Stitc
ST: Lock Stitch

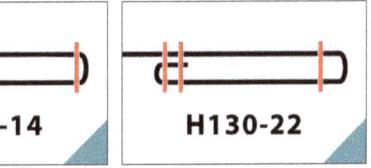

TST: Double Topstitch
Off-edge + Basic Topstitch
ST: Lock Stitch

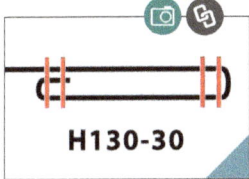

TST: Double Topstitch
Off-edge + Double Topstitch
ST: Lock Stitch

H150
FACED HEM / SELF POLISHED

MAIN PROPERTIES

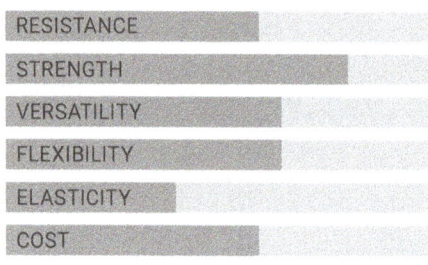

RESISTANCE
STRENGTH
VERSATILITY
FLEXIBILITY
ELASTICITY
COST

COMMON USES

- Unlined clothing.
- Curved and bias-cut edges.
- Bottoms in general.
- Necklines of tops and dresses.
- Armholes of sleeveless tops and dresses.
- Plackets of tops, pants, and outerwear.
- Cuffs and cuff vents.
- Waistband of skirts and formal pants.
- Pocket opening.
- Bags, accessories, and home decor.

ADDITIONAL NOTES

- A piece of interfacing might be needed.
- Reversible Seam (exposed): The backside can be used as the right side.

3D VIEW

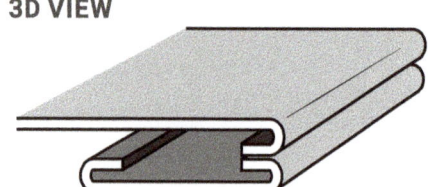

RELATED SEAMS

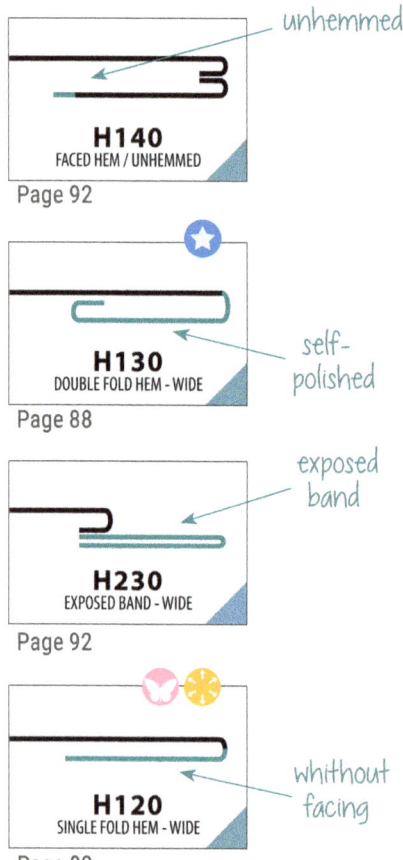

H140
FACED HEM / UNHEMMED
Page 92
— unhemmed

H130
DOUBLE FOLD HEM - WIDE
Page 88
— self-polished

H230
EXPOSED BAND - WIDE
Page 92
— exposed band

H120
SINGLE FOLD HEM - WIDE
Page 82
— whithout facing

H101
BOUND HEM (1)
Page 72
— narrower
— (bias) binding

Strong Seams

H150 — FACED HEM / SELF POLISHED

STITCH OPTIONS

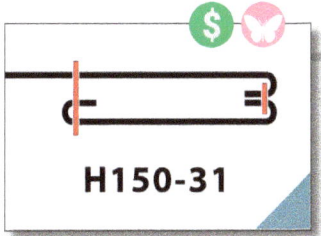

H150-31
TST: Basic Topstitch Off-edge
ST: Lock Stitch

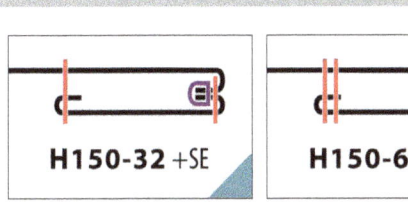

H150-32 +SE
TST: Basic Topstitch Off-edge + Understitch
ST: Lock Stitch + Serged Edge

H150-62 +SE
TST: Double Topstitch Off-edge + Understitch
ST: Lock Stitch + Serged Edge

STITCH OPTIONS

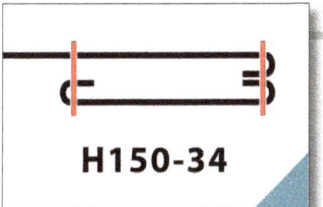

H150-34
TST: Basic Topstitch Off-edge + Edge Stitch
ST: Lock Stitch

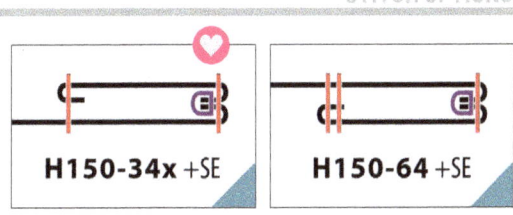

H150-34x +SE
TST: Basic Topstitch Off-edge + Edge Stitch
ST: Lock Stitch + Serged Edge

H150-64 +SE
TST: Double Topstitch Off-edge + Edge Stitch
ST: Lock Stitch + Serged Edge

STITCH OPTIONS

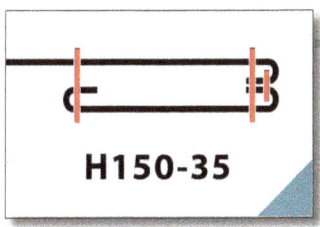

H150-35
TST: Basic Topstitch Off-edge + Basic Topstitch
ST: Lock Stitch

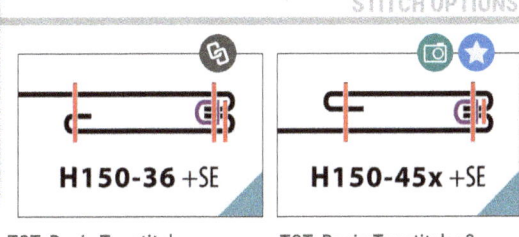

H150-36 +SE
TST: Basic Topstitch Off-edge + Basic Topstitch + Understitch
ST: Lock Stitch + Serged Edge

H150-45x +SE
TST: Basic Topstitch x2 (each edge)
ST: Lock Stitch + Serged Edge

ABC Seams®

H150
FACED HEM / SELF POLISHED

BONUS

H140
FACED HEM / UNHEMMED

STITCH OPTIONS

H140-5 +SE

H140-12 +SE

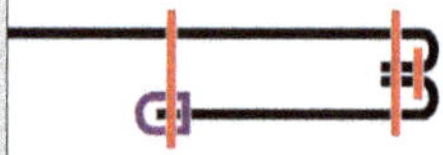

H140-15 +SE

H140-21 (CS-OS4)

H230
EXPOSED BAND - WIDE

STITCH OPTIONS

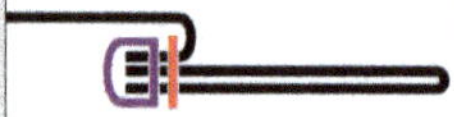

H230-1 +SE

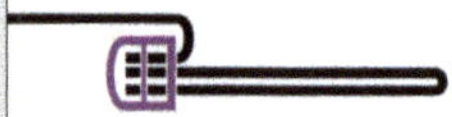

H230-1 (OS4)

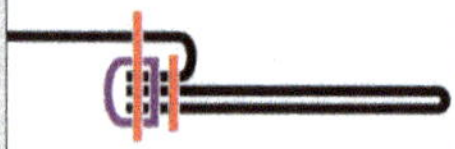

H230-3 +SE

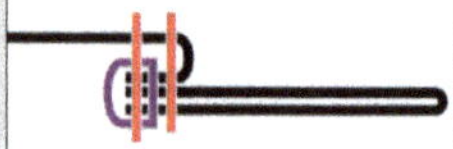

H230-4 +SE

Strong Seams

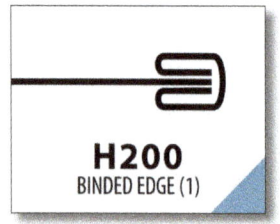

MAIN PROPERTIES

RESISTANCE
STRENGTH
VERSATILITY
FLEXIBILITY
ELASTICITY
COST

COMMON USES

- Casual clothing and sportswear.
- Lingerie and swimsuits.
- Curved and bias-cut edges.
- Edges with decorative trimming.
- Necklines.
- Narrow plackets.
- Cuffs and cuff slits.
- Keyhole cut-out edges.
- Bags, footwear, accessories such as hats, and home decor products.

ADDITIONAL NOTES

- Ideal for edges that need stability and stretching resistance.
- Regular Binding Width (finished): 0.6 cm (or 1/4").

3D VIEW

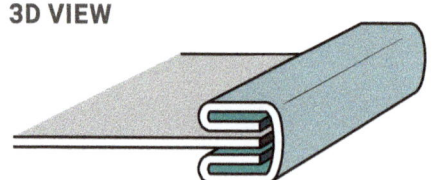

RELATED SEAMS

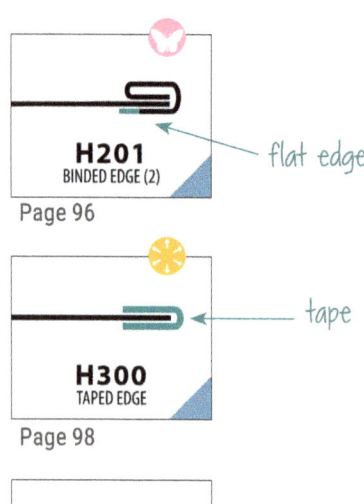

Strong Seams

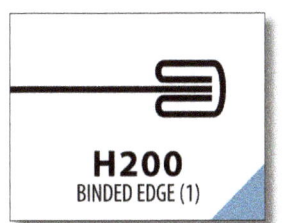

H200 BINDED EDGE (1)

STITCH OPTIONS

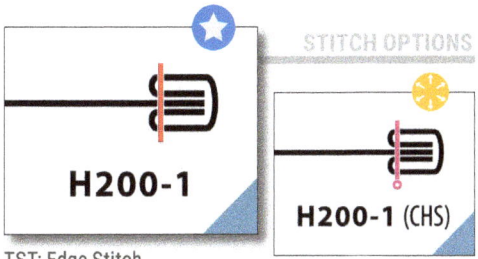

H200-1
TST: Edge Stitch
ST: Lock Stitch

H200-1 (CHS)
TST: Edge Stitch
ST: Chain Stitch

STITCH OPTIONS

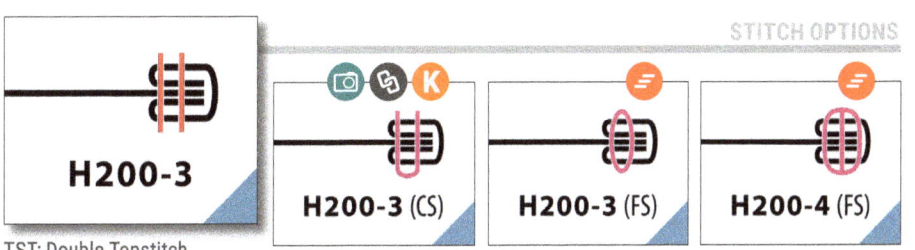

H200-3
TST: Double Topstitch
ST: Lock Stitch

H200-3 (CS)
TST: Double Topstitch
ST: Cover Stitch (2N)

H200-3 (FS)
TST: Cover Topstitch
ST: Flatlock Stitch (2N)

H200-4 (FS)
TST: Cover Topstitch
ST: Flatlock Stitch (3N)

BONUS

STITCH OPTIONS

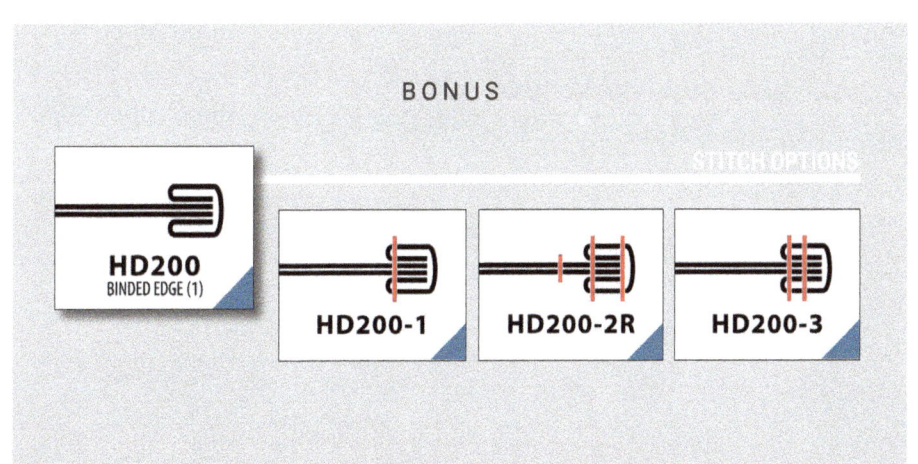

HD200 BINDED EDGE (1)

HD200-1

HD200-2R

HD200-3

Page | 95

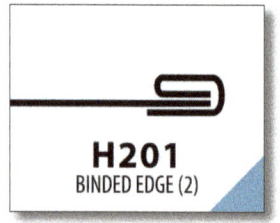

MAIN PROPERTIES

RESISTANCE
STRENGTH
VERSATILITY
FLEXIBILITY
ELASTICITY
COST

COMMON USES

- Mostly used on woven fabrics.
- Medium to heavy-weight fabrics.
- Edges with decorative trimming.
- Curved and bias-cut edges.
- Bags, accessories like wallets, footwear, and home decor products.
- Upholstery.

ADDITIONAL NOTES

- The binding should be made of a material/fabric that does not fray.
- Regular Binding Width (finished): 0.6 cm (or 1/4").

3D VIEW

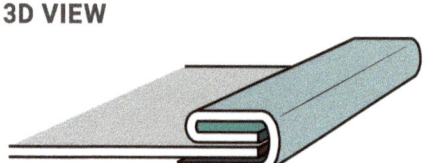

RELATED SEAMS

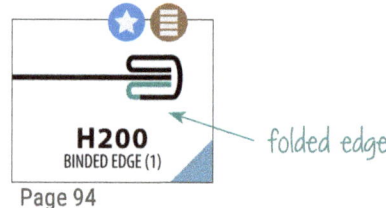
← folded edge

Page 94

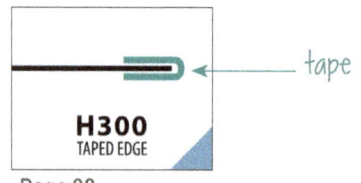
← tape

Page 98

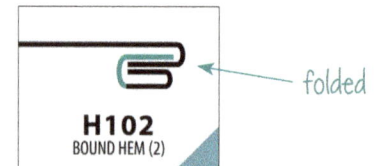
← folded

Strong Seams

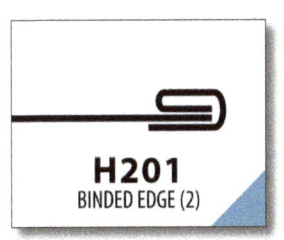

H201 BINDED EDGE (2)

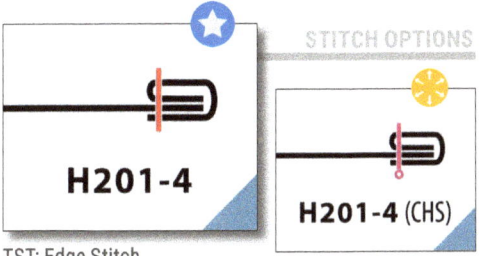

H201-4
TST: Edge Stitch
ST: Lock Stitch

H201-4 (CHS)
TST: Edge Stitch
ST: Chain Stitch

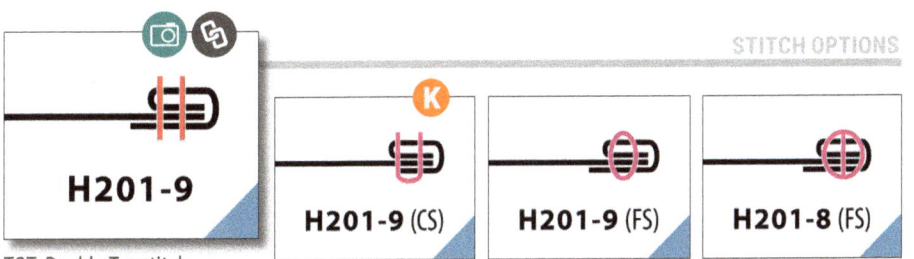

H201-9
TST: Double Topstitch
ST: Lock Stitch

H201-9 (CS)
TST: Double Topstitch
ST: Cover Stitch (2N)

H201-9 (FS)
TST: Cover Topstitch
ST: Flatlock Stitch (2N)

H201-8 (FS)
TST: Cover Topstitch
ST: Flatlock Stitch (3N)

BONUS

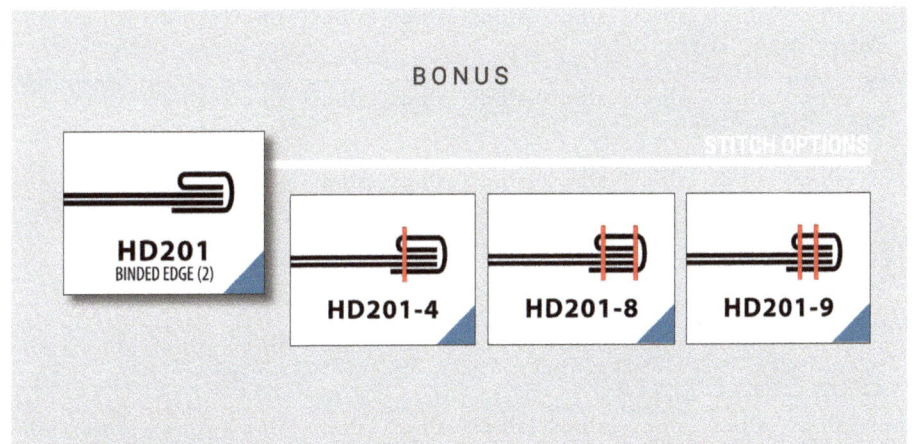

HD201 BINDED EDGE (2)

HD201-4

HD201-8

HD201-9

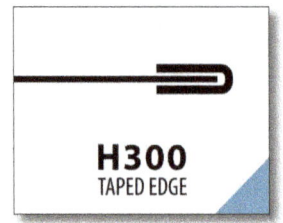

MAIN PROPERTIES

| RESISTANCE |
| STRENGTH |
| VERSATILITY |
| FLEXIBILITY |
| ELASTICITY |
| COST |

COMMON USES

- Ideal for heavy-weight fabrics.
- Ideal for heavy-weight fabrics.
- Straight or slightly curved edges.
- Lingerie and swimsuits.
- Plackets and slits.
- Edges with decorative trimming.
- Bags, footwear, accessories like wallets, and home decor products.
- Upholstery.

ADDITIONAL NOTES

- Good option to avoid thickness when using heavy-weight fabrics.
- Regular Tape Width (finished): 0.6 cm (or 1/4").

3D VIEW

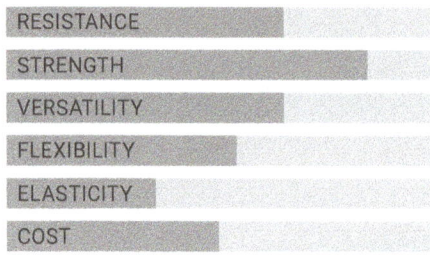

RELATED SEAMS

H200 BINDED EDGE (1) ← (bias) binding
Page 94

H105 BOUND HEM (5) ← folded
Page 75

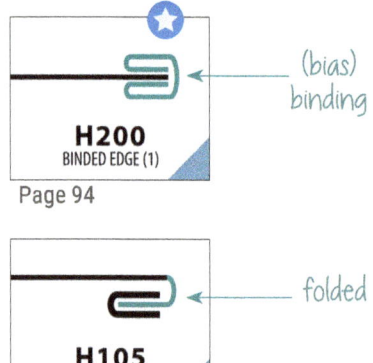

Strong Seams

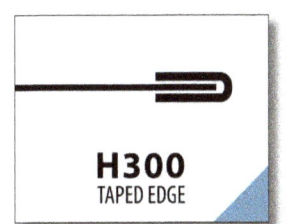

H300 — TAPED EDGE

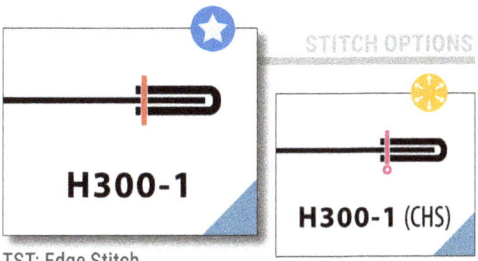

H300-1
TST: Edge Stitch
ST: Lock Stitch

H300-1 (CHS)
TST: Edge Stitch
ST: Chain Stitch

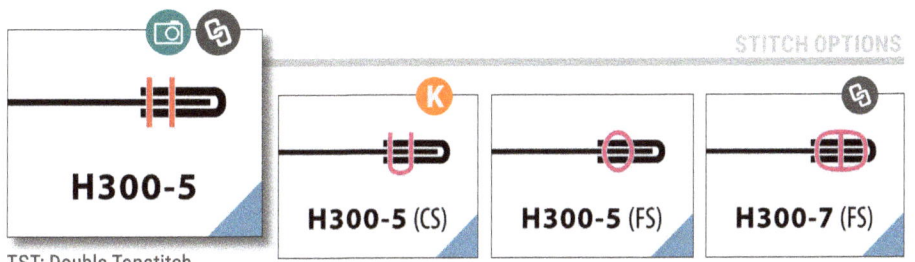

H300-5
TST: Double Topstitch
ST: Lock Stitch

H300-5 (CS)
TST: Double Topstitch
ST: Cover Stitch (2N)

H300-5 (FS)
TST: Double Topstitch
ST: Flatlock Stitch (2N)

H300-7 (FS)
TST: Double Topstitch
ST: Flatlock Stitch (3N)

BONUS

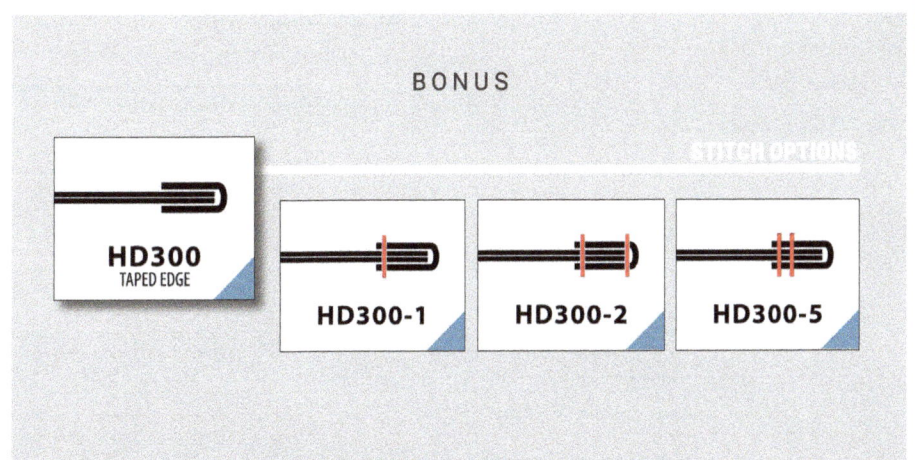

HD300 — TAPED EDGE

HD300-1

HD300-2

HD300-5

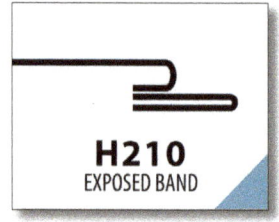

MAIN PROPERTIES

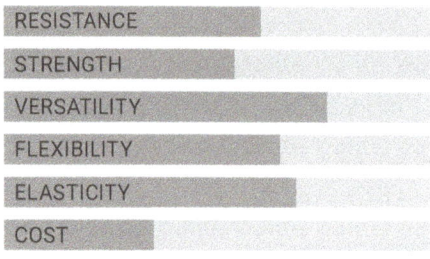

COMMON USES

- Widely used on garments made of knit fabrics.
- Casual clothing.
- Curved and bias-cut edges.
- Necklines of tops and dresses.
- Armhole of sleeveless garments.
- Cuffs of shirts and blouses.
- Waistbands with an elastic band.

ADDITIONAL NOTES

- The band stabilizes the edge.
- When sewing curved edges, it works better to use a bias-cut band.

3D VIEW

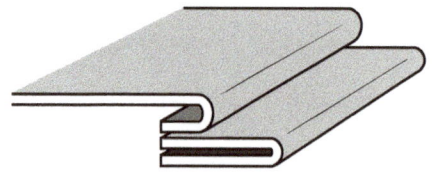

RELATED SEAMS

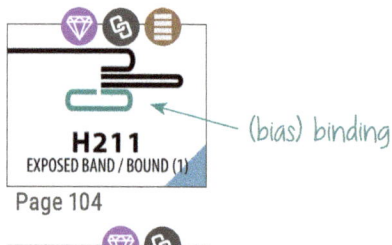

Page 104

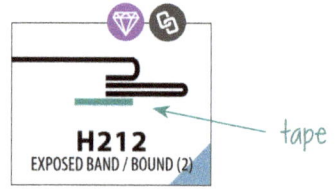

Page 106

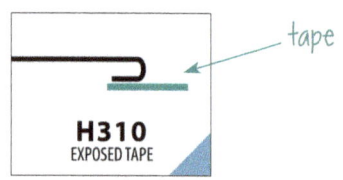

Page 102

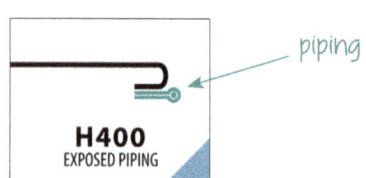

Page 102

Strong Seams

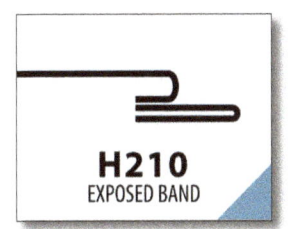

H210 EXPOSED BAND

STITCH OPTIONS

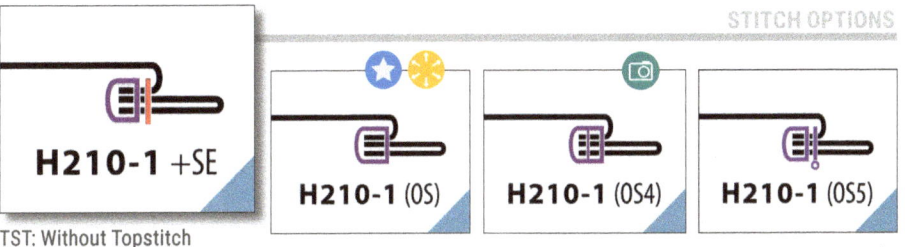

H210-1 +SE
TST: Without Topstitch
ST: Lock Stitch + Serged Edge

H210-1 (OS)
TST: Without Topstitch
ST: Overlock (3T)

H210-1 (OS4)
TST: Without Topstitch
ST: Overlock (4T)

H210-1 (OS5)
TST: Without Topstitch
ST: Overlock (5T)

STITCH OPTIONS

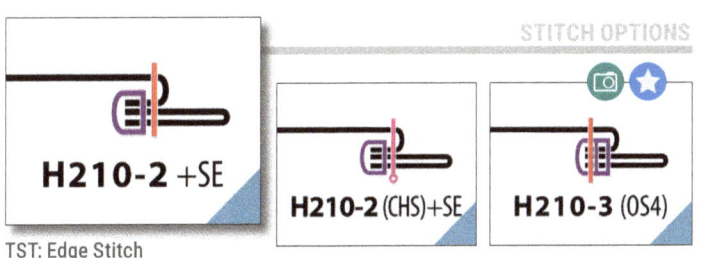

H210-2 +SE
TST: Edge Stitch
ST: Lock Stitch + Serged Edge

H210-2 (CHS)+SE
TST: Edge Stitch
ST: Chain Stitch + Serged Edge

H210-3 (OS4)
TST: Basic Topstitch
ST: Lock Stitch + Overlock (4T)

STITCH OPTIONS

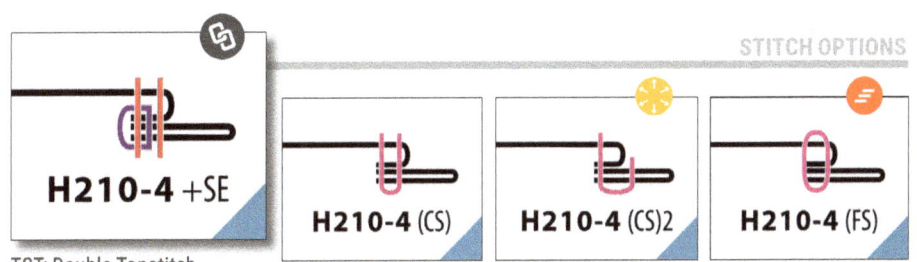

H210-4 +SE
TST: Double Topstitch
ST: Lock Stitch + Serged Edge

H210-4 (CS)
TST: Double Topstitch
ST: Cover Stitch (2N)

H210-4 (CS)2
TST: Double Topstitch
ST: Cover Stitch (2N)

H210-4 (FS)
TST: Cover Topstitch
ST: Flatlock Stitch (2N)

ABC Seams®

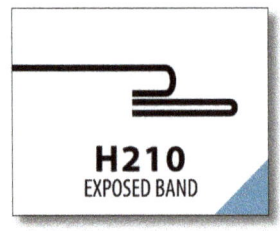

H210
EXPOSED BAND

BONUS

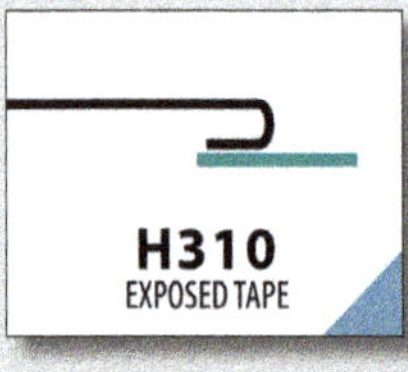

H310
EXPOSED TAPE

STITCH OPTIONS

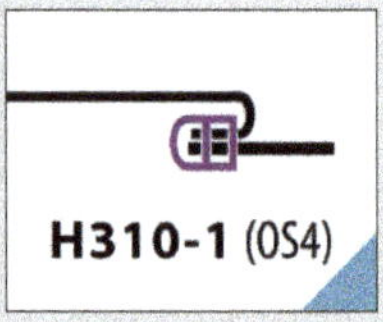

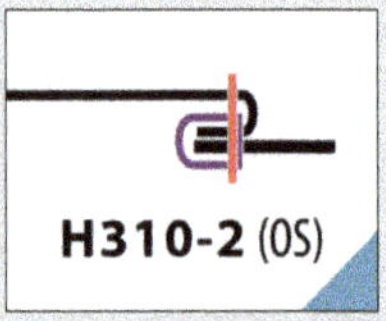

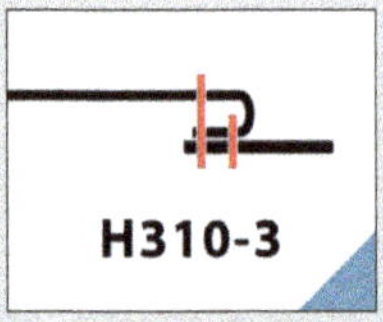

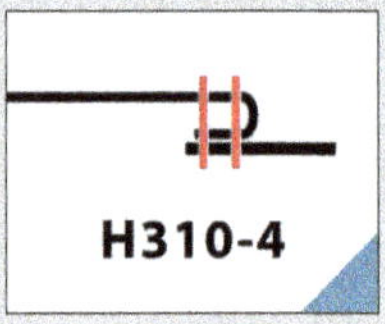

H310-1 (OS4) **H310-2** (OS) **H310-3**

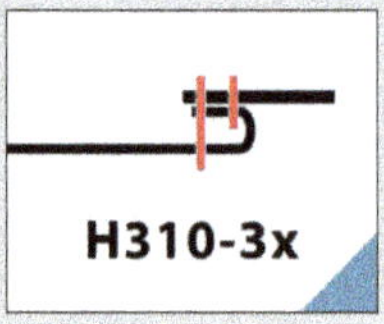

H310-3x **H310-4**

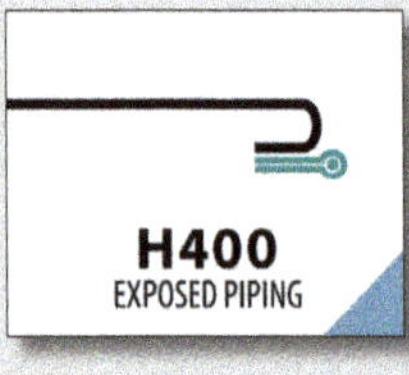

H400
EXPOSED PIPING

STITCH OPTIONS

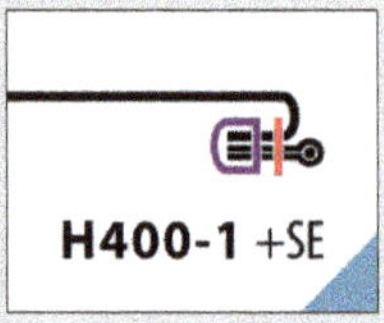

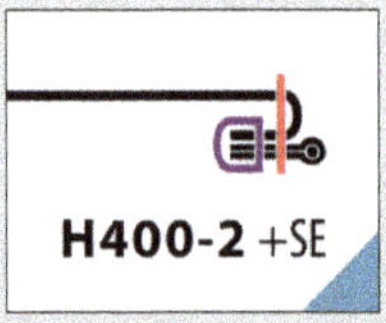

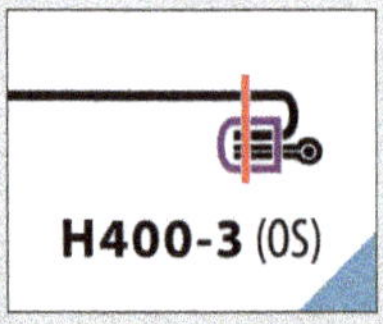

H400-1 +SE **H400-2** +SE **H400-3** (OS)

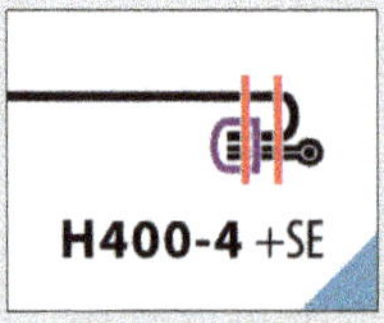

H400-4 +SE

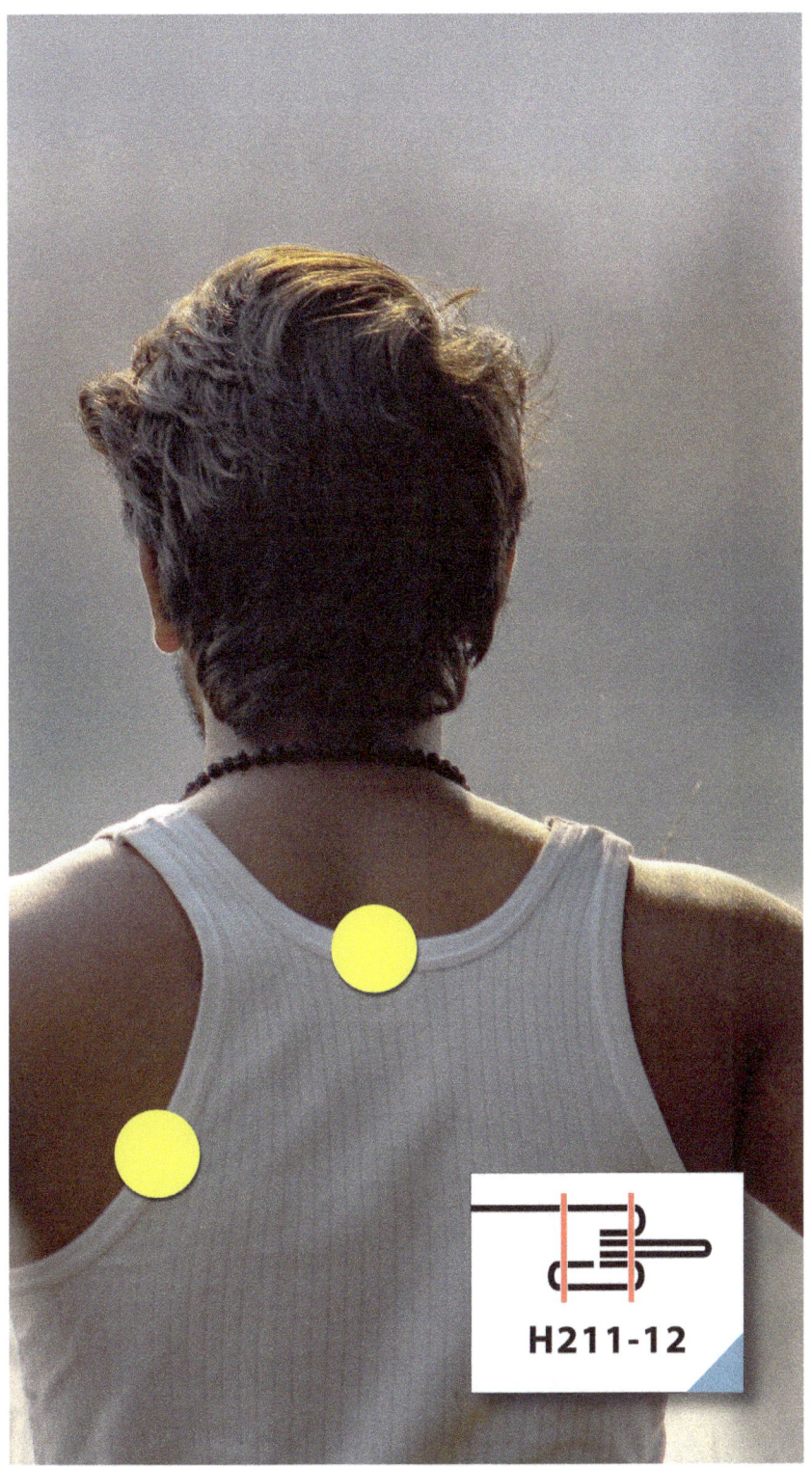

ABC Seams®

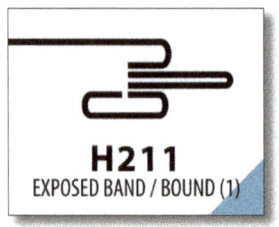

H211
EXPOSED BAND / BOUND (1)

MAIN PROPERTIES

RESISTANCE	
STRENGTH	
VERSATILITY	
FLEXIBILITY	
ELASTICITY	
COST	

COMMON USES

- Curved and bias-cut edges.
- Back neckline of t-shirts.
- Armhole of sleeveless garments.
- Sleeve hems of shirts and blouses.
- Cuffs and bottoms.
- Edges with decorative trimming.

ADDITIONAL NOTES

- Excellent stretch resistance

- It could be too bulky and stiff if using heavy-weight fabrics.

- Reversible Seam (exposed): The backside can be used as the right side.

- Regular Binding Width: 1.2 cm (or 1/2").

3D VIEW

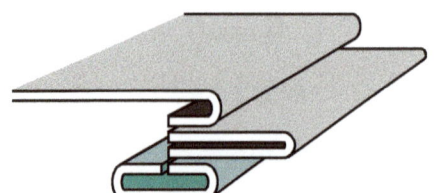

RELATED SEAMS

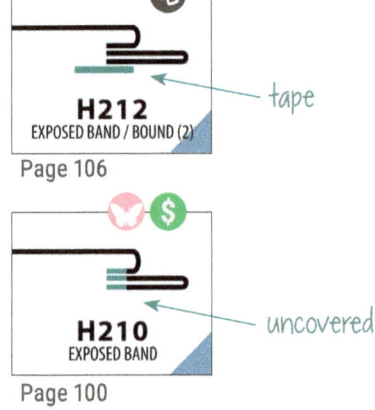

Page 106

Page 100

Strong Seams

H211
EXPOSED BAND / BOUND (1)

STITCH OPTIONS

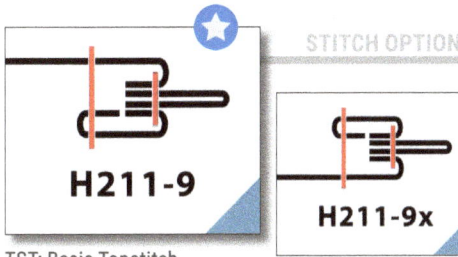

H211-9
TST: Basic Topstitch
ST: Lock Stitch

H211-9x
TST: Edge Stitch
ST: Lock Stitch

STITCH OPTIONS

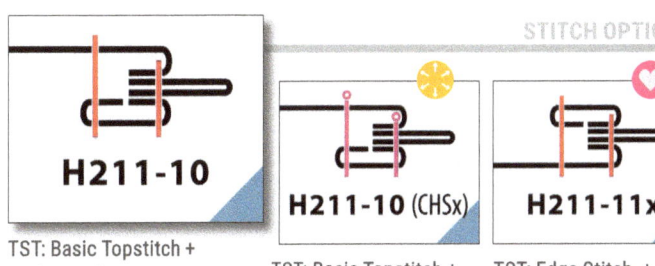

H211-10
TST: Basic Topstitch + Understitch
ST: Lock Stitch

H211-10 (CHSx)
TST: Basic Topstitch + Understitch
ST: Exposed Chain Stitch

H211-11x
TST: Edge Stitch + Understitch
ST: Lock Stitch

STITCH OPTIONS

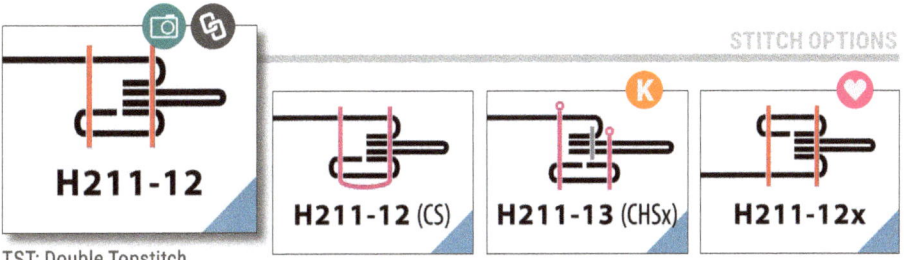

H211-12
TST: Double Topstitch
ST: Lock Stitch

H211-12 (CS)
TST: Double Topstitch
ST: Cover Stitch (2N)

H211-13 (CHSx)
TST: Double Topstitch
ST: Exposed Chain Stitch

H211-12x
TST: Double Edge Stitch
ST: Lock Stitch

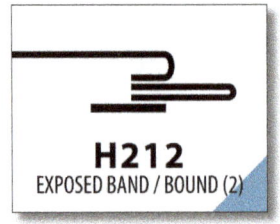

H212
EXPOSED BAND / BOUND (2)

MAIN PROPERTIES

- RESISTANCE
- STRENGTH
- VERSATILITY
- FLEXIBILITY
- ELASTICITY
- COST

COMMON USES

- Straight edges or slightly curved.
- Back necklines of t-shirts.
- Sleeve hems of shirts and blouses.
- Cuffs and bottoms made of rib.
- Edges with decorative trimming.
- Bags and footwear.

ADDITIONAL NOTES

- The band and the tape underneath stabilize the edge and strengthen it.
- Reversible Seam (exposed): The backside can be used as the right side.
- Regular Tape Width: 1.2 cm (or 1/2").

3D VIEW

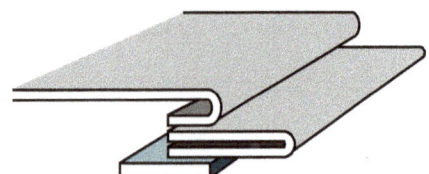

RELATED SEAMS

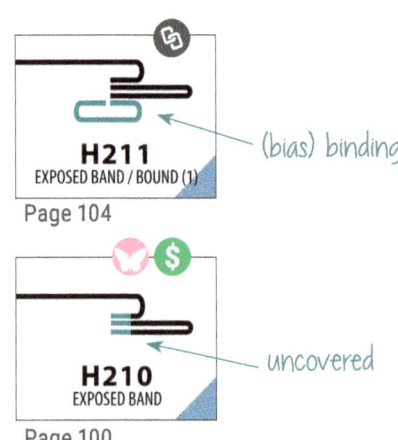

H211 — EXPOSED BAND / BOUND (1) — Page 104 — (bias) binding

H210 — EXPOSED BAND — Page 100 — uncovered

Strong Seams

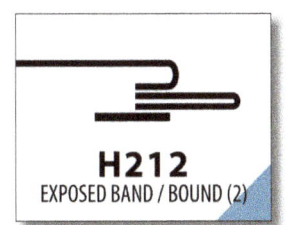

H212 EXPOSED BAND / BOUND (2)

STITCH OPTIONS

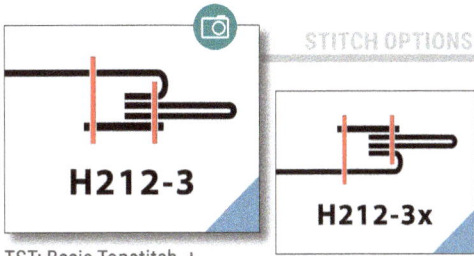

H212-3
TST: Basic Topstitch + Understitch
ST: Lock Stitch

H212-3x
TST: Double Edge Stitch
ST: Lock Stitch

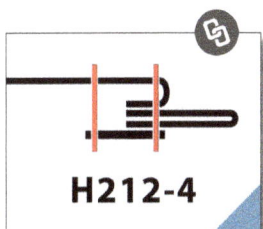

H212-4
TST: Double Topstitch
ST: Lock Stitch

STITCH OPTIONS

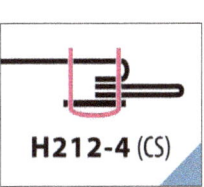

H212-4 (CHS)
TST: Double Topstitch
ST: Chain Stitch

H212-4 (CS)
TST: Double Topstitch
ST: Cover Stitch (2N)

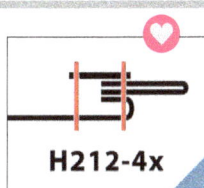

H212-4x
TST: Double Edge Stitch
ST: Lock Stitch

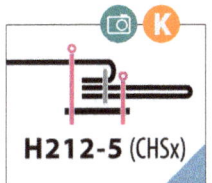

H212-5 (CHSx)
TST: Double Topstitch
ST: Exposed Chain Stitch

MY NOTES
FINISHES

Strong Seams

MY SAMPLES
FINISHES

GLUE	GLUE

GLUE	GLUE

GLUE	GLUE

DETAILS

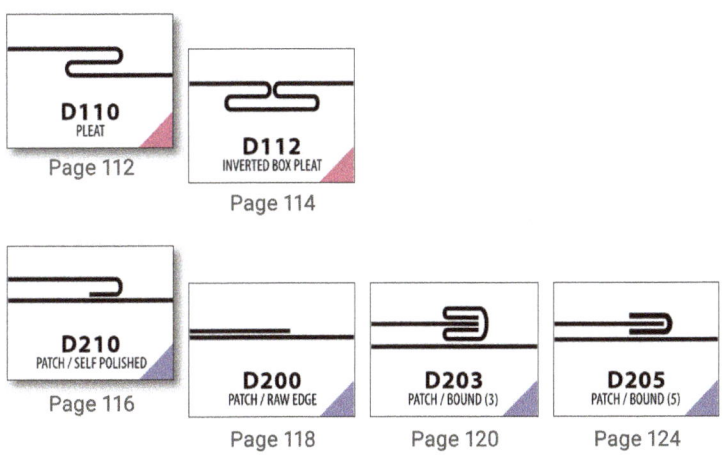

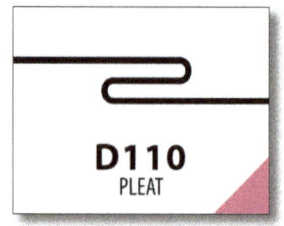

MAIN PROPERTIES

RESISTANCE
STRENGTH
VERSATILITY
FLEXIBILITY
ELASTICITY
COST

COMMON USES

- Widely used on woven garments.

- Commonly used on waist, hip, and bust areas of women's clothing.

- Children wear.

- Cuff seam of shirts and blouses.

- Back yoke of shirts, blouses, and outerwear (especially for men's clothing).

- Inner back of lined outerwear.

- Accessories such as bags and hats.

ADDITIONAL NOTES

- When it is open, it gives volume to the garment. And when it is closed, it reduces its volume.

3D VIEW

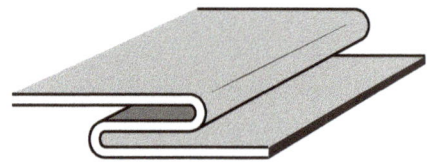

RELATED SEAMS

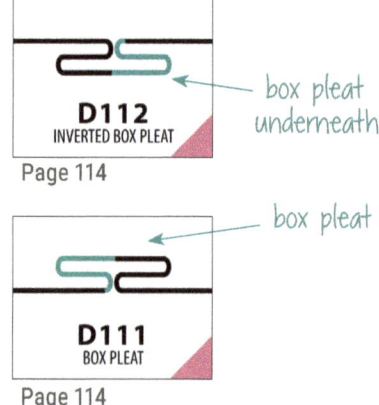
Page 114

Page 114

Strong Seams

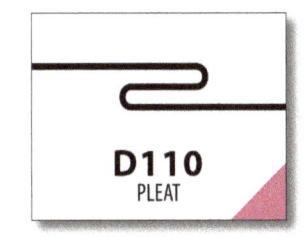

D110
PLEAT

STITCH OPTIONS

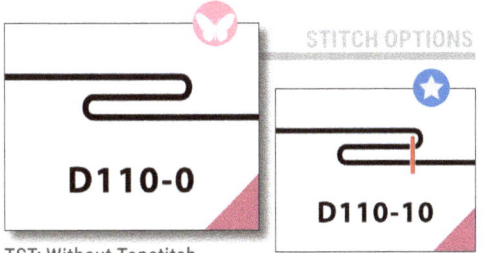

D110-0
TST: Without Topstitch
ST: - - -

D110-10
TST: Without Topstitch
ST: Lock Stitch

STITCH OPTIONS

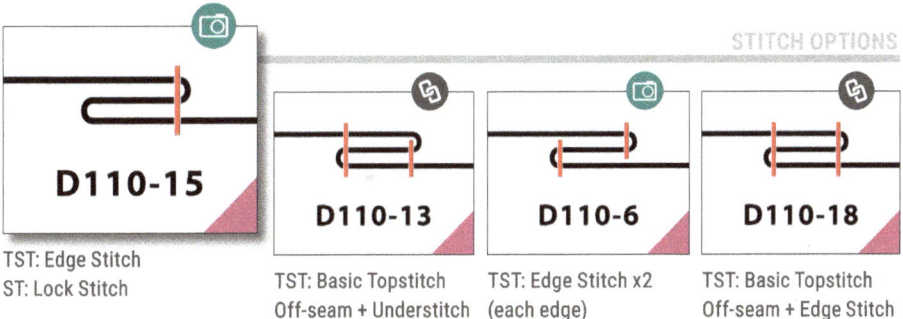

D110-15
TST: Edge Stitch
ST: Lock Stitch

D110-13
TST: Basic Topstitch
Off-seam + Understitch
ST: Lock Stitch

D110-6
TST: Edge Stitch x2
(each edge)
ST: Lock Stitch

D110-18
TST: Basic Topstitch
Off-seam + Edge Stitch
ST: Lock Stitch

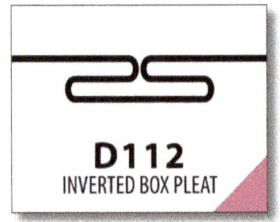

MAIN PROPERTIES

RESISTANCE	
STRENGTH	
VERSATILITY	
FLEXIBILITY	
ELASTICITY	
COST	

COMMON USES

- Widely on woven garments.
- Areas that need ease of movement.
- Front waist area of skirts and pants.
- Patch pockets of cargo pants.
- Inner back of lined outerwear.
- Back yoke of shirts, blouses, and outerwear (especially for men's clothing).

ADDITIONAL NOTES

- It strengthens when using a shorter stitch length to join the centre.
- Reversible Seam (exposed): The backside can be used as the right side.
- The box underneath will be visible from the outside of the garment.

3D VIEW

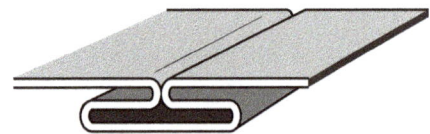

RELATED SEAMS

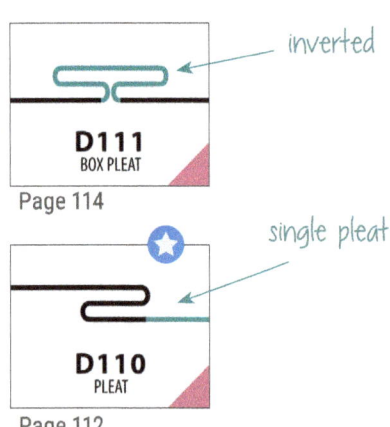

inverted

Page 114

single pleat

Page 112

Strong Seams

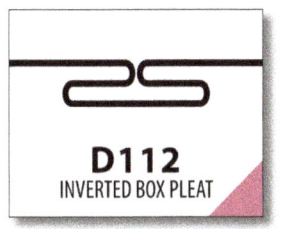

D112 — INVERTED BOX PLEAT

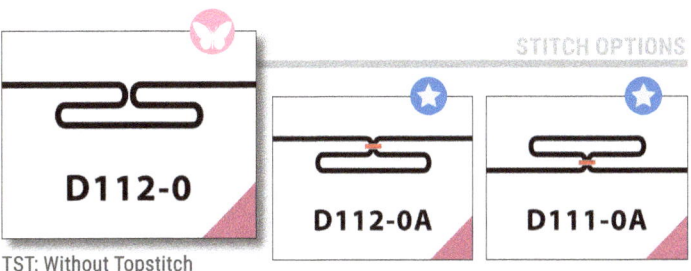

STITCH OPTIONS

D112-0
TST: Without Topstitch
ST: ---

D112-0A
TST: Without Topstitch
ST: Lock Stitch

D111-0A
TST: Without Topstitch
ST: Lock Stitch

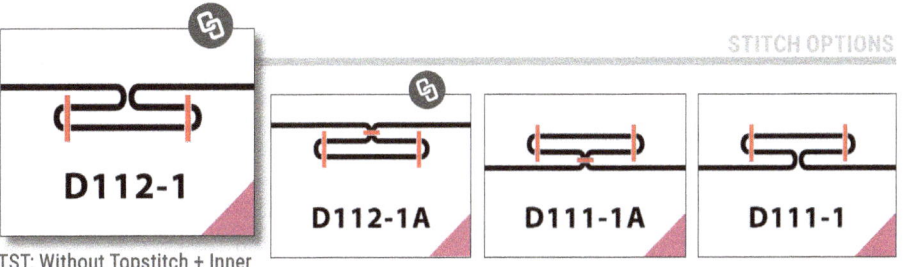

STITCH OPTIONS

D112-1
TST: Without Topstitch + Inner Edge Stitch x2 (each side)
ST: Lock Stitch

D112-1A
TST: Without Topstitch + Inner Edge Stitch x2 (each side)
ST: Lock Stitch

D111-1A
TST: Double Edge Stitch
ST: Lock Stitch

D111-1
TST: Double Edge Stitch
ST: Lock Stitch

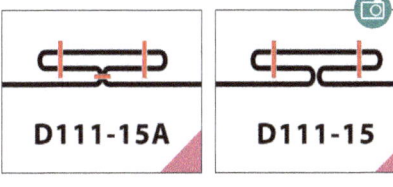

D111-15A
TST: Basic Topstitch x2 (each side)
ST: Lock Stitch

D111-15
TST: Basic Topstitch x2 (each side)
ST: Lock Stitch

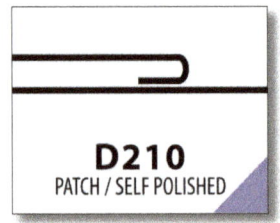

MAIN PROPERTIES

- RESISTANCE
- STRENGTH
- VERSATILITY
- FLEXIBILITY
- ELASTICITY
- COST

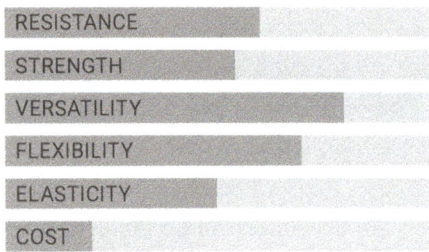

COMMON USES

- Work and casual clothing.
- Side seam of patch pockets.
- Facing edge of side pockets of pants.
- Inner back yoke of polo shirts.
- Appliqués, especially for fabrics that easily fray.
- Bags, footwear, and accessories such as hats.
- Upholstery.

ADDITIONAL NOTES

- The most common type of patch seam.
- Both fabrics must have the same care techniques (shrinkage, wash and dye fastness, etc.).

3D VIEW

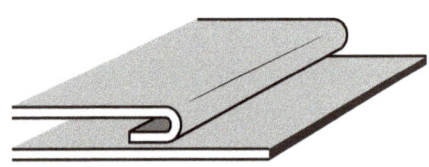

RELATED SEAMS

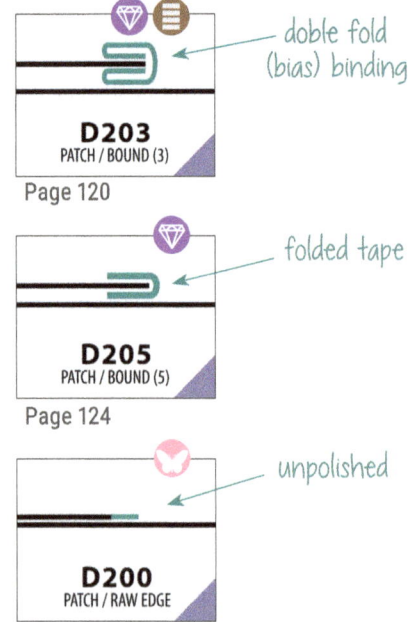

— doble fold (bias) binding
Page 120

— folded tape
Page 124

— unpolished
Page 118

Strong Seams

D210 PATCH / SELF POLISHED

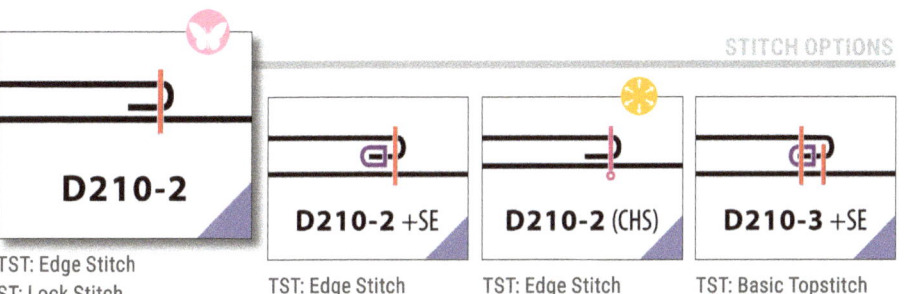

D210-2
TST: Edge Stitch
ST: Lock Stitch

D210-2 +SE
TST: Edge Stitch
ST: Lock Stitch + Serged Edge

D210-2 (CHS)
TST: Edge Stitch
ST: Chain Stitch

D210-3 +SE
TST: Basic Topstitch
ST: Lock Stitch + Serged Edge

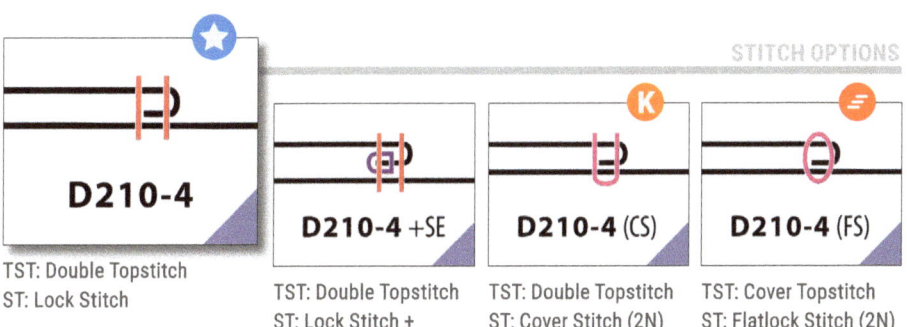

D210-4
TST: Double Topstitch
ST: Lock Stitch

D210-4 +SE
TST: Double Topstitch
ST: Lock Stitch + Serged Edge

D210-4 (CS)
TST: Double Topstitch
ST: Cover Stitch (2N)

D210-4 (FS)
TST: Cover Topstitch
ST: Flatlock Stitch (2N)

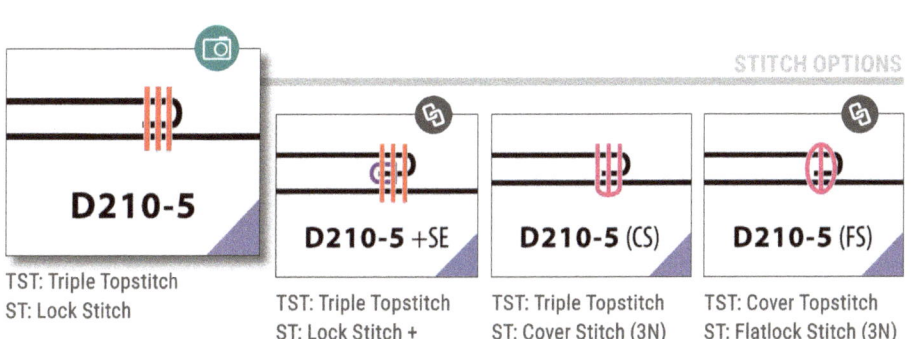

D210-5
TST: Triple Topstitch
ST: Lock Stitch

D210-5 +SE
TST: Triple Topstitch
ST: Lock Stitch + Serged Edge

D210-5 (CS)
TST: Triple Topstitch
ST: Cover Stitch (3N)

D210-5 (FS)
TST: Cover Topstitch
ST: Flatlock Stitch (3N)

MAIN PROPERTIES

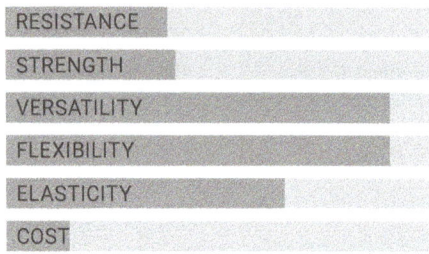

COMMON USES

- Fabrics/materials that do not fray, such as leather, suede, and laces.

- Garment made of knit fabric.

- Lingerie and sportswear.

- Facing edge of side pockets of pants.

- Inner back yoke of polo shirts.

- Elbow patches.

- Appliqués and embroideries.

- Bags, footwear, and accessories such as wallets and gloves.

- Upholstery.

ADDITIONAL NOTES

- Good option to avoid thickness when using heavy-weight fabrics.

3D VIEW

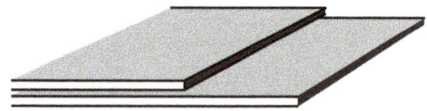

RELATED SEAMS

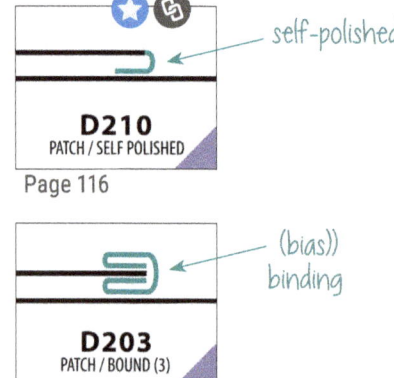

Strong Seams

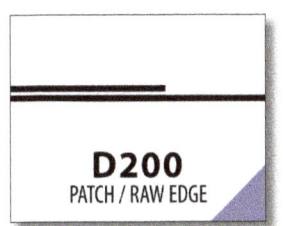

D200
PATCH / RAW EDGE

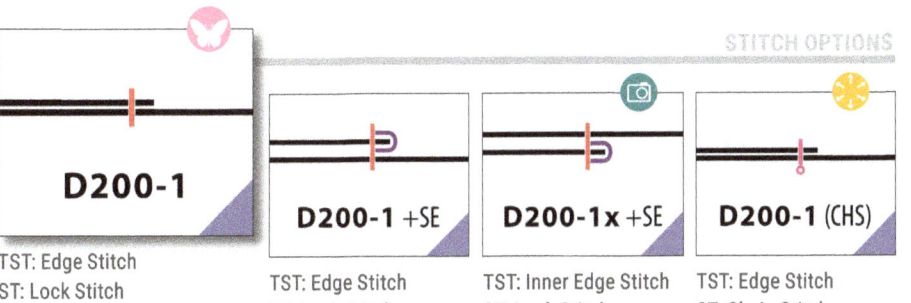

STITCH OPTIONS

D200-1

TST: Edge Stitch
ST: Lock Stitch

D200-1 +SE

TST: Edge Stitch
ST: Lock Stitch +
Serged Edge

D200-1x +SE

TST: Inner Edge Stitch
ST: Lock Stitch +
Serged Edge

D200-1 (CHS)

TST: Edge Stitch
ST: Chain Stitch

STITCH OPTIONS

D200-4

TST: Double Topstitch
ST: Lock Stitch

D200-4 +SE

TST: Double Topstitch
ST: Lock Stitch +
Serged Edge

D200-4 (CS)

TST: Double Topstitch
ST: Cover Stitch (2N)

D200-4 (FS)

TST: Cover Topstitch
ST: Flatlock Stitch (2N)

STITCH OPTIONS

D200-5

TST: Triple Topstitch
ST: Lock Stitch

D200-5 +SE

TST: Triple Topstitch
ST: Lock Stitch +
Serged Edge

D200-5 (CS)

TST: Triple Topstitch
ST: Cover Stitch (3N)

D200-5 (FS)

TST: Cover Topstitch
ST: Flatlock Stitch (3N)

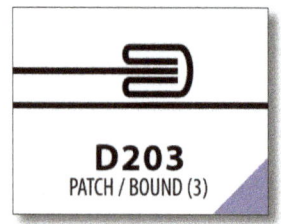

MAIN PROPERTIES

RESISTANCE
STRENGTH
VERSATILITY
FLEXIBILITY
ELASTICITY
COST

COMMON USES

- Garment made of woven fabric.
- Fabrics that easily fray.
- Edges with decorative trimming.
- Side seam of patch pockets.
- Elbow patches.
- Appliqués.

ADDITIONAL NOTES

- Regular Binding Width (finished): 0.6 cm (or 1/4").

3D VIEW

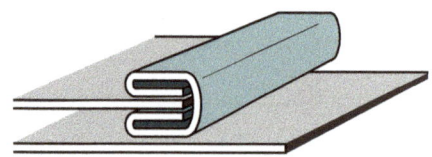

RELATED SEAMS

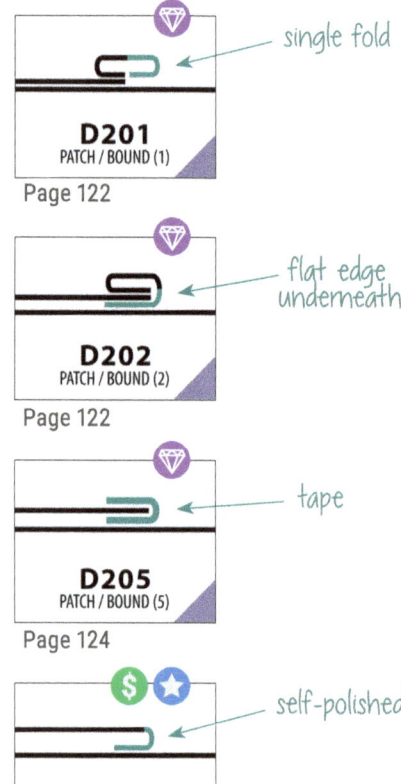

D201 — PATCH / BOUND (1) — single fold — Page 122

D202 — PATCH / BOUND (2) — flat edge underneath — Page 122

D205 — PATCH / BOUND (5) — tape — Page 124

D210 — PATCH / SELF POLISHED — self-polished — Page 116

Strong Seams

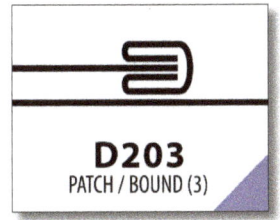

D203
PATCH / BOUND (3)

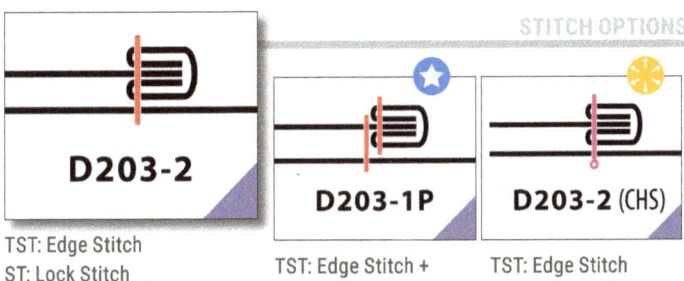

STITCH OPTIONS

D203-2
TST: Edge Stitch
ST: Lock Stitch

D203-1P
TST: Edge Stitch +
Stitch In-the-Ditch
ST: Lock Stitch

D203-2 (CHS)
TST: Edge Stitch
ST: Chain Stitch

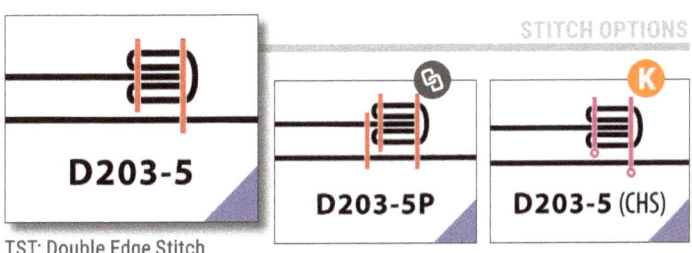

STITCH OPTIONS

D203-5
TST: Double Edge Stitch
ST: Lock Stitch

D203-5P
TST: Double Edge Stitch
+ Stitch In-the-Ditch
ST: Lock Stitch

D203-5 (CHS)
TST: Double Edge Stitch
ST: Chain Stitch

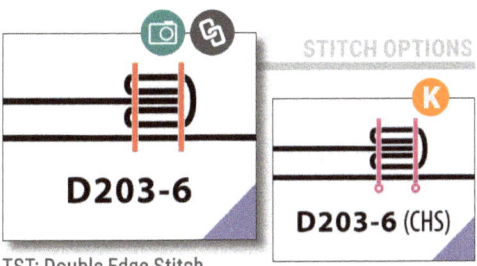

STITCH OPTIONS

D203-6
TST: Double Edge Stitch
ST: Lock Stitch

D203-6 (CHS)
TST: Double Edge Stitch
ST: Chain Stitch

D203
PATCH / BOUND (3)

BONUS

D201
PATCH / BOUND (1)

STITCH OPTIONS

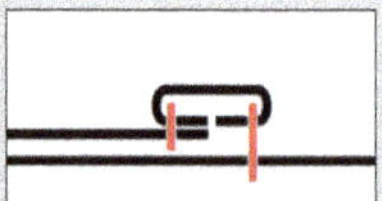

D201-5

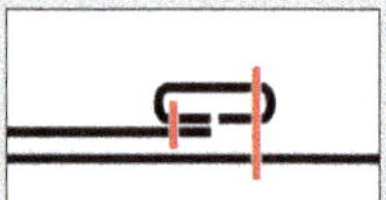

D201-13

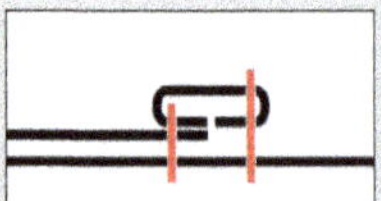

D201-14

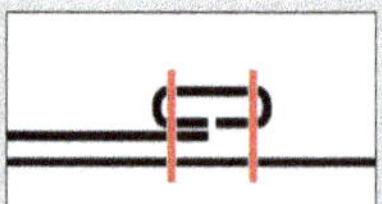

D201-16

D202
PATCH / BOUND (2)

STITCH OPTIONS

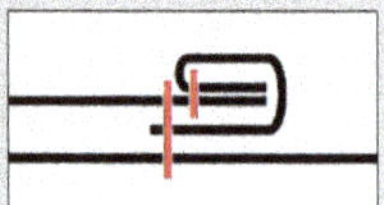

D202-1P

D202-4

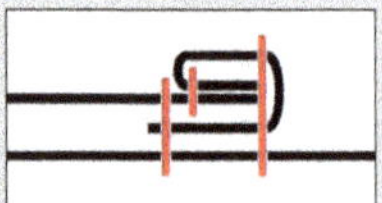

D202-9P

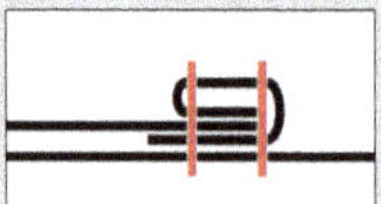

D202-12

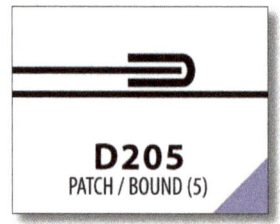

MAIN PROPERTIES

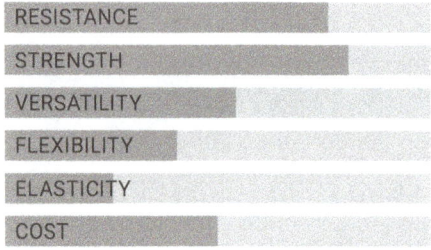

COMMON USES

- Fabrics that easily fray and knit fabrics.
- Ideal for heavy-weight fabrics.
- Sport-wear and lingerie.
- Elbow patches.
- Edges with decorative trimming.
- Bags, footwear, and accessories.
- Appliqués.

ADDITIONAL NOTES

- It works better on straight or slightly curved edges.
- Regular Tape Width (finished): 0.6 cm (or 1/4").

3D VIEW

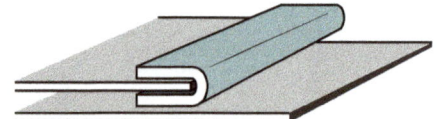

RELATED SEAMS

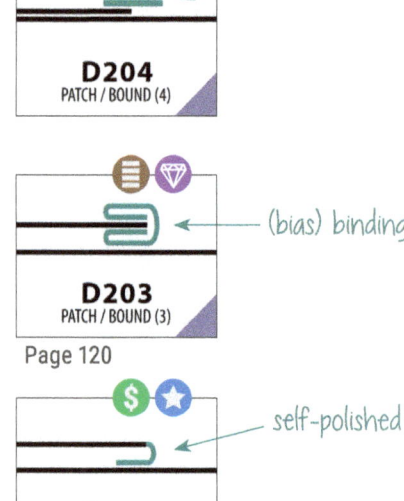

Strong Seams

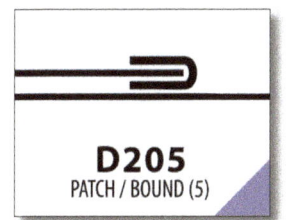

D205
PATCH / BOUND (5)

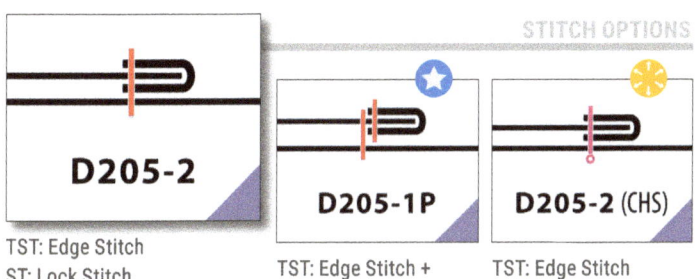

D205-2
TST: Edge Stitch
ST: Lock Stitch

D205-1P
TST: Edge Stitch +
Stitch In-the-Ditch
ST: Lock Stitch

D205-2 (CHS)
TST: Edge Stitch
ST: Chain Stitch

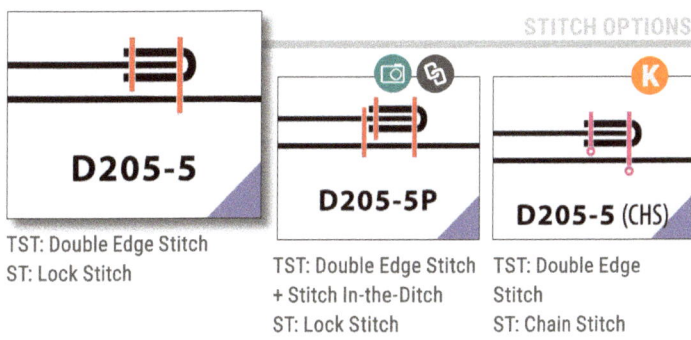

D205-5
TST: Double Edge Stitch
ST: Lock Stitch

D205-5P
TST: Double Edge Stitch
+ Stitch In-the-Ditch
ST: Lock Stitch

D205-5 (CHS)
TST: Double Edge
Stitch
ST: Chain Stitch

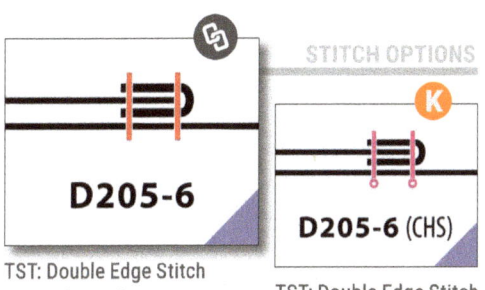

D205-6
TST: Double Edge Stitch
ST: Lock Stitch

D205-6 (CHS)
TST: Double Edge Stitch
ST: Chain Stitch

MY NOTES
DETAILS

Strong Seams

MY SAMPLES
DETAILS

GLUE	GLUE

GLUE	GLUE

GLUE	GLUE

OVERVIEW

Strong Seams

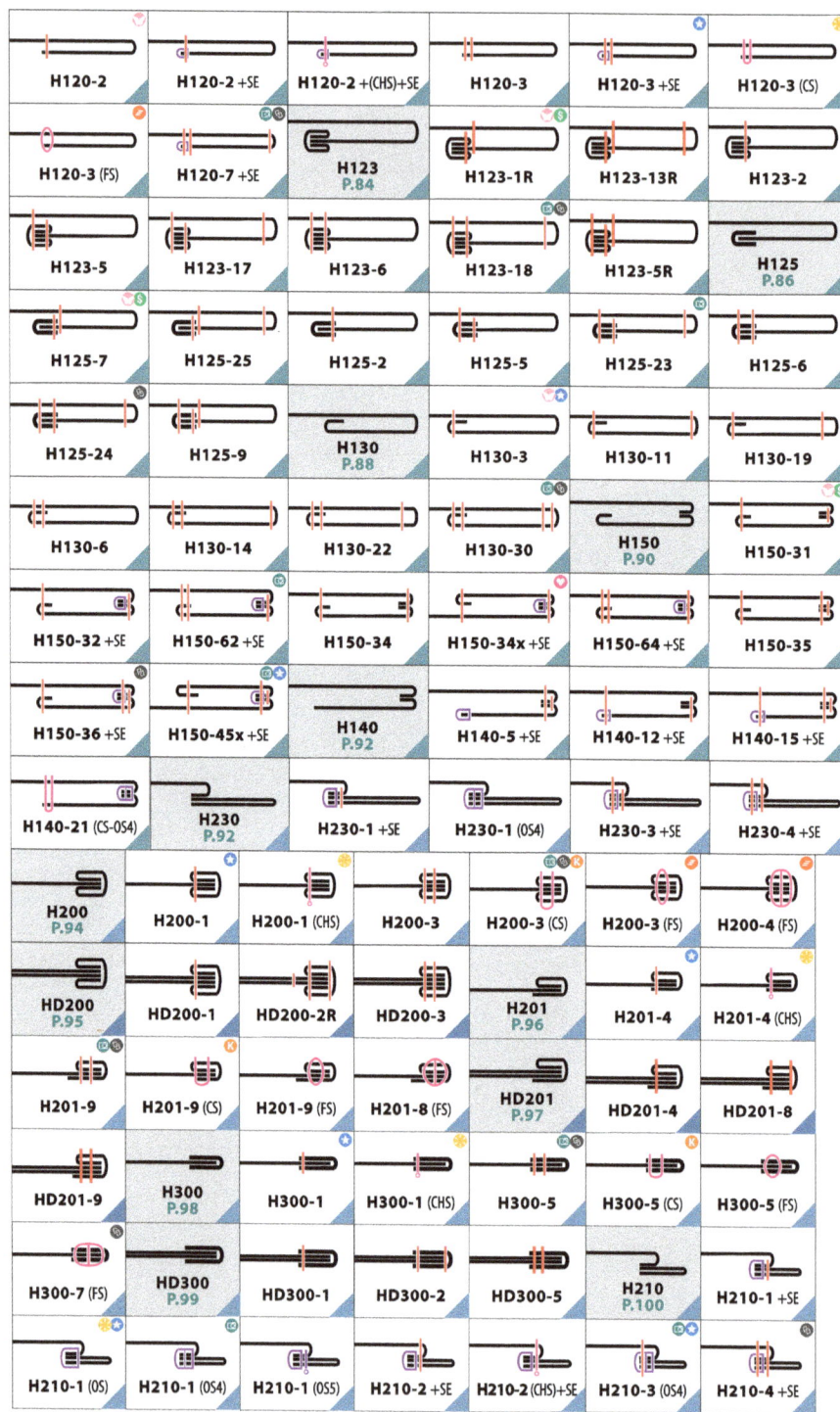

Strong Seams

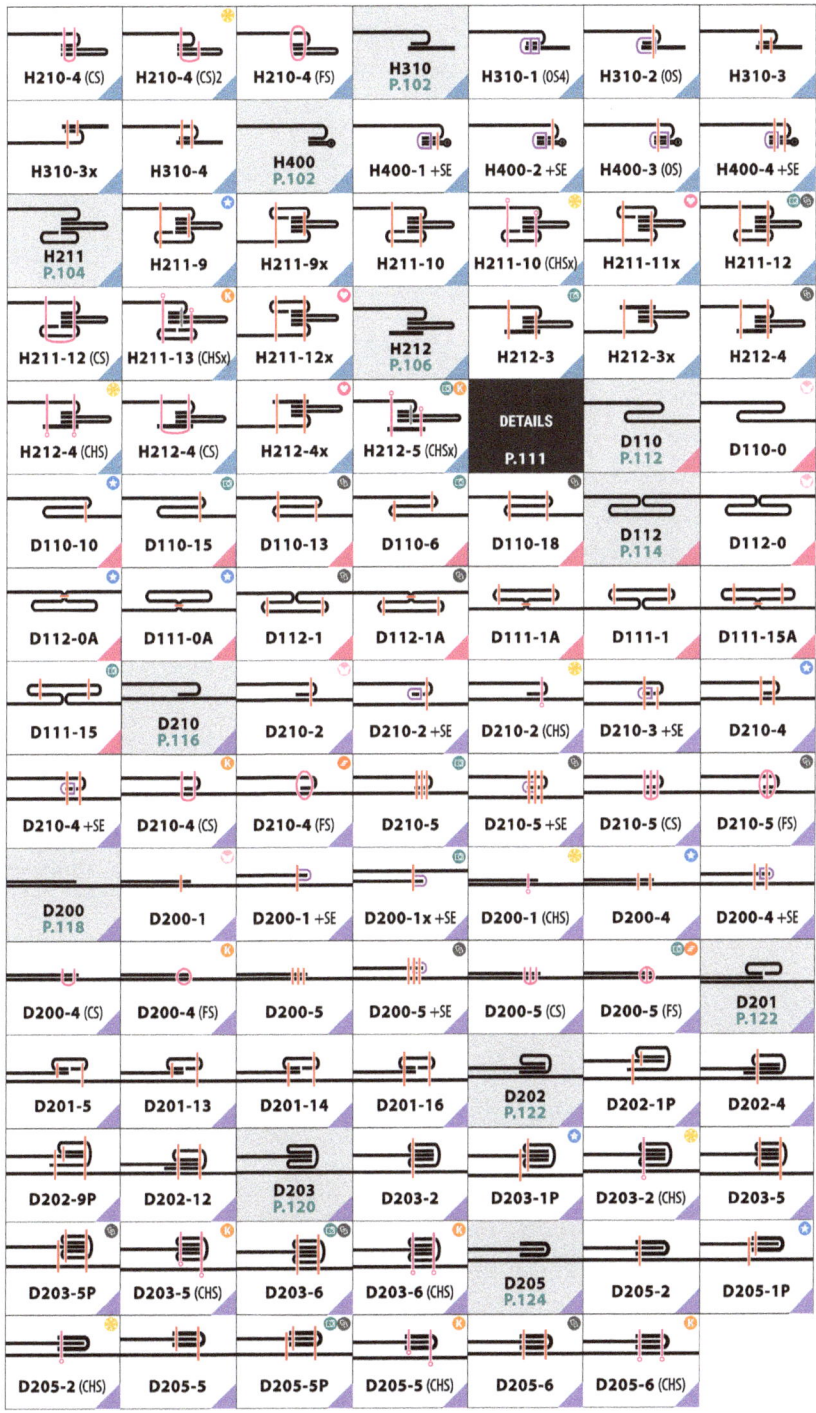

Note: Download this chart at *www.abcseams.com/strong-seams-overview*

Part Three

REFERENCE MATERIAL

PICTURES

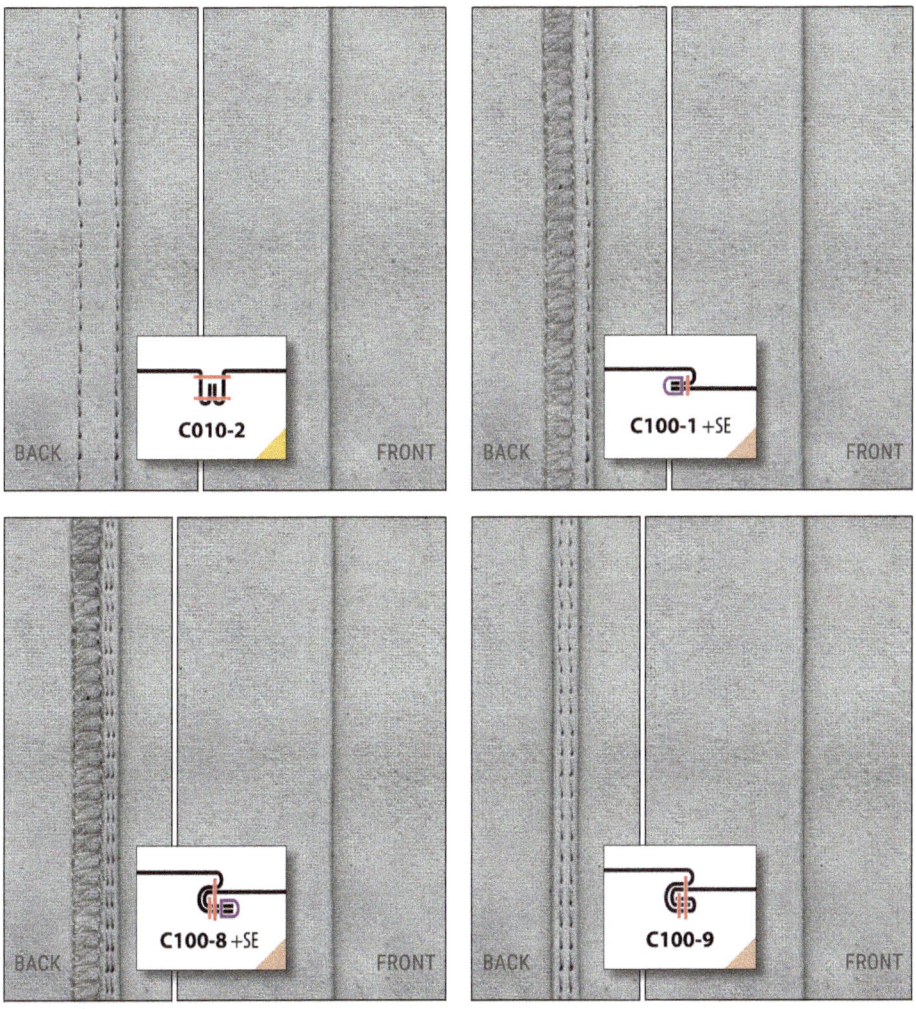

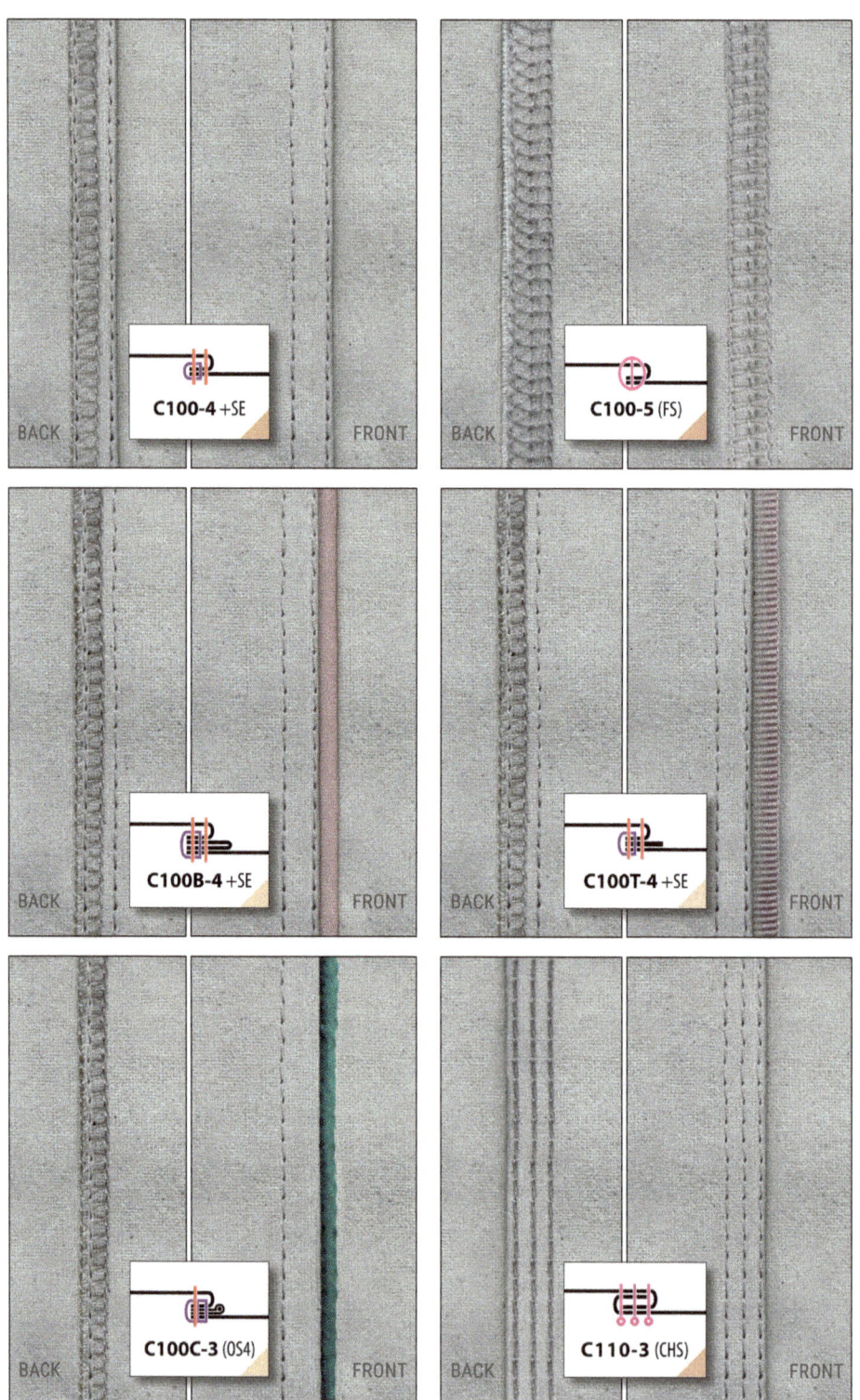

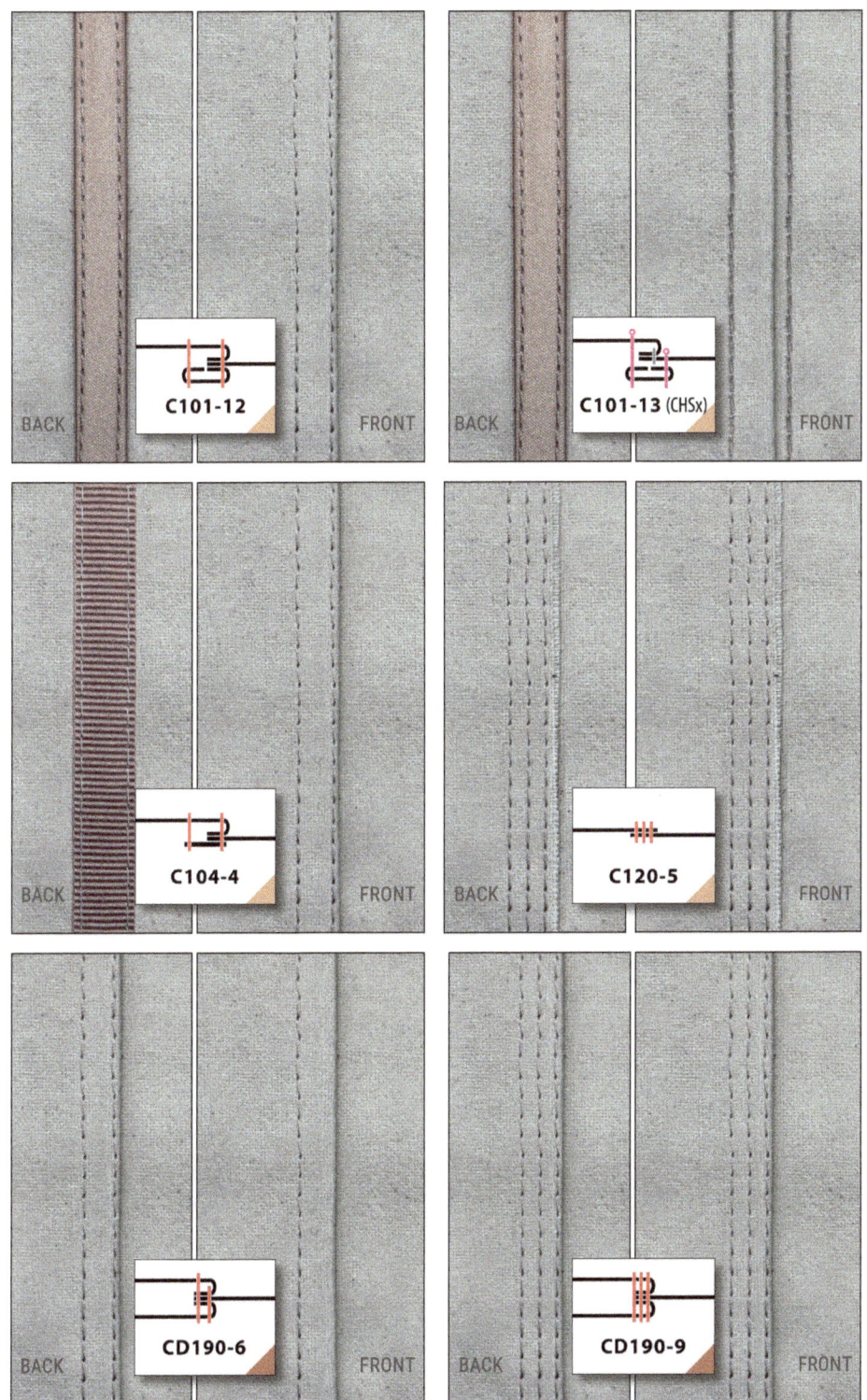

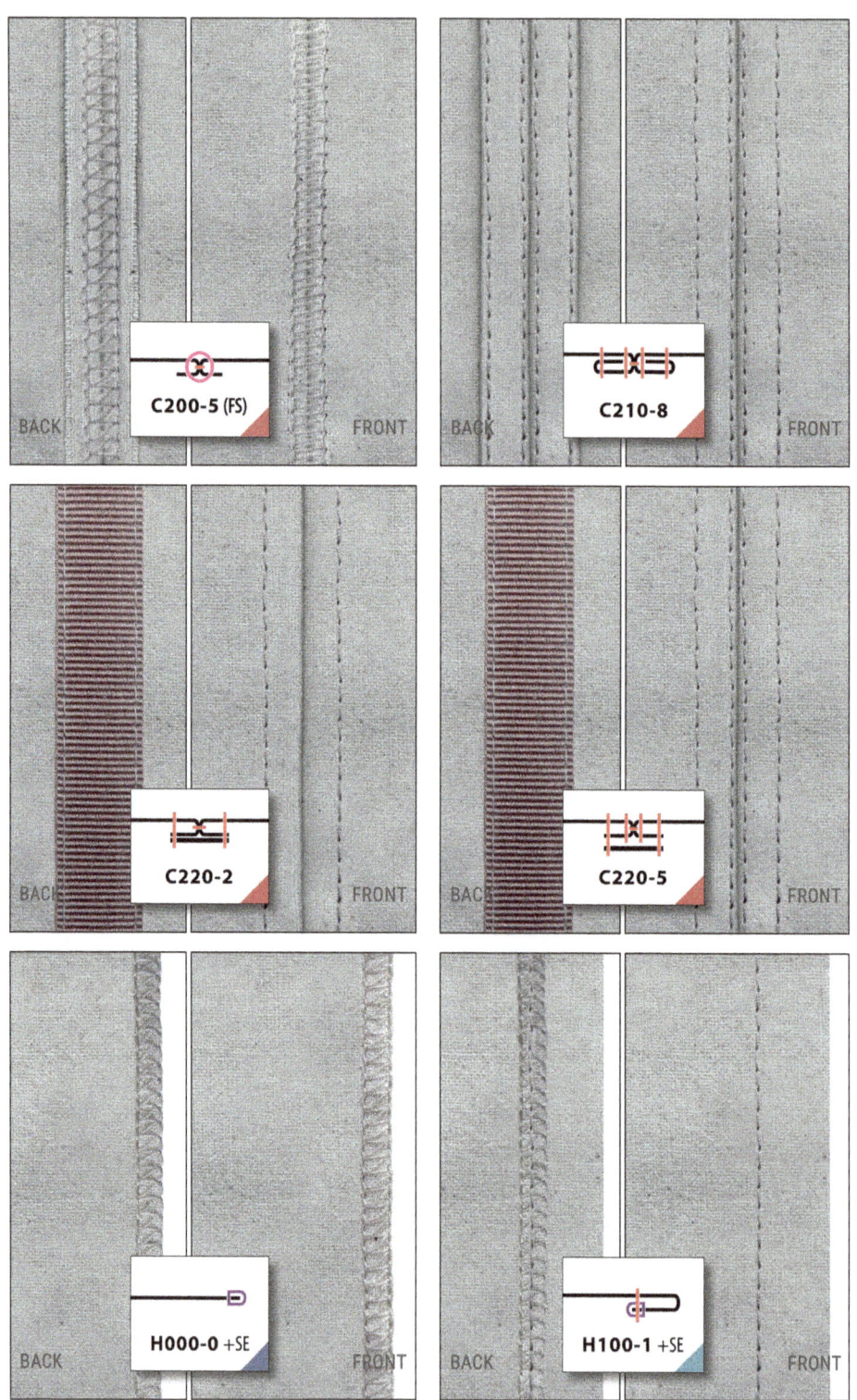

Strong Seams

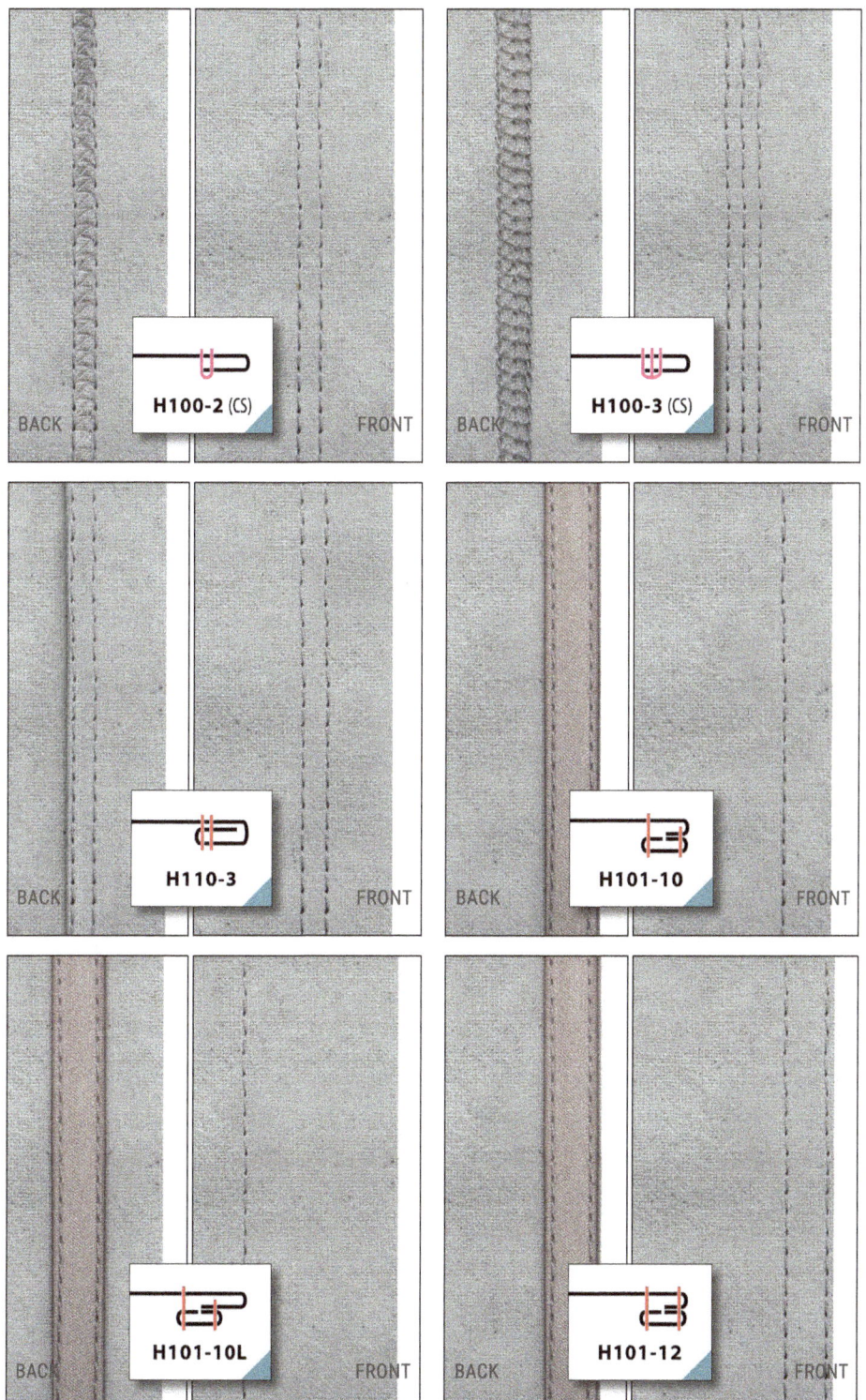

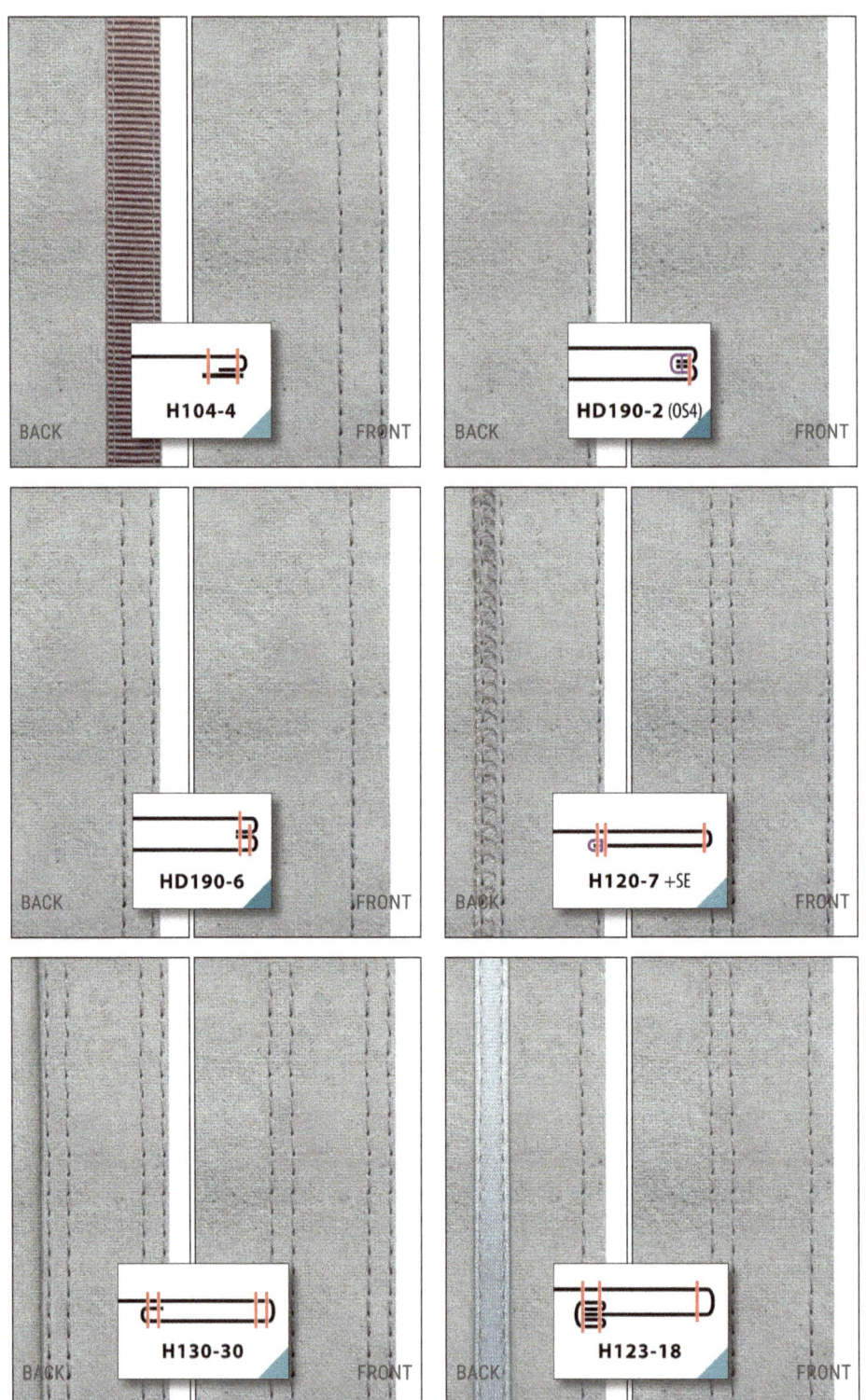

Strong Seams

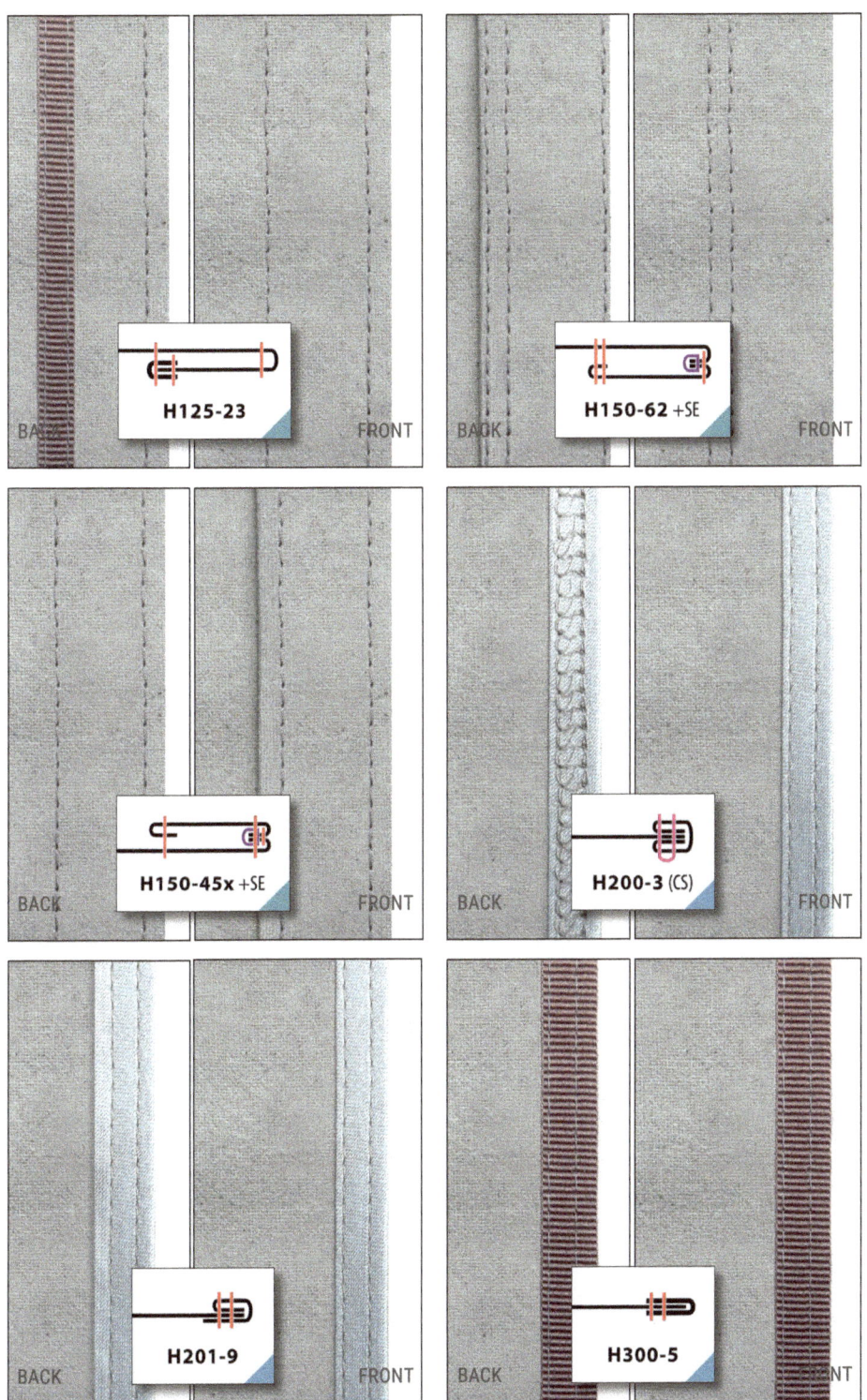

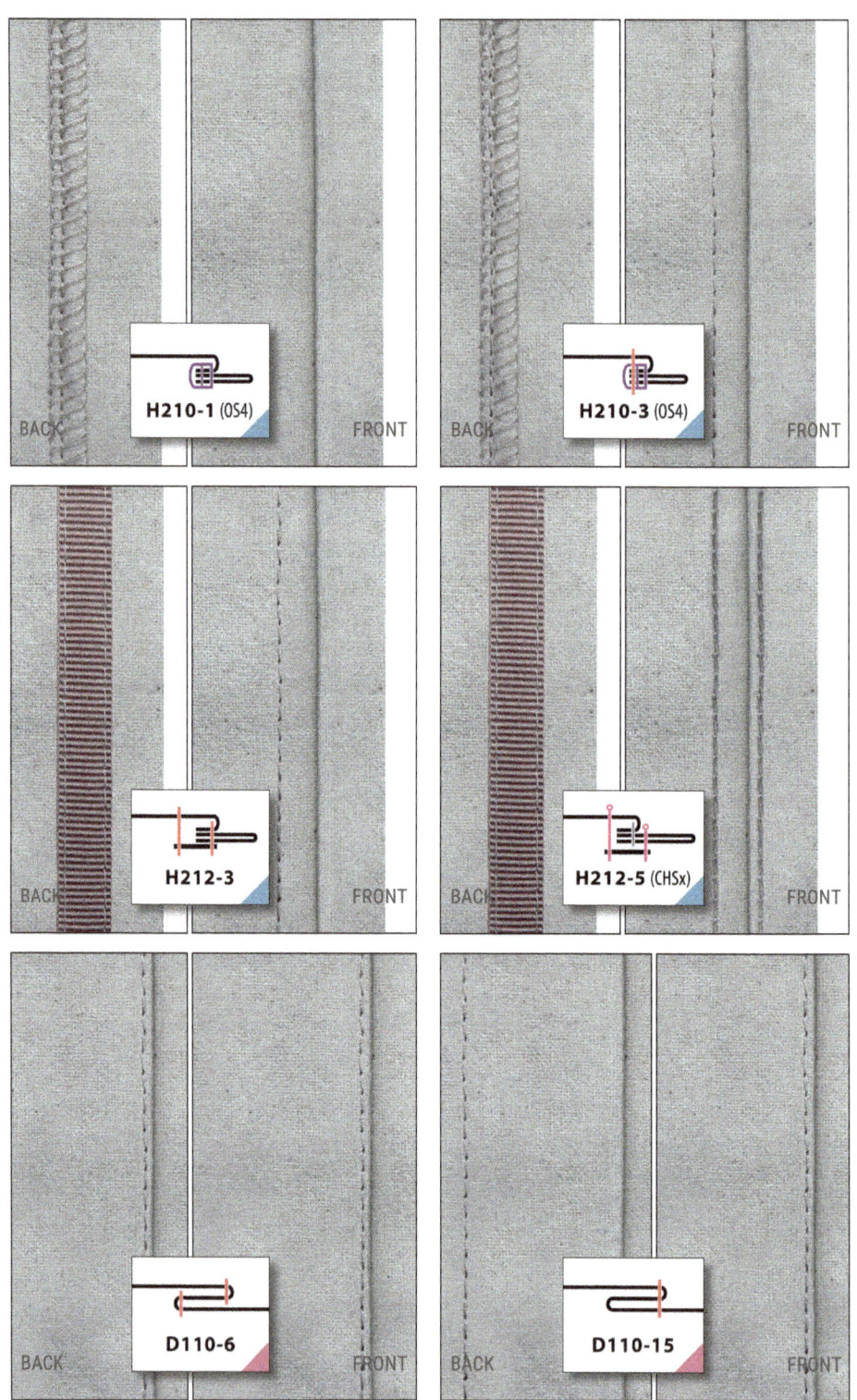

Strong Seams

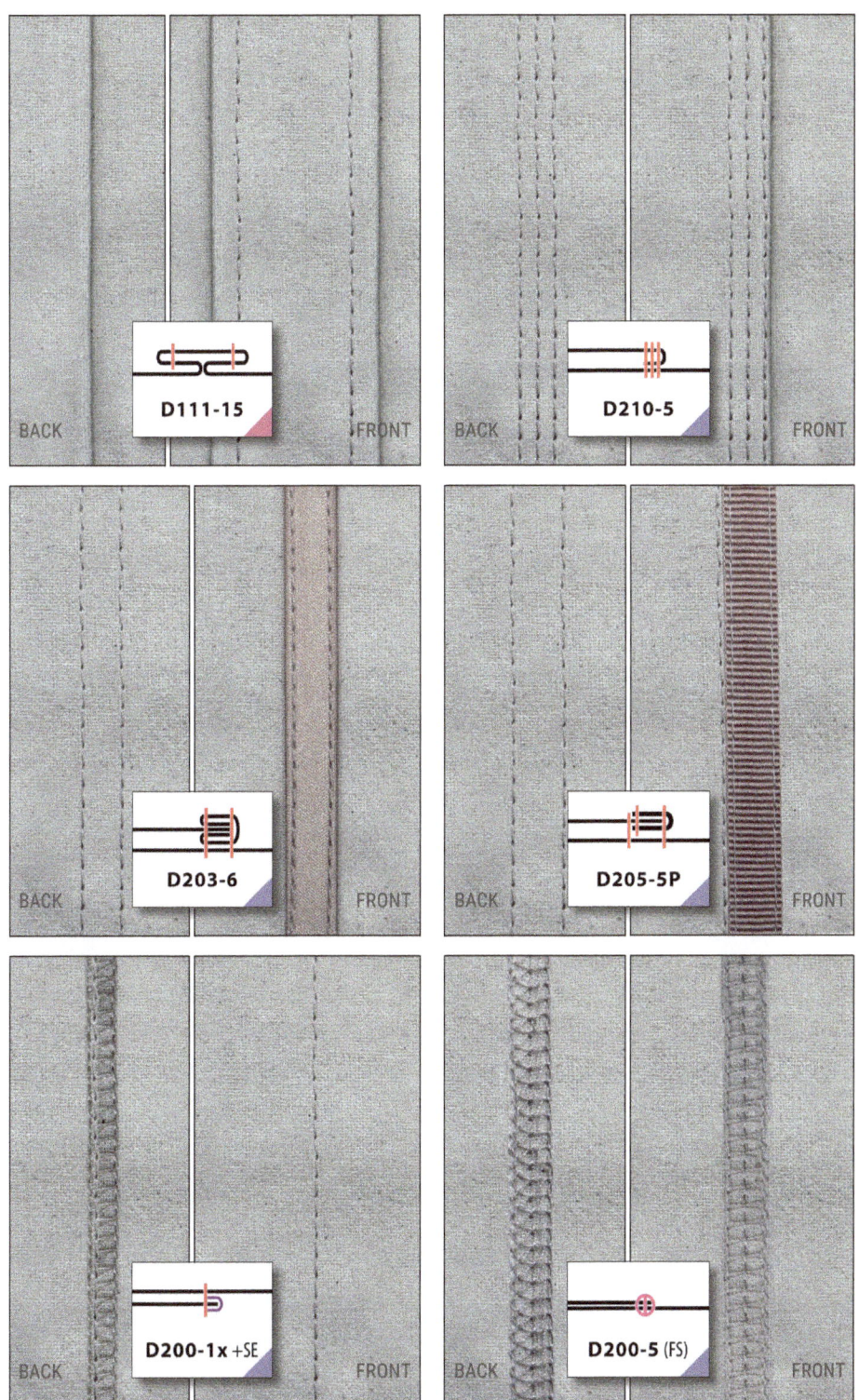

WHAT MAKES A SEAM STRONG

SEAM STRENGHT	
1. Materials & processes	**2. Garment assembly**
1.1 - Fabric 1.2 - Sewing thread 1.3 - Trimmings 1.4 - Chemical Treatments	2.1 - Seams structure, topstitch and stitch 2.2 - Machinery 2.3 - Operator Skills

Figure 3.1: Factors that affect the strength of a seam

1. Materials and Processes

1.1 - Fabrics

Fabrics of diverse kinds have different characteristics that can significantly impact the strength of seams. For instance, denim, which has a tightly woven and dense structure, provides high strength and a sturdy base for seams. Meanwhile, fabrics with fine fibers typically produce smoother and more even seams, although those with extremely light fibers may lack the tensile strength needed to withstand stress.

When choosing fabrics, seam strength should be your top priority. Here are some **characteristics to consider, in order of importance**:

Characteristic	Definition
Tensile strength (high priority)	The ability of a fabric to resist fraying, tearing or breaking when pulled in opposite directions. Conducting a tensile strength test on the fabric and seam, including a seam slippage test before buying the fabric is highly recommended. *Notes for reference:* *- Low tensile strength: Below 400 N/tex* *- Moderate tensile strength: 400 N/tex to 800 N/tex* *- High tensile strength: Above 800 N/tex*
Weave structure	The way threads are interlaced to create the fabric. Different weaves (plain, twill, satin) affect properties like strength, slippage, drape and breathability.
Shrinkage	The tendency of a fabric to decrease in size after washing or drying. Fabrics with low shrinkage stay closer to their original size. *Notes for reference:* *- Low Shrinkage Fabrics: below 3%* *- Moderate Shrinkage Fabrics: from 3 to 5%* *- High Shrinkage Fabrics: above 5%*
Thread count	The number of threads per square inch of fabric. More threads generally indicate a denser, heavier fabric, though quality and weave also matter. Additionally, smooth and slippery surfaces are more prone to seam slippage. *Notes for reference:* *- Low Thread Count: below 150 threads per in2.* *- Medium Thread Count: between 150 and 300 threads per in2.* *- High Thread Count: above 300 threads per in2.*
Fabric weight	The weight of the fabric per unit area, measured in grams per square meter (gsm). Heavier fabrics are more stable and durable, while lighter, free-flowing fabrics may require more delicate techniques to prevent seam distortion. *Notes for reference:* *- Extra Light weight: below 135 gsm / 4 osy* *- Light weight: from 135 to 200 gsm / 4 to 6 osy* *- Medium weight: from 200 to 305 gsm / 6 to 9 osy* *- Heavy weight: from 305 to 370 gsm / 9 to 11 osy* *- Extra Heavy weight: above 370 gsm / 11 osy*
Abrasion resistance	How well a fabric withstands rubbing and friction without wearing down or pilling. A higher abrasion resistance means the fabric lasts longer without becoming fuzzy or thin.

Abrasion resistance	Notes for reference on Martindale Abrasion Test: - *Light weight: 6,000 to 9,000 double rubs* - *Medium weight: 9,000 to 15,000 double rubs* - *Heavy weight: 15,000 double rubs and above*
Other factors to consider	- Stretch and elasticity - Bias stretch - Texture and pile - Colorfastness

1.2 - Sewing thread

Just as the fabric provides the structural foundation for the seam, **the thread works as the force that holds it all together**. However, not all threads are the same. While natural fibers such as cotton are inherently strong, they may weaken during processes like dyeing.

The selected sewing thread must match the fabric's characteristics, such as composition, weight and shrinkage. Heavier fabrics require thicker threads, while thinner ones will work better for lighter fabrics. Balancing fabric and thread shrinkage helps to avoid seams puckering, especially for garments with post-sewing treatments.

Tip 1: Purchasing threads from well-established brands known for producing high-quality threads. Examples include Gütermann, Coats & Clark, Mettler, and A&E.

Tip 2: Use specialty threads when needed. For instance, leggings made of a stretchable and moisture-wicking fabric such as spandex or a blend of polyester and elastane might need a high-tenacity polyester thread designed for stretch fabrics. Or, choose flame-resistant thread for garments that require fire resistance.

1.3 - Trimmings

The type and quality of trimming used in seams can directly impact their strength and performance. **Seams that utilize trims such as tapes, bias binding, corded piping, or stay tape require a balance between fabric**

and trimming characteristics. For instance, similarities in shrinkage are necessary to maintain seam appearance after washing. However, the trimming weight should be lighter than the fabric to prevent excessive thickness, particularly for heavy-weight fabrics.

1.4 - Chemical treatments

Fabrics and finished products often undergo coating and finish treatments such as enzymes, dyes, washing, bleaching, and softeners. These treatments may either be part of the design or applied to improve the garment's overall appearance, hand feel, and hanging. However, **most chemical processes affect the fabric and seam properties, potentially affecting their strength.** For example, dyed finished products may experience additional shrinkage due to the effects of heat and moisture. Or, anti-shrink treatments, such as resin finishes, may alter the fabric's flexibility, potentially impacting seam strength. A similar situation happens with softeners and fabric conditioners, which alter the fabric's hand feel and surface characteristics, making the fabric prone to slippage.

2. Garment Assembly

2.1 - Seam Types

Before selecting the seams for a new style, there are a few things to consider, including the brand's quality standards, the garment's intended use, the seam location, and the fabric type. For example, some areas prone to tension or movement, such as the shoulders or knees in workwear, may require reinforced seams to withstand stress, especially if the fabric is prone to fraying. Areas like the back neckline, which are usually exposed, may require the seam allowance to be carefully polished using tape or bias binding to provide stability and a clean look to the overall garment.

To select the right seam, you need to **break down the process into three correlative steps: selecting the seam structure, the topstitch type, and the stitch type** (see the **3 Steps Method** in page 18).

Steps	Description
1. Seam structure C110	The **arrangement of fabric layers** is known as the seam structure. When selecting the most suitable seam structure, the first thing to consider is the type of seam you need, whether it is for **construction, edge finishing, or a detail** such as pleats. Once we have determined this, we can move on to other **structural factors like how the seam allowance will be arranged and finished** (for instance, serged edge, enclosed edges, or encasing edges with binding or tape). That decision will significantly impact the seam's flexibility, strength, elasticity, appearance and production cost. It's also crucial to avoid making the seam too thick by balancing the fabric's thickness with the number of layers in the structure.
2. Topstitch type C110-2 (CHS)	An excellent example of how the topstitch can enhance the strength of a seam is the double topstitch. It **provides significant stability**, particularly useful in areas of high stress, such as the inseams of pants and patch pockets. In contrast, edge stitching and single topstitching provide less strength than double topstitching. Both types of topstitches create a more polished appearance. They are commonly used on light-weight fabrics or areas where additional strength is not a primary concern, like the collar edges of shirts. *Note*: Find more details on this Topstitch Types on page 178. *Tip*: Maintain an accurate and even seam allowance width to provide fabric for the topstitch to secure the seam.
3. Stitch Type	Different types of stitching offer different levels of strength, each with specific purposes and unique characteristics such as stretchiness and tear resistance. It is essential to **match the stitch type to the fabric type, and when doing so, we will consider the seam location needs carefully**. The *lockstitch* is commonly used on woven fabrics due to its stability. However, garments made of woven fabrics with a high shrinkage rate, such as denim, require a chain stitch to adjust the dimensional changes (shrinkage). This is especially noticeable in long seams such as the side seams of jeans. On the other hand, the *zig-zag* and stretch stitches, like overlock and cover stitches are a "must" for knit and stretchable fabrics that require certain elasticity to avoid potential thread breakage. A *Stitch Selection Guide* can be found on page 174.

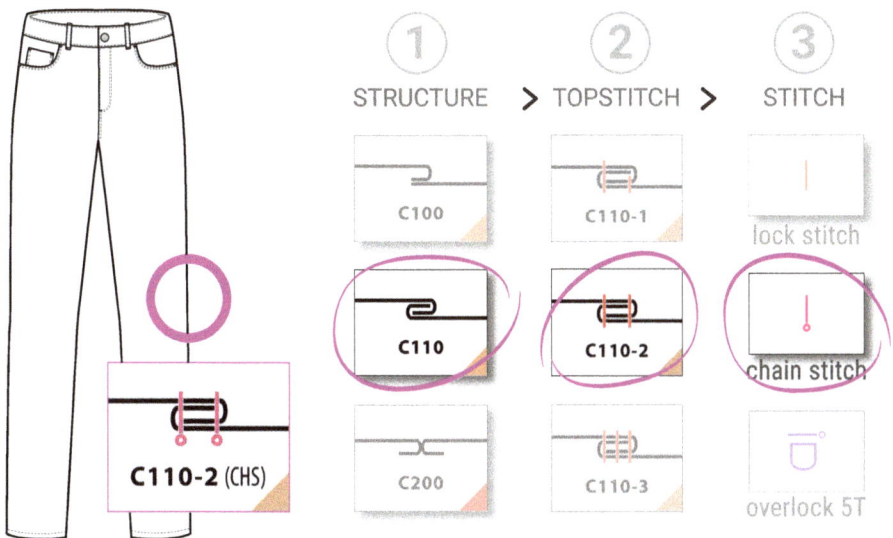

Figure 3.2: 3-Steps Method to select the right seam.

2.2 - Machinery Type and Setting

The type of machinery and its settings play a vital role in determining the overall strength of a seam. **The sewing machine case, presser foot, and feed dog system must meet the seam's requirements.**

Some *machine cases* are better suited for specific seams or techniques. For example, seam H200-3 (CS) is made by a 2-needle cover stitch with a 34mm binder accessory to wrap the edge. If we are sewing a bikini top, the machine will have a flat-bed case, but

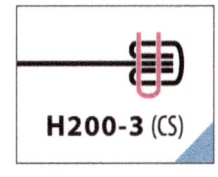

if we are sewing a tubular seam, such as a sleeve bottom, the case will be a cylinder bed. Also, the presser foot must be adjusted (raised or lowered) depending on the thickness of the fabric and seam structure. Higher pressure is suitable for thicker fabrics, while lighter pressure prevents distortion of light-weight fabrics.

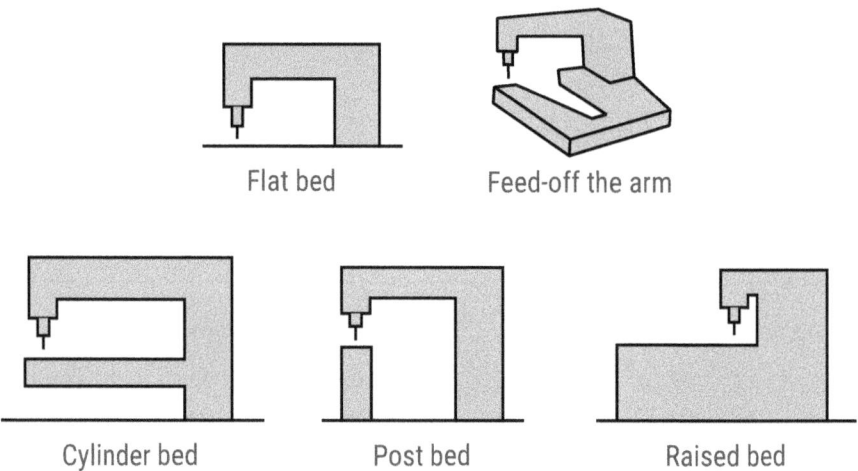

Figure 3.5: Sewing machine bed types

Controlling the machine speed to match complex seams positively influences the creation of a strong and well-constructed seam. Slower speeds allow the operator greater precision, especially for tricky parts requiring more detail.

As mentioned above, the thread type and quality play a vital role. However, **the correct thread tension is equally important** to ensure the stitches are secure. The tension is adjusted based on the type of fabric and the number of layers involved in the seam structure.

Matching the stitch length with the fabric's weight and seam thickness is also crucial. Light-weight and stretchable fabrics such as sheers and jerseys require shorter stitches. On the other hand, longer stitches work better for heavy-weight and thick fabrics like PU.

However, excessively long (e.g., over 2 SPCM / 5 SPI) or short stitches (e.g., under 6 SPCM / 15 SPI) may compromise seam durability by providing poor thread coverage or excessive perforations in the fabric, thus weakening its structure.

GARMENT TYPE	MM	SPCM	SPI
T-shirt	2.0 - 2.5	4.0 - 5.0	10.0 - 13.0
Shirt	2.0 - 3.0	3.5 - 5.0	8.5 - 13.0
Dress	2.0 - 3.0	3.5 - 5.0	8.5 - 13.0
Skirt	2.0 - 3.0	3.5 - 5.0	8.5 - 13.0
Denim	3.0 - 4.0	2.5 - 3.5	6.5 - 8.5
Pants	2.5 - 3.5	3.0 - 4.0	7.5 - 10.0
Sweatshirt	3.0 - 4.0	2.5 - 3.5	6.5 - 8.5
Swimming & lingerie	1.5 - 2.0	5.0 - 6.5	12.0 - 16.0
Lycra	2.0 - 3.0	3.5 - 5.0	12.5 - 17.0
Childrenswear	2.0 - 2.5	4.0 - 5.0	10.0 - 13.0

Figure 3.4: General reference to stitch length.

Note: Please keep in mind that the stitch length might vary depending on fabric weight and seam structure.

It is vital to **use the appropriate needle type, size and quality according to the fabric**. That helps to prevent fabric damage and issues such as skipped stitches. Using a needle that is too large for the fabric can leave visible holes, compromising the seam's integrity. For heavier fabrics, thicker needles work best, while finer needles are ideal for delicate fabrics. Ballpoint needles are suitable for knit fabrics, while universal or sharp needles work well for woven fabrics.

2.3 - Operator Skills

Proper handling of the machine, accurate stitching, and meticulous attention to detail all play a significant role in ensuring the overall durability of the seam. For instance, skilled operators can precisely align seams and stitches while also managing the tension applied to the fabric. However, along with technical skills, effective communication and adaptability to change are also valuable.

REINFORCEMENTS AND SEWING TECHNIQUES

Two types of methods can be used to strengthen areas of garments that are prone to stress, such as necklines and pocket openings. **The first type is used to finish seam allowances** and includes methods such as serging and encasing the seam allowance. **The second type secures and stabilizes seams**, and involves techniques like adding bar tacks or stay tape.

Using these techniques will make the product stronger and more durable, enhancing its overall visual appeal.

REINFORCEMENTS & SEWING TECHNIQUES	
1. Seam allowance finishing	2. Securing & stabilizing seams
1.1 - Serged or stitched Edge	2.1 - Topstitching
1.2 - Self-Enclosed Edge	2.2 - Stay Tape (or Silicon Tape)
1.3 - Trimmings	2.3 - Bar tacks
1.4 - Piece of Fabric	2.4 - Backstitching

Figure 3.5: Types of reinforcements

1. Seam Allowance Finishing

Well-finished seams not only enhance the product's appearance but also ensure the durability of the garment. To prevent fraying and unravelling, effective seam allowance finishing is crucial. Below, we explore the four methods commonly used to finish seam allowances.

1.1 - Serged Edge: A stitch wraps the edge of the seam allowance.

Properties	- Low cost (time-efficient). - Easy and fast to execute. - This technique is not considered as a clean finishing.
Common uses	- Applicable to most fabric types, especially those prone to fraying and unravelling. - Widely used on knit garments. - Suitable for various types of clothing. - Ideal for edges of flowy skirts cut on the bias.
Common stitches	- Overlock Stitch: this is the most popular choice for construction seams due to its affordability, ease of execution, and resistance. - Cover Stitch: primarily applied on the hems of knitted garments. - Flatlock Stitch: offers a clean appearance on both sides, resembling an embroidery. Typically found in activewear due to its soft touch and resistance. - Zigzag Stitch: the 1-step version is suitable for woven fabrics, while the 3-step version is mainly used on knit fabrics, especially in lingerie and underwear.
Common seams	C100-1 +SE, C200-1 +SE, C120-5 (FS), H000-0 +SE, H100-1 +SE, H100-2 (CS), H100-3 (FS)
Notes	If the backside of the seam is visible, such as the back neckline seam of a t-shirt, a serged edge will lower the perceived quality of the garment.

1.2 - Self-Enclosed Edge: The seam allowance is polished by folding at least one seam allowance edge inwards and enclosing the other inside.

Properties	- Clean appearance and cost-effectiveness. - Considered as a type of clean finishing. - Versatile.

Common uses	- Primarily used on woven fabrics, from light-weight sheers to heavy-weight fabrics like denim. - Commonly employed in unlined jackets, workwear, and accessories. - Applied to hems, shoulder seams, crotch seams of jeans, cuff vents, and pockets.
Common seams	C010-1 C110-2 (CHS) H110-2
Notes	The best-known seams within this technique are the French Seam, Welt Seam, and Double Fold Hem.

1.3 - Edge Polished with a Trim:
The edge of the seam allowance is wrapped or covered by trimming (tape or binding).

Properties	- Also known as Hong Kong finish. - Considered as a high-quality technique. - The trim increases strength and stabilizes the seam. - The garment gains an elegant finish from the trim. - Medium to high cost: the trim increases its cost. Also, some variants of this technique type require added machine passes, making them even more expensive.
Common uses	- Better suitable for medium to heavy-weight fabrics. - Perfect option for fabrics that fray easily. - Commonly seen in high-quality garments. - Widely used on unlined garments. - Ideal for curved or bias-cut edges.
Common seams	C101-10 C220-2 H101-10 H211-10

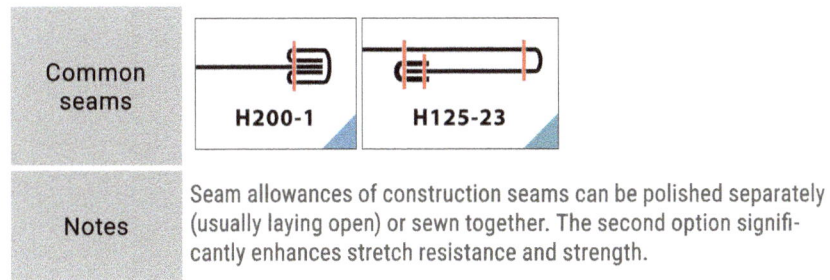

Common seams	H200-1, H125-23
Notes	Seam allowances of construction seams can be polished separately (usually laying open) or sewn together. The second option significantly enhances stretch resistance and strength.

1.4 - Edge Covered with a Piece of Fabric: An additional pattern piece, such as a facing, lining or fabric layer, is sometimes used to polish the seam allowance.

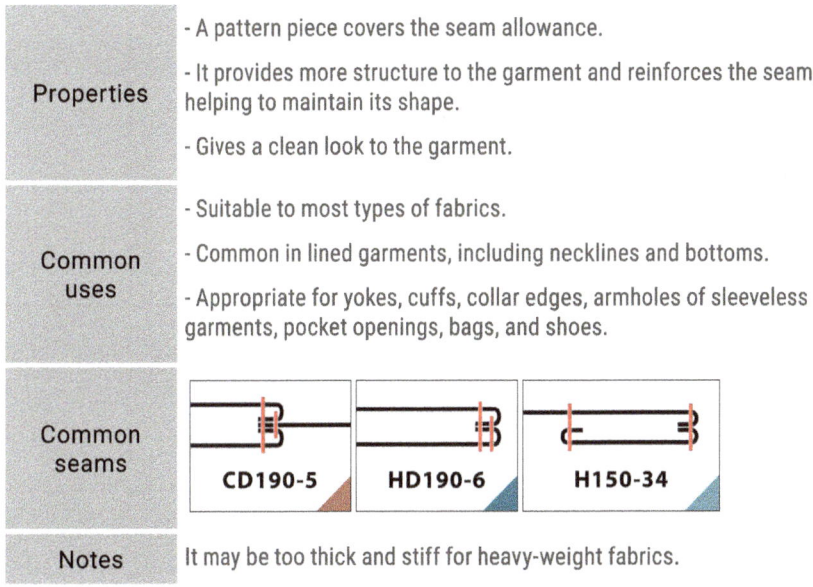

Properties	- A pattern piece covers the seam allowance. - It provides more structure to the garment and reinforces the seam, helping to maintain its shape. - Gives a clean look to the garment.
Common uses	- Suitable to most types of fabrics. - Common in lined garments, including necklines and bottoms. - Appropriate for yokes, cuffs, collar edges, armholes of sleeveless garments, pocket openings, bags, and shoes.
Common seams	CD190-5, HD190-6, H150-34
Notes	It may be too thick and stiff for heavy-weight fabrics.

2. Securing and Stabilizing Seams

This section will go beyond seam allowance finishings to explore the four techniques used to secure and stabilize seams.

2.1 - Topstitching:
One or more stitch lines are sewn on the right side of the fabric. Usually, the topstitch attaches the seam allowance to the fabric, keeping it stable underneath.

Properties	- Visible on the right side of the garment. - Serves functional and aesthetic purposes: it increases the strength and stability of the seam and gives a decorative effect to the garment, emphasizing specific design details. - Usually is placed parallel to a seamline or along the fabric edge. - Varies in width.
Common uses	- Versatile, applicable to most types of fabric and products. - Widely used in denim, workwear, sportswear, ready-to-wear garments, bags, and shoes. - Applied in high-stress areas such as pocket edges and pants crotch. - Used for edge finishing and to attach elements such as pockets and flaps.
Common stitches	- Lockstitch: widely used on woven fabrics. - Chain stitch: typically applied to large construction seams in woven fabrics with a high shrinkage rate, such as the side seam of jeans. It is also suitable for use on knit and stretchable fabrics. - Cover stitch: used for edge finishing on knit fabrics. - Flatlock stitch: applied to construction or finished seams in knit fabrics, particularly for sportswear.
Common seams	C100-2 +SE, C100-3 +SE, C110-2, C110-3, H100-2 +SE, H100-2 (CS), H101-12
Notes	Achieving consistent and straight topstitching demands precise sewing machine settings and advanced operator skills, especially when working with contrasting thread colours.

2.2 - Stay tape (including Silicon Tape):

A stay tape is attached to the inner side of the seam for additional support and to prevent stretching along seamlines.

Properties	- Prevent stretching and distortion. - The additional layer of fabric increases the seam stability.
Common uses	- Applied on high-stress points such as necklines and shoulders. - Used in areas around zippers and closures. - Ideal for curved seams, like armholes.
Common seams	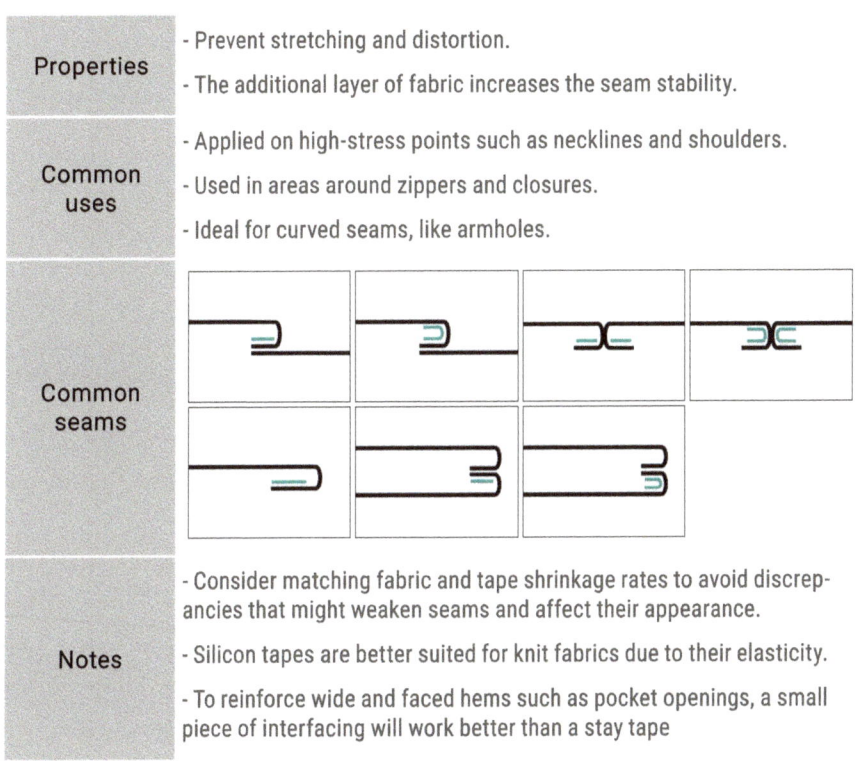
Notes	- Consider matching fabric and tape shrinkage rates to avoid discrepancies that might weaken seams and affect their appearance. - Silicon tapes are better suited for knit fabrics due to their elasticity. - To reinforce wide and faced hems such as pocket openings, a small piece of interfacing will work better than a stay tape

2.3 - Bar tacks:

Stitches sewn closely together create a bar tack.

Properties	- Short, dense stitches provide exceptional strength and stability. - Offers additional strength to specific points. - Withstands constant pulling and strain.
Common uses	- Ideal for heavy-duty garments such as denim, jackets, and workwear. - Applied in areas subject to repeated stress and strain, like pocket openings, flaps, and belt loops. - Used at zipper corners and on pants flies.

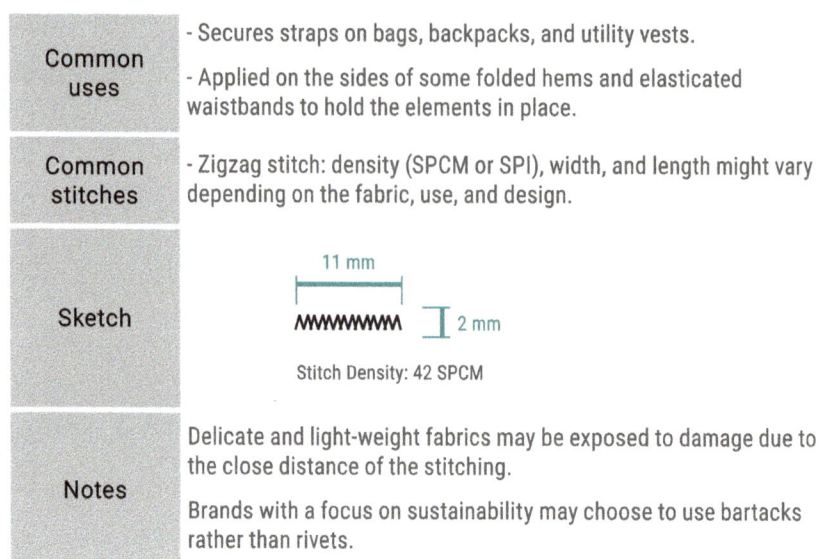

Common uses	- Secures straps on bags, backpacks, and utility vests. - Applied on the sides of some folded hems and elasticated waistbands to hold the elements in place.
Common stitches	- Zigzag stitch: density (SPCM or SPI), width, and length might vary depending on the fabric, use, and design.
Sketch	11 mm 〰〰〰〰〰 2 mm Stitch Density: 42 SPCM
Notes	Delicate and light-weight fabrics may be exposed to damage due to the close distance of the stitching. Brands with a focus on sustainability may choose to use bartacks rather than rivets.

2.4 - Backstitching: The seam is sewn backward and forward at the beginning and end.

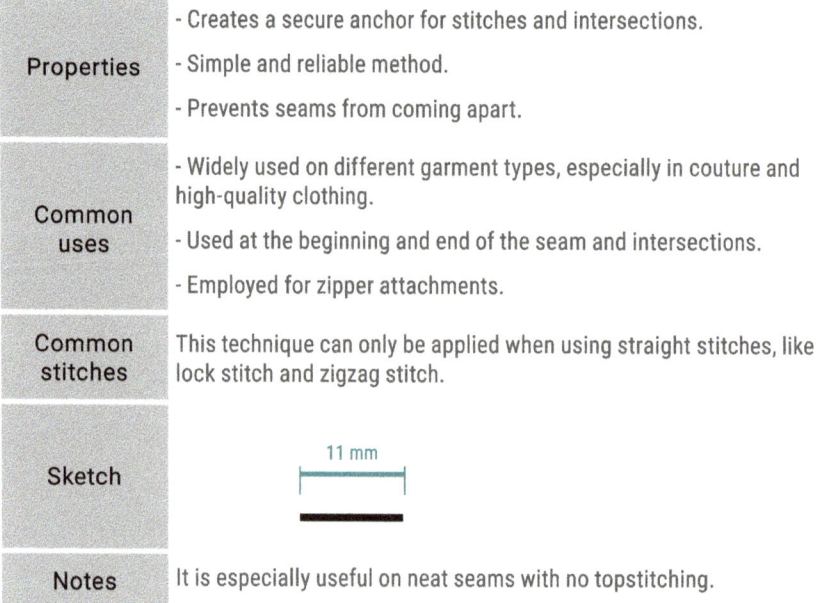

Properties	- Creates a secure anchor for stitches and intersections. - Simple and reliable method. - Prevents seams from coming apart.
Common uses	- Widely used on different garment types, especially in couture and high-quality clothing. - Used at the beginning and end of the seam and intersections. - Employed for zipper attachments.
Common stitches	This technique can only be applied when using straight stitches, like lock stitch and zigzag stitch.
Sketch	11 mm
Notes	It is especially useful on neat seams with no topstitching.

Note: Find examples of **Seams Implementation** at *www.abcseams.com/strong-seams-implementation*

STRESSED AREAS

Stressed areas are **those parts of a garment that undergo more wear and tear due to frequent use and movement**. These areas are more prone to seam failure, tearing or ripping if not designed with special considerations. Some examples of such areas include shoulders, crotch seams, and pocket openings.

The nature of stressed areas varies depending on the seam location, garment type and fit. For instance, the crotch seam of climbing pants undergoes different stress than the crotch of formal pants. Additionally, **fabric selection is crucial** in determining seam strength, as different fabrics react differently to stress. For example, the elbow area of a tight coat of woven fabric undergoes more stress than the elbows of a running T-shirt made of high-stretch fabric.

Therefore, reinforcing stressed areas requires a holistic approach and special attention to selecting appropriate seams. Reinforced seams, like bound seams for the back neckline of T-shirts and welt seams for the crotch of some pants, help strengthen these areas.

Figure 3.6: Factors that affect the level of stress

Stress Levels

Based on the degree of strain that the seam experiences, **stress areas are categorized into three levels: high, medium, and low.**

Strong Seams

Stress level	Description
High	These seams are exposed to significant tension, compression or abrasion. They are usually found in areas prone to movement or friction, such as shoulder straps, scoop T-shirt necklines, pocket openings, pants crotches, or waistbands.
Medium	These seams endure moderate tension, typically due to body movement. Examples include inseams in pants, shoulders and some armholes.
Low	Seams exposed to minimal strain. These seams may include most side seams, relaxed-fit bottoms, and open necklines.

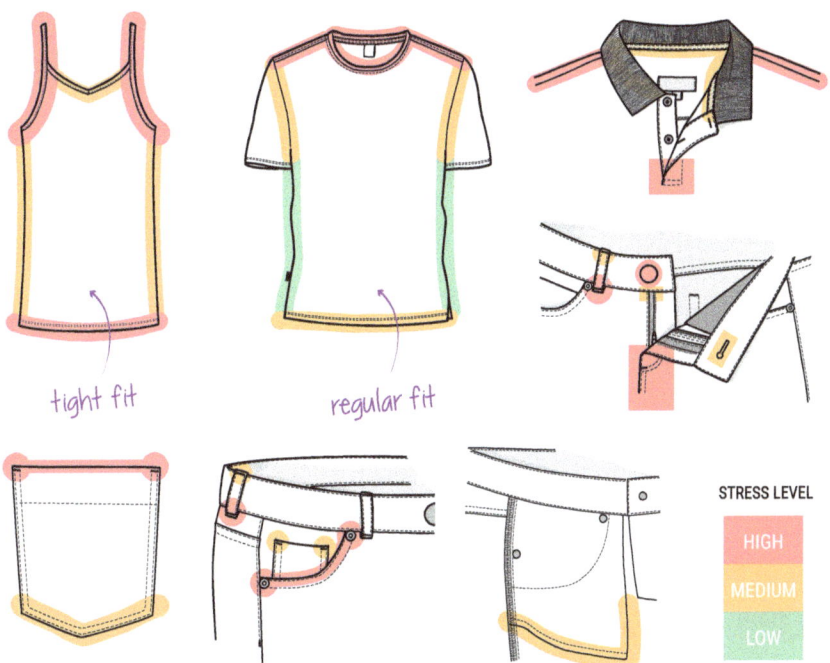

Figure 3.7: Classification of stressed areas and locations

Note: Remember, this classification is a general guideline. It's always best to analyze each style and fit before determining the stress level.

CHECKING SEAMS & QUALITY CONTROL

Garment inspection plays an essential role to ensure durable products. The materials, measurements, labelling and packaging require thorough testing to ensure our customers receive only high-quality products that meet our standards.

One of the critical aspects of the garment inspection is **testing seams for strength and durability**. This is important to **prevent seam defects and ensure that the garment will remain strong, dimensionally stable, and attractive** over time. Proper seam inspection can also **save time and money**.

Types of evaluations

There are two ways to evaluate the quality of seams: **visual inspection and mechanical testing**.

Visual inspection involves **examining the construction and appearance of seams by sight**. Examples of regular visual inspections include checking whether the seam lays flat (without any overstretched or puckered areas) and whether the stitch length is correct and even.

Mechanical testing involves subjecting seams to physical stress, such as tension. **Mechanical tests can be conducted either manually or with the help of specialized machines**. An example of manual testing is gently pulling a T-shirt neckline to assess the stitch resistance without breaking. Meanwhile, a tensile pull test machine applies a specific pulling force to check the seam strength for a precise period of time. Such machines are often more complex but provide more accurate results.

Additionally, **mechanical tests are applied to either a piece of fabric or the finished product**, depending on the stage of the product (creation, development, or production) and the required level of precision. Specific fabric tests will be applied to a piece of cloth *before approving the material*, and we will require new tests to be applied *to the garment before approving the production shipment*.

COMMON LABORATORY TESTS	
1. Chemical tests	2. Physical tests
1.1 - Formaldehyde 1.2 - Azo dyes 1.3 - Phthalates 1.4 - Heavy metals	2.1 - Tensile strength 2.2 - Washing performance (dimensional stability, general look, color fastness, etc) 2.3 - Fiber composition 2.4 - Pilling Resistance (knit fabrics)

Figure 3.8: Example of common tests required by most European fashion brands.

Note: While this chart highlights common laboratory tests required in Europe, clothing safety regulations and mandatory chemical testing vary between countries. For more information on **RSL** (Restricted Substances List), visit the AFIRM Group website (*www.afirm-group.com*).

Visual and mechanical checks are usually carried out at the **fashion brand's offices** during prototype and sample evaluations, and in **factories** during production inspections. However, some mechanical tests, such as slippage and pilling resistance, are performed in **specialized laboratories**.

Test type	Description
Tensile strength	Assesses the overall seam strength, resistance and integrity. It evaluates the ability to withstand stretching and pulling forces.
Slippage resistance	Analyses how well the seam maintains its original alignment after applying a certain amount of tension for a specific time. It evaluates the seam's resistance to slipping and fabric layers shifting.

Test type	Description
Washing resistance	This test mimics the repeated stress of regular laundering and provides insights into how seams withstand mechanical actions and chemical exposure during washing cycles. This is one of the most important tests regarding durability. The results cover a significant range of points to consider, including seam integrity, dimension stability, shrinkage, and changes in colour and texture. The test must follow the care instructions label.
Bursting strength	Indicates how well the seam can withstand splitting under pressure.
Abrasion resistance	Assesses the durability of seams in areas prone to friction, like the inseams of pants. It measures the resistance to abrasion, simulating wear and tear.
Shear strength	Evaluates the ability of a seam to withstand forces acting parallel to the seam line. This test is relevant for seams subjected to lateral stresses, such as some workwear and sportswear garments subject to significant movement.

Quality Manual

To maintain the quality of their products, fashion brands need to **establish clear standards that will act as a uniform criterion for designing, testing and acceptance**. These standards are specified in a *quality manual*, which helps guide the entire team, including designers, product developers, manufacturers and inspectors.

The manual **outlines design requirements and inspection details**, covering procedures, sample size (or AQL), and the tools necessary for on-site inspections. For example, for wash testing, the finished garment must undergo a predetermined number of wash cycles using a standard washing machine. These cycles may include agitation, temperature variations, and exposure to specific detergents.

The use of a quality manual **ensures quality consistency and uniformity among all products**, regardless of who designs or produces them. The certainty of knowing the brand's standards and priorities will help everyone work efficiently. As a result, the main **benefits** of using this tool are **saving valuable resources, like time and money**, from the creative stage to production.

Strong Seams

QUALITY MANUAL / Rev.: 2022

BARTULOS

Part 3: Standards and Specifications

3.5 - Seam Slippage

Figure 3.9: Example of the quality manual. Seam slippage test instructions 1 of 5

QUALITY MANUAL / Rev.: 2022   Part 3: Standard Specifications (Rev.: 2022)

Standard: **Slippage Resistance - ISO 13936-1: 2004**

ISO 13936-1: 2004
Textiles — Determination of the slippage resistance of yarns at a seam in woven fabrics
Part 1: Fixed seam opening method

Scope   This part of ISO 13936 is intended for the determination of the resistance offered by thread systems of woven fabric, to slippage at a sewn seam.

This method is not suitable for stretch fabrics or for industrial fabrics, e.g. beltings.

Principle   An unseamed and a seamed part of a test specimen are separately extended by using a tensile testing machine, fitted with grab test jaws, to produce, in the case of the use of a chart recorder, two force/extension curves originating from the same abscissa. The force required to produce a specified distance between the curves, equivalent to a specified seam opening is determined.

Results Include
- Seam Slippage (warp and weft)
- Seam Breakdown (seam opening)

MINIMUM ACCEPTANCE LEVEL
- Applied Force: 55 N
- Max. Seam Opening: 5 mm. / min.
- Standard: ISO 13936-1: 2004

Figure 3.9: Example of the quality manual. Seam slippage test instructions 2 of 5

QUALITY MANUAL / Rev.: 2022   Part 3: Standard Specifications (Rev.: 2022)   BARTULOS

Standard: **Slippage Resistance - ISO 13936-1 : 2004**

Apparatus, materials, and preparation

CRE Machine: as ISO 13936-1 : 2004
- tensil testing machine
- the machine shall be capable of constant rate of extension of 50 mm/min
- the machine shall be capable of setting the gauge length to 100 mm.

Equipment for sewing test specimens: as ISO 13936-1 : 2004
- sewing machine: electrical, single needle, lock stitch, 2 threads (needle and bobin)
- stitch type: 301 (Lock Stitch 2 Threads), as described in ISO 4915:1991

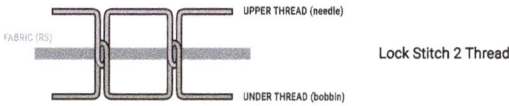

Lock Stitch 2 Threads

- sewing thread: 100% polyester - core spun (filament core, staple sheath) - size 45 tex
- calibrated rule: graduated in 0,5 millimetres divisions

Adjustment of sewing machine:
- throat-plate and feed-dog: as ISO 13936-1:2004
- needle size: 14/90 (ensure the needle is undamaged by examining under magnification)
- stitch length: 4 SPCM (or 10 SPI)

Fabric sample sizes: as ISO 13936-1 : 2004
a) warp slippage: 100 mm (warp) x 200 mm (weft) - x8 pieces = 4 samples (2 pieces per sample)
b) weft slippage: 100 mm (weft) x 200 mm (warp) - x8 pieces = 4 samples (2 pieces per sample)
Note: no test specimen shall be cut from within of either edge of the laboratory sample. Wherever possible, no two specimens in any group of five shall contain the same warp or weft threads

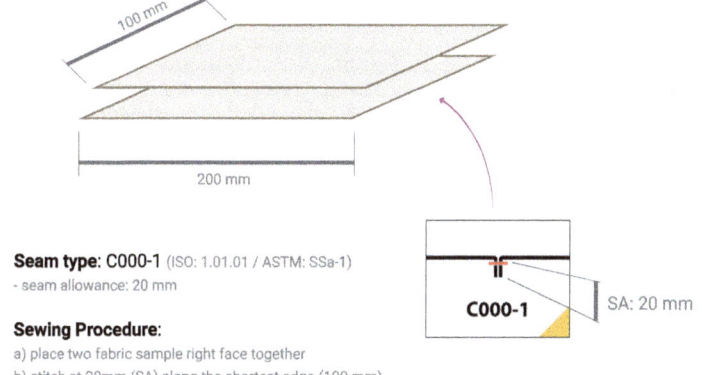

Seam type: C000-1 (ISO: 1.01.01 / ASTM: SSa-1)
- seam allowance: 20 mm

Sewing Procedure:
a) place two fabric sample right face together
b) stitch at 20mm (SA) along the shortest edge (100 mm)

Figure 3.9: Example of the quality manual. Seam slippage test instructions 3 of 5

Standard: **Slippage Resistance - ISO 13936-1: 2004**

PROCEDURE GUIDE
APPROVAL & MONITORING

The material has to be approved BEFORE its purchase (including the purchase of the style).

The material has to be checked by a certified laboratory and it must pass the minimum standard required on the previous page.

Suppliers must provide the required information (see *General Requirements* on page 11) on its technical specifications sheet.

3.5-A1 (Rejected Materials) - **Fabrics with a lower level of slippage resistance are REJECTED.** They has to be treated accordingly (anti-slippage process) to be approved. Otherwise, they have to be replaced.

(Rev.: 2019) **If the information is not provided nor accurate** and the fabric was approved, it is the supplier responsibility to replace the material, or proceed according to the contract conditions.

During the garment developing and production processes (including pre-shipping), prototypes and inspection garments must be re-checked on-site by the product developer and/or inspector.

(Rev.: 2018) - Procedure for manual/visual inspection on-site: pull the seam by hand to a reasonable strength to check slippage resistance.

If the material do not pass the hand pull test:

3.5-A2 (Legal Responsibilities) - The material must be re-send to a certified laboratory to be tested again. Then, the new result must be compared with the technical specification of the material. The legal responsibilities and following steps are specified on the purchase contract.

3.5-A3 (Approved and Uncut Materials) - Treat the fabric accordingly and test it again to approve it.
The anti-slippage process applied to the material should not change its appearance.
Also, consider if the type of seams used on the product are accurate.
Change seam construction if necessary: see seams C100-9 or C100-8 +SE

3.5-A4 (Approved and Cut Materials) - Reinforce stressed areas such as shoulders, necklines, and crotch seams. See *Reinforcement. Common Sewing Techniques* on page 83).

Also, consider using seams C100-9 or C100-8 +SE on side seams of tops and dresses and apply new test.

3.5-A5 - For **bulk productions that can not be fixed or improved**, the case must be studied and evaluated according to each particular circumstances.

Rev.: 2019 - INSPECTION NOTES: a new sample with the improvements should be tested by the *Wear and Wash On-Site Test* (see page 47)

Figure 3.9: Example of the quality manual. Seam slippage test instructions 4 of 5

QUALITY MANUAL / Rev.: 2022   Part 3: Standard Specifications (Rev.: 2022)   SNS BARTULOS

Standard: **Slippage Resistance - ISO 13936-1: 2004**

PROCEDURE GUIDE
ROUTE MAP

MATERIAL SELECTION (fashion designer)
- FABRIC → rejected → 3.5-A1
- approved → PURCHASE

Laboratory Test on Materials
KEY STEPS (prevention)

PRODUCT DEVELOPMENT (product developer)
- PROTO → rejected → 3.5-A3 or 3.5-A1 / 3.5-A2
- approved
- SMS (SALESMAN SAMPLE) → rejected → 3.5-A3 / 3.5-A2
- approved

PRODUCTION (inspector)
- PP (PRE-PRODUCTION) → rejected → 3.5-A3 or 3.5-A4 / 3.5-A2
- approved
- PS (PRE-SHIPPING) → rejected → 3.5-A4 or 3.5-A5 / 3.5-A2

Page 19 of 77

Figure 3.9: Example of the quality manual. Seam slippage test instructions 5 of 5

Seams and common defects

Some typical faults arise when checking the seam's quality. Those issues include puckered or overstretched seams, unbalanced thread tension, lack of elasticity, skipped and uneven stitches, unfinished edges, amended stitches, seam slippage, missed elements like stay tapes, and inconsistent seam allowances.

The severity of these defects depends on their type, size, and location. Therefore, defects are categorized into **three levels**, each with varying significance:

Defect level	Description
Critical	These defects directly affect the garment's durability and performance and may harm the end user. Critical defects include seam slippage, stitches prone to break due to lack of elasticity, and holes in the fabric (other than pinholes).
Major	Major defects are noticeable and can cause the garment to be sold as "defective". Some defects include open seams and amended, missed or broken stitches placed in zone A.
Minor	These defects have little impact on the performance or appearance of the product. Minor defects include uneven stitches in zones B and C and uncut threads shorter than 1.3 cm (longer ones can be major defects, especially if located in zone A.

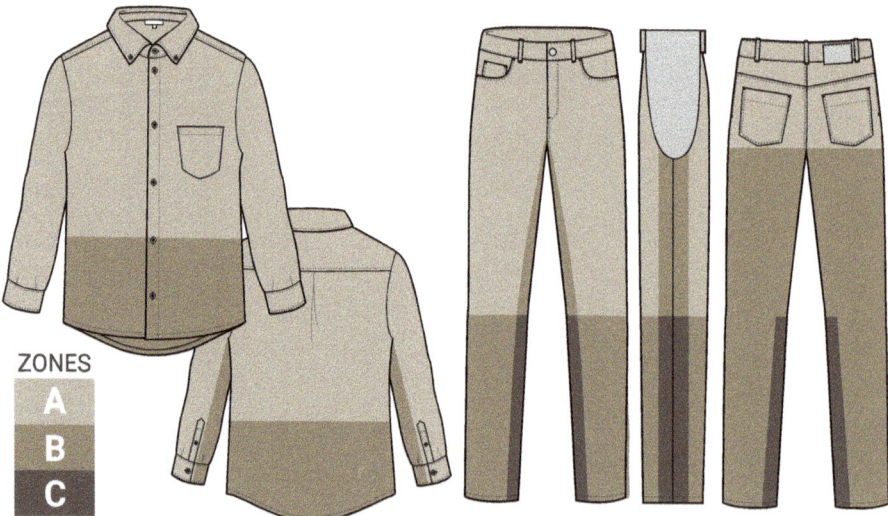

Figure 3.10: Defect locations in garments

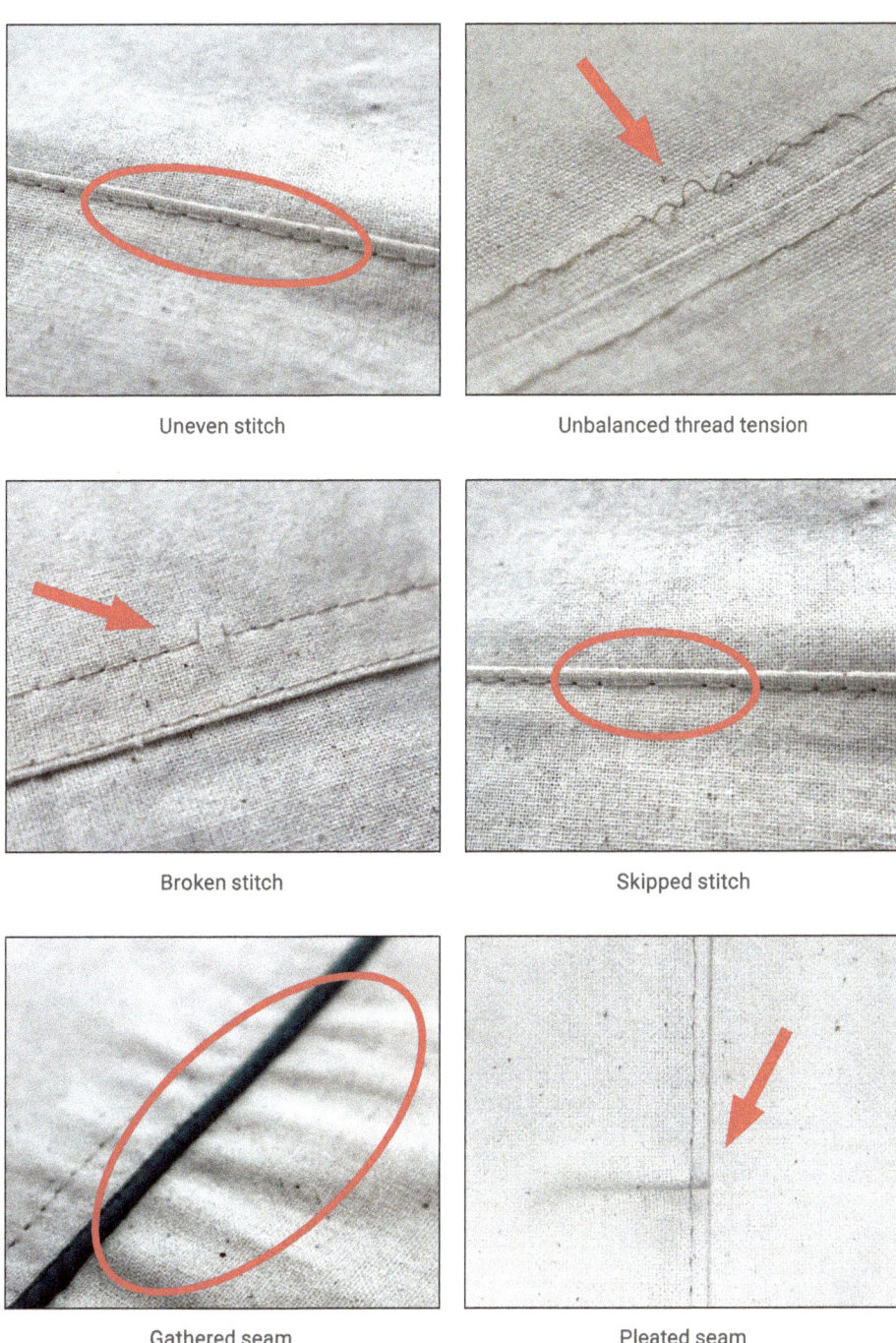

Figure 3.11: Examples of common seam defects

Seam Inspection Checklist

Visual inspection: Appearance

- **Required seam type** (structure, stitch, and topstitch type, SPCM or SPI) ☐
- **Flat seam** (no wrinkles, puckering, waved, overstretched, pleats, fabric caught up, twisted, or needle damages) ☐
- **Even stitching** (consistent length, no skipped or missed stitch) ☐
- **Symmetry** (parallel to the seamline or edge) ☐
- **Required thread** (quality, size, and color) ☐
- **Clean finishing** (no loose, uncut, or bunched-up thread; no amended stitch) ☐
- **Required trimmings** (bands, tapes, pipings, or bias bindings) ☐

Strength: Pull Test

- **Correct braking strength** (no cracked thread) ☐
- **Slippage resistance** ☐
- **Elasticity, stretch resistance, and elongation recovery** (for knit fabrics) ☐
- **Balanced thread tension** (no open seam, gathering, or looped thread) ☐

Reinforcements

- **Seam allowance** (correct finishing technique, no frying edges, or uneven SA width) ☐
- **Interfacing, stay or clear tape** (correct quality, attachment strength, and location) ☐
- **Bar tacks -or rivets** (correct location, length, and stitch density) ☐

Special Techniques (if applicable)

- **Pleats** (correct construction, symmetry, and measures) ☐
- **Buttonholes** (correct location, type, length, stitch width and density, and balanced thread tension) ☐
- **Hardware functionality and attachment strength** (zippers, buttons, etc.) ☐
- **Pattern matching** (if applicable) ☐
- **Labeling** (correctness and attachment) ☐

Figure 3.12: Seam Inspection Checklist

Note: Bear in mind that **defect levels can vary depending on the quality standards of each brand**.

BOOK CONVENTIONS & TECHNICAL VOCABULARY

1. STITCH TYPES (page 174)

Lockstitch	Overlock	Chain stitch	Cover stitch	Flatlock

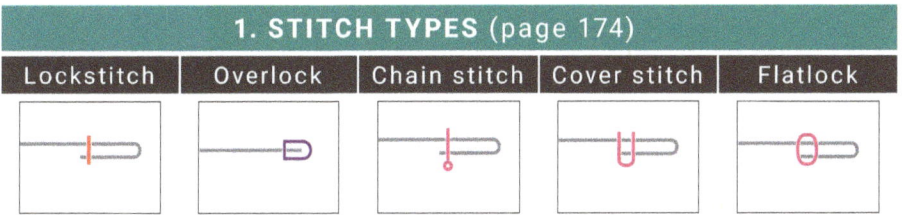

2. TOPSTITCH TYPES (page 178)

Hidden		Visible			

3. TRIMMING TYPES (page 180)

Band	Tape	Piping	Binding

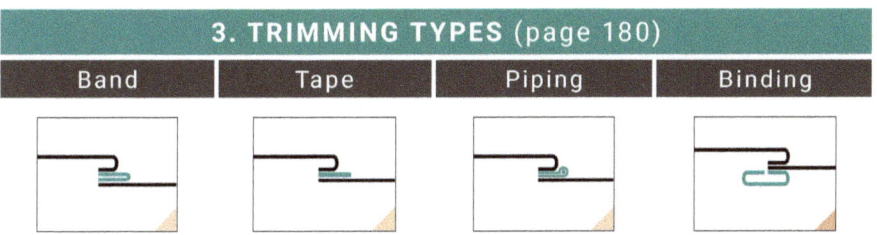

4. SEWING THREADS (page 184)

Regular uses	Special purposes
- Cotton	- Silk
- Cotton-wrapped & polyester core	- Serged thread
- Polyester	- Topstitching
- Nylon	

1. STITCHES

Types	Characteristics	Common uses
Lockstitch ISO 301 (2T)	- Strong and secure. - Not stretchable. - Versatility: Different woven fabrics, garments, and locations. - Neat appearance on both sides: straight stitch line. - It is the most common type of stitch. - It can be backstitched. - Also called Plain Stitch and Straight Stitch. BACK FRONT	- Woven fabrics. - Not suitable for knit and stretchy fabrics. - General purposes: constructions, finishes, and details. - A wide range of garments, accessories, and upholstery. - Topstitching and decorative use. - Zippers applications.
Chain stitch ISO 101 (1T) ISO 401 (2T)	- Flexible and stretchy. - Relatively weak: it can unravel easily by pulling one end. - The 2-thread stitch is the most common and the strongest option. BACK FRONT	- Knit and stretchy fabrics. - Woven fabrics with high shrinkage rates, like denim. - Hemming and joins. - Attaching elastic. - Basting.
Overlock stitch - GENERAL	- Secure and stretchy. - The looped threads encase the fabric edge, minimizing the risk of unravelling and fraying. - The machine can trim the SA, reducing bulk and creating an even edge.	- Knit and stretchable fabrics. - Ready-to-wear garments. - Joining pieces of fabric (construction). - Edge finishing, especially useful for wovens that fray easily (seams with serged edges). - Stitch width varies

Strong Seams

Stitch	Characteristics	Common uses
Overlock 3T ISO 504	- Stitch width varies depending on the sewing machine type and model. - Weaker than a 4T overlock due to single-needle thread. - The most flexible and stretchable overlock stitch due to less thread density. - It is less bulky than a 4T overlock. - Standard stitch width: 3mm (narrow) to 6mm (wide).	depending on the sewing machine type and model. - Light-weight and delicate fabrics: woven and knit fabrics. - Not suitable for heavy-weight fabrics. - High-stretch fabrics. - Lingerie and underwear. - Decorative raw edge finish on light-weight fabrics: narrow version.
Overlock 4T ISO 514	- A straight stitching is placed in the middle of the stitch. - Balance between strength and flexibility: the additional stitch line adds strength and stability, but it makes it less flexible than a 3T overlock. - Standard width: 4mm (narrow) to 7mm (wide).	- Woven fabrics. - Not suitable for knit and stretchy fabrics. - General purposes: constructions, finishes, and details. - A wide range of garments, accessories, and upholstery. - Topstitching and decorative use. - Zippers applications.
Overlock 5T ISO 516	- Combines a 3T overlock stitch with a 2T chain stitch running parallel to the overlock. - The strongest overlock stitch. - The less stretchable overlock stitch. - Slightly bulkier than a 3T and 4T overlock. - Standard width: 6mm (narrow) to 9mm (wide).	- Heavy-weight fabrics. - High-stressed seams. - Woven fabrics with high shrinkage rates, like denim. - Not recommended for light-weight fabrics. - Jogging pants, outerwear, and upholstery.

ABC Seams®

Stitch	Characteristics	Common uses
	BACK / FRONT	
Cover stitch - GENERAL	- Stretchable and flexible. - Flat finishing, reducing bulk and irritation on the skin. - Tidied finish on both sides: enclosed seam allowance. - Secure and comfortable. - Stitch width varies depending on the sewing machine.	- All kinds of knit and stretchy fabrics. - Versatile: even though it's less common, they work well on woven fabrics. - All types of knitwear garments. - Hemming. - Joining overlapped knit pieces (reduces bulk).
Cover 2N 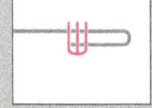 ISO 406	- Creates two parallel rows of straight stitching on the right side. - Highly elastic due to the stitch on the reverse. - Moderate strength. - Less bulky than a 3N cover stitch. - Standard width: 4mm (narrow) to 7mm (wide).	- Light to medium-weight fabrics. - Single fold hems. - Underwear, lingerie, and swimwear. - Belt loops of jeans. - Attach binding.
	BACK / FRONT	
Cover 3N ISO 407	- Create three parallel rows of straight stitching on the right side. - Slightly bulkier than a 3T cover due to the additional needle stitch. - Standard width: 4mm (narrow) to 8mm (wide).	- Medium to heavy-weight fabrics. - Stretchable seams that require maximum strength and comfort. - High-stress seams requiring additional stability. - Athletic gear. - Decorative.

Strong Seams

Stitch	Characteristics	Common uses
Flatlock stitch - GENERAL	- Secure, stretchable, and flat. - Serged stitch on both sides: flat look. - The additional looper thread on top adds reinforcement, increasing the strength and stability compared to standard cover stitches; however, they are less stretchable.	- Seams that require additional strength and stability. - Decorative and functional uses.
Flatlock 2N ISO 602	- Stronger than cover 2N. - Less stretchable than cover 2N. - Slightly bulkier than cover 2N. - Standard width: 4mm (narrow) to 7mm (wide).	- Light to medium-weight fabrics. - Not suitable for extra heavy fabrics or when high-stretchiness is required. - Sportswear and activewear. - Sweatshirts and leggings.
Flatlock 3N ISO 605	- The additional needle thread in the middle makes it the steadiest and least stretchable of all cover and flatlock stitches. - Stronger than cover 3N. - Slightly bulkier than flatlock 2N. - Standard width: 4mm (narrow) to 8mm (wide).	- Medium to heavy-weight fabrics. - Not suitable for delicate and very light fabrics or when high stretchiness is required. - Sportswear and activewear. - Bold decorative topstitching.

2. TOPSTITCHE TYPES

Hidden	Visible
- Understitch - Stitch in-the-ditch	- Edge Stitch - Basic Topstitch - Double Topstitch - Triple Topstitch

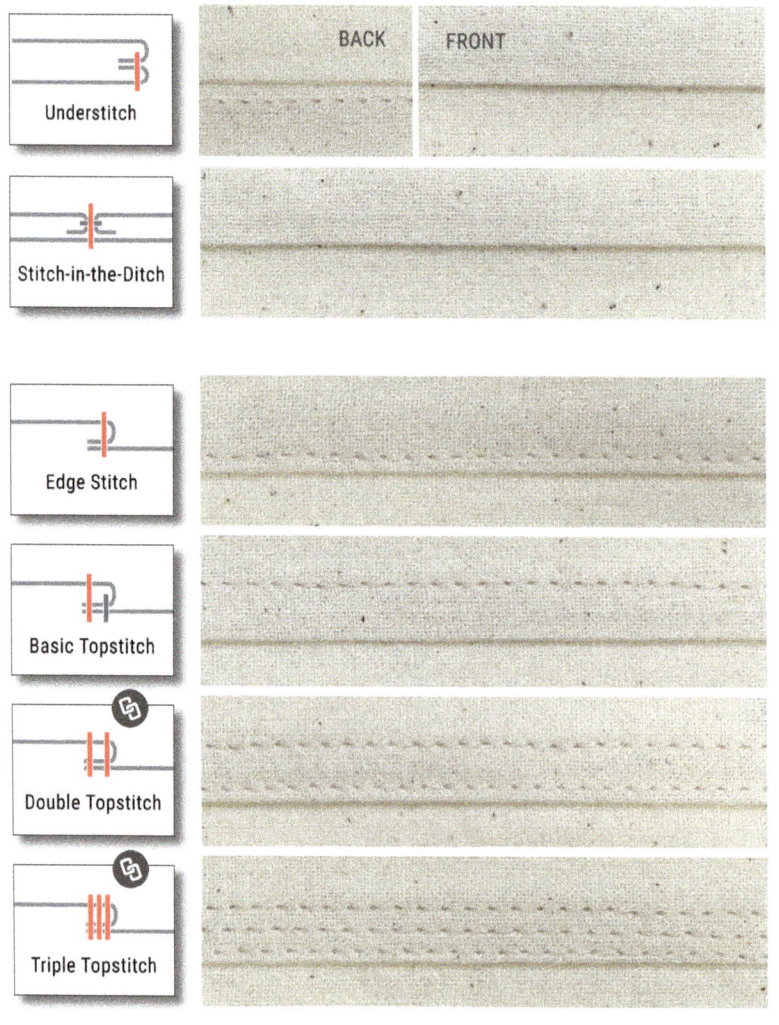

BONUS

FABRIC: WEIGHT					
	Extra Light	Light	Medium	Heavy	Extra Heavy
	- 135 gsm - 4 osy	135-200 gsm 4-6 osy	200-305 gsm 6-9 osy	305-370 gsm 9-11 osy	+ 370 gsm + 11 osy

GSM: Grams per square meter
OSY: Ounces per square yard

FABRIC: SHRINKAGE		
1. Low	2. Moderate	3. High
below 3%	from 3 to 5%	above 5%

FABRIC: TENSILE STRENGTH		
1. Low	2. Moderate	3. High
below 400 N/tex	400 N/tex to 800 N/tex	above 800 N/tex

FABRIC: THREAD COUNT		
1. Low	2. Medium	3. High
below 150 threads per in2	between 150 and 300 threads per in2.	above 300 threads per in2.

Note: Please notice that these measures may vary depending on the standards of each brand.

3. TRIMMING TYPES

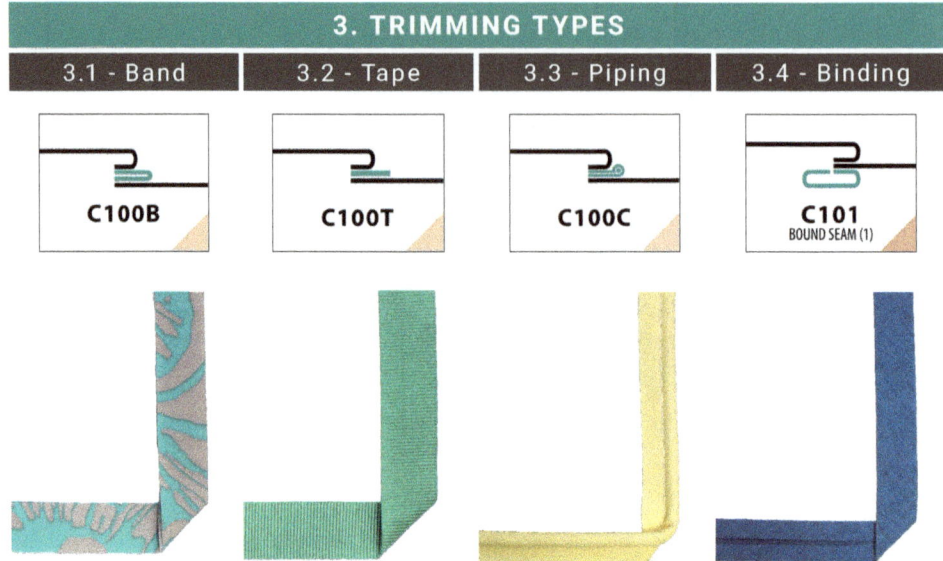

Figure 3.13: Trimming types for sewing seams

	3.1 - Band
Properties	- It is a strip of woven fabric with a folded edge along one side - The two raw edges line up together. - Often cut on the straight grain, but it can be cut on the bias. - The band cut on the grain provides more stability and prevents the seam from stretching. - When cut on the bias, it offers stretch and recovery. - It has a seam allowance to be sewn into the seam. - It can be purchased ready-made or custom-made. - Come in various widths, colours, patterns, and materials, being the most suitable light-weight fabrics to avoid bulkiness. - Provides colour and texture to the seam. - The band reinforces the seam, adding structure and strength.
Common uses	- Decorative purposes. - Cuffs, patch pockets, plackets, waistbands, side seams. - Bed sheets.

Common seams	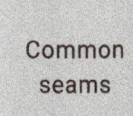 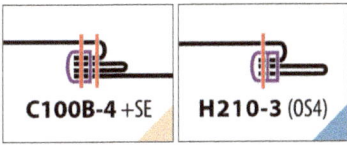 C100B-4 +SE H210-3 (OS4)

3.2 - Tape

Properties	- Flat strip of fabric made of woven or knit. - Edges are polished with diverse techniques. - Come in diverse materials, widths, colours, and patterns: laces offer delicate looks, ribbons provide a smooth finish, and grosgrain gives a robust texture. - Multiple purposes: from functional, like reinforcing seams and polishing fabric edges, to purely decorative use. - It provides structure to the seam and increases its strength. - The most common types applied on seams are herringbone twill tape, lace, grosgrain tape, webbing tape, fringe, and stay and silicone tape.
Common uses	- Finish raw edges. - Reinforce seams. - Laces are used for lingerie, underwear, and childrenswear. - Grosgrain and herringbone reinforce necklines, plackets, and waistbands. - Stay and silicone tapes are used inside the seam to strengthen stressed areas, like shoulders. - Corsetry and accessories such as bags and shoes. - Upholstery. - Casing for elastic or drawstrings.
Common seams	C002-1 C100T-4 +SE C220-2 H310-4

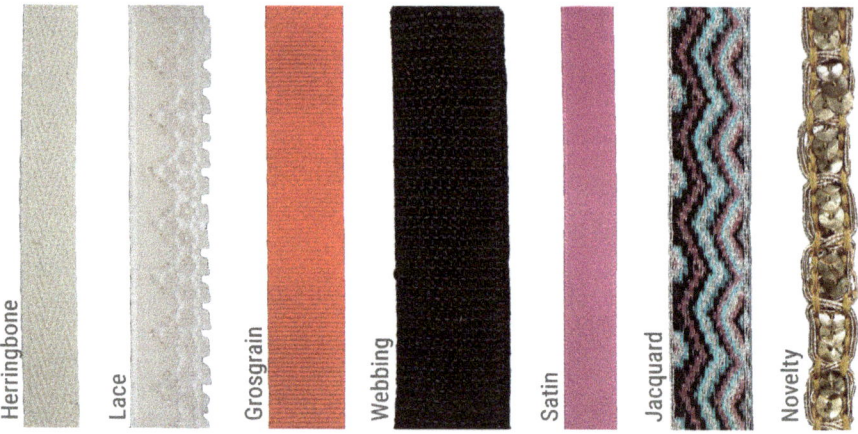

Figure 3.14: Tapes classification

	3.3 - Piping
Properties	- Made by encasing a cord within a folded fabric strip, then stitching it closed. - The strip of fabric can be cut straight on the bias to add some stretchiness. - Fabric edge/s are lined up together and can be raw or polished. - It has SA to be sewn into the seam, exposing only the rounded edge. - The fabric comes in different materials (usually woven), colours, and patterns. - The cord comes in various thicknesses. - It can be purchased ready-made or custom-made. - The cord creates a raised decorative seam/edge, adding tailored detail. - It adds structure to seams and edges and defines silhouettes. - It increases the strength.
Common uses	- Decorative and functional purposes. - Pyjamas and many other types of clothing like womenswear and outerwear. - Collars, pockets, plackets, and hems. - Accessories like shoes and bags. - Upholstery and home décor accessories like cushions.
Common seams	C100C-3 (0S4) H400-4 +SE

3.4 - (Bias) Binding

Properties	- It is a strip of woven fabric with both edges folded inwards, creating a clean finish on the outside. - Seam allowances placed on the backside. - When cut on the bias, it offers stretch and recovery, preventing the seam from stretch or distortion. - It can be purchased ready-made or custom-made. - Come in various widths, colours, patterns, and materials. - It polishes and reinforces seams and edges, adding structure, and colour.
Common uses	- Decorative and functional purposes. - When on the bias, it is perfect for curved edges or areas requiring flexibility. - Finish raw edges. - Most types of clothing, accessories and home décor items like blankets. - Casing for elastic or drawstrings.
Common seams	C101-10 H101-10 H200-1

Additional Notes:

- Trimming selection depends on: the garment use, fabric, and design aesthetic.

- The trim must match the performance and care needs of the main fabric: colourfastness to washing and crocking, abrasion resistance, and shrinkage.

4. SEWING THREADS		
Type	Characteristics	Uses
Cotton	- Regular strength. - Usually mercerized: may fade or crock - Absorbent - Can shrink if not pre-washed. - Adds a natural, matte finish.	- Light-weight to medium-weight wovens. - Not good for high-stress seams. - Post dyed garments. - Zippers and buttonholes. - Quilting, patchwork and applique.
Cotton-wrapped & polyester core	- Stronger than mercerized cotton. - Combines the breathability of cotton with the strength of polyester. - More durable and wrinkle-resistant than pure cotton.	- Woven and some knits. - Garments that require frequent washing. - Ready-to-wear and childrenswear. - Accessories and home decor.
Polyester	- Strong, durable, and resistant to abrasion. - Versatile - Water-resistant and dries quickly. - Wide variety of colours available. - Can melt under high heat (ironing). - Not as breathable as cotton.	- Natural and synthetic fabrics. - Woven and knit. - Not good for delicate fabrics. - Most types of garments - High-stress seams, like pockets. - Sportswear, swimwear, bags. - Embroidery.
Nylon	- Very strong and abrasion-resistant, - Stretchy and elastic. - Water-resistant and dries quickly. - Can be slippery and difficult to sew with.	- Woven and knit. - Heavy-weight fabrics, like jeans. - Ideal for high-stress seams. - Activewear and acessories - Upholstery and outdoor gear.
Silk	- Luxurious, soft, and shiny. - Delicate (not very strong). - More expensive than other thread types.	- Light-weight and delicate fabrics. - Not for gral. sewing - Decorative stitching. - Embroidery. - Buttons and buttonholes.

Serged thread	- Light-weight - Stretchable. - Often textured (woolly nylon or air-core) to create a bulkier seam for better coverage and finishing edges. - Available in a variety of colours - Functional and decorative use.	- Knit and woven fabrics. - Serged edges. - Seaming light to medium-weight fabrics. - Decorative hemming.
Topstitching	- It is not a specific thread type but a functional thread for decorative topstitching. - Usually thicker than regular threads for better visibility. - May have a slight sheen or texture depending on the material.	- Visible topstitch lines. - Adding structure and reinforcement to specific areas of a garment. - Decorative and functional uses. - Buttons and buttonholes on heavy-weight fabrics.

THREAD		NEEDLE	FABRIC
Size: Tex (ISO)	Tensile strength (LBS)	Size (Singer)	Weight
16	2.1	10-12	Light
30	3.7	12-14	
45	7.1	14-16	Medium
70	10.1	16-18	
90	13.5	18-20	
135	20.6	20-22	Heavy
210	30.7	22-24	
270	40.1	24-26	Extra heavy
350	51.5	26-28	

Figure 3.15: Threads, needles, and fabric correlation's chart.

INDEX

A
abbreviations, 20
abrasion resistance, 145, 164
apparel industry, 25
AQL, 29

B
back-stitching, 158
band, 180
bar tacks, 157
basic seam, 34-35
    bounded, 36
binded edge, 94-97
binding, 182
boning seam, 60-61
bound hem, 72-75
    wide, 84-87
bound seam, 44-47
bursting strength, 164

C
chain stitch, 174
chemical tests, 163
chemical treatments, 144, 147
constructions, 8, 33, 128
cover-stitch, 153, 176

D
design, 19
details, 9, 111, 131
double fold hem, 76-77
    wide, 88-89
durability, 25, 27-28
    definition & types, 27
    physical, 28

E
exposed band, 100-102
    bound, 104-107
    wide, 92, 90
exposed piping, 102
exposed tape, 102

F
fabric, 29, 144
    type, 19, 159
    weight, 185
faced hem
    self-polished, 90-92
    unhemmed, 92
felled seam, 39-43
finishes, 8, 65, 129
fit, 29, 170
flatlock stitch, 153, 177
french seam, 37-38

G
garment assembly, 29, 144, 147
garment inspection, 162

H
hairline seam, 36
hong kong seam, 59

I
icons, 21
inspections, 161, 172
inverted box pleat, 114-15

J

K

L
laboratory tests, 163
lapped seam, 50-51
lining, 155
lockstitch, 174

M
machinery, 29, 149
    bed types, 150
Martindale abrasion test, 145

N
needle size, 185

O
open seam, 56-59

operator skills, 144, 151
overlock stitch, 153, 174
overview, 17, 128

P
patch
    bound, 120-125
    raw edge, 118-119
    self-polished, 116-117
piping, 182
pleat, 112-113

Q
quality
    control, 162 -172
    manual, 165
    types, 25

R
reinforcements, 29, 152, 172

S
sandwich hem, 78-80
sandwich seam, 52-54
seam
    allowance, 152
    catalogue, 14, 15, 16, 31
    classification, 14
    defects, 170
    inspection checklist, 172
    location, 19, 161
    quality checks, 170
    quality control, 162
    selection, 18, 28-29, 149
    strength, 144
    structure, 16, 148
    types, 147
    stabilizing, 152, 155
self-enclosed edge, 153
self-polished, 153
serged edge, 152
sewing techniques, 152
sewing thread, 144, 146, 173, 184
shear strength, 164
shrinkage, 145
single fold hem, 70-71

wide, 82-83
slippage, 165
    resistance, 163
stay tape, 157
stitch
    length, 151
    type, 148, 173
stress, types & levels, 160
stressed areas, 160

T
tape, 181
taped edge, 98-99
technical vocabulary, 173
tensile strength, 145, 163, 185
test
    mechanical, 162
    physical, 162
    pull, 172
    and methods, 29
    thread size, 185
topstitch type, 148, 173, 178
topstitching, 156
trimming, 29, 144, 146, 154
    types, 173, 180

U
unhemmed edge pp. 66-68
    2 layers, 68
    reinforced, 68

V

W
washing resistance, 164
welt seam, 48-49

X

Y

Z
zigzag stitch, 153

SEAM CODES | INDEX

C

C000: 34-35, 37, 56
C001: 36, 34
C002: 36, 34
C010: 37-38, 34, 48
C011: 36, 34, 37
C100: 39-43, 44, 46, 48, 50, 52, 55, 56, 103
C101: 44-45, 39, 46, 81
C103: 45, 44
C104: 46-47, 39, 44
C105: 47, 46
C110: 48-49, 37, 39, 69
C120: 50-51, 39
C200: 56-57, 58
C202: 59, 58
C210: 58-59, 56
C220: 60-61, 46, 56, 58
CD190: 52-54, 39

D

D110: pp. 112-113, 114
D112: pp. 114-15, 112, 123
D200: pp. 118-119, 116
D201: pp. 122, 120
D202: pp. 122, 120
D203: pp. 120-121, 116, 124
D205: pp. 124-125, 116, 120
D210: pp. 116-117, 118, 120, 124

H

H000: 66-68
H001: 68, 66, 70
H002: 68, 66, 74
H100: 70-71, 66, 72, 74, 76, 78
H101: 72-73, 74, 76, 90
H104: 74-75, 70, 72
H105: 75, 74, 86, 98
H110: 76-77, 70, 88
H120: 82-83, 70, 84, 86, 88, 90
H123: 84-85, 82, 86
H125: 86-87, 82, 84
H130: 88-89, 76, 82, 84, 86, 90
H140: 92, 90
H150: 90-92, 72, 78, 82, 88
H200: 94-95, 96, 98
H201: 96-97, 94
H210: 100-102, 104, 106
H211: 104-105, 93, 100, 106
H212: 106-107, 100, 104
H230: 92, 90
H300: 98-99, 94, 96
H310: 102, 100
H400: 102, 10
HD000: 68, 66
HD190: 78-80, 70

BIBLIOGRAPHY & SOURCES CONSULTED

ABC Seams® Pty. Ltd. (2021). *101 Sewing Seams: The Most Used Seams by Fashion Designers* (2nd ed.). ABC Seams® Pty. Ltd. ISBN 978-0-6482734-6-2.

ABC Seams® Pty. Ltd. (2020). *Sewing Seams for Tech Packs: A visual guide to produce clothing*. ABC Seams® Pty. Ltd. ISBN 978-0-6482734-4-8.

Askaroff, A. (2019). *The Complete Guide To Sewing Machine Tension Adjustment: Sewing Machine Tension Made Easy*. Independently published. ISBN 978-1703009845.

Askaroff, A. (2022). *A Perfect Stitch*. Independently published. ISBN 979-8789426159.

ASTM International. (2004). *ASTM D Test Method 1776: Standard practice for conditioning and testing textiles*. Philadelphia, PA: ASTM International.

ASTM International. (2021). *ASTM-D5034: Standard Test Method for Breaking Strength and Elongation of Textile Fabrics (Grab Test)*.

Black, S. (2012). *The Sustainable Fashion Handbook*. Thames and Hudson Ltd. ISBN 978-0500290569.

Brown, P., & Rice, J. (2001). *Ready to wear apparel analysis*. Prentice Hall. ISBN 0130254347.

British Standards Institution. (1991). *BS3870: Part 1 and Part 2: Classification and Terminology of Stitch Types*.

Bubonia, J. E. (2014). *Apparel Quality: A Guide to Evaluating Sewn Products*. Fairchild. ISBN 978-1609015123.

Bubonia, J. E. (2017). *Apparel Production Terms and Processes* (2nd ed.). Fairchild. ISBN 978-1501315571.

Burns, L. D., Mullet, K. K., & Bryant, N. O. (2012). *The Business of Fashion: Designing, Manufacturing and Marketing* (4th ed.). Fairchild Books. ISBN 978-1609011101.

Carr, H., & Latham. (2008). *Technology of Clothing Manufacture* (4th ed.). Blackwell Science. ISBN 978-1405161985.

Cole, J., & Czachor, S. (2008). *Professional Sewing Techniques for Designers*. Fairchild Books. ISBN 978-1563675164.

Delgado Luque, M. L., & Gardetti, M. Á. (2019). *Manual de Moda Sostenible*. Arcopress Ediciones. ISBN 978-8417057791.

Eberle, H. (2008). *Clothing Technology: From Fibre to Fashion* (5th ed.). Verlag Europa-Lehrmittel Nourn. ISBN 978-3808562256.

Editors of Creative Publishing. (2009). *Singer Complete Photo Guide to Sewing*. Creative Publishing. ISBN 978-1589234345.

Fischer, A., & Gobin, K. (2017). *Construction for Fashion Design*. Bloomsbury Visual Arts. ISBN 978-1472538755.

Fletcher, K. (2020). *Sustainable Fashion and Textiles: Design Journeys* (2nd ed.). Taylor & Francis Ltd. ISBN 978-0415644561.

Friend, R. L. (1977). *Sewing Room Technical Handbook: Lock-stitch and Overlock Seams*. Hatra. ISBN 0901056022.

Gerry Cooklin. (2006). *Introduction to Clothing Manufacture* (2nd ed.). Blackwell Science. ISBN 978-0632058464.

Ghiuzan, L. (2024). *Manufacturing Excellence and Quality Management in Sustainable Fashion Apparel*. VersaCharm Books. ISBN 978-0975645605.

Glock, R., & Kunz, G. (2004). *Apparel Manufacturing: Sewn Product Analysis* (4th ed.). Pearson Higher Ed USA. ISBN 978-0131119826.

Golizia, D. (2021). *The Fashion Business: Theory and Practice in Strategic Fashion Management*. Routledge. ISBN 978-0367490552.

Gwilt, A., & Rissanen, T. (2011). *Shaping Sustainable Fashion: Changing the Way We Make and Use Clothes*. Routledge. ISBN 978-1849712422.

Gwilt, A. (2020). *A Practical Guide to Sustainable Fashion*. Bloomsbury Academic. ISBN 978-1350067043.

Gwilt, A., Payne, A., & Anicet Ruthschilling, E. (2019). *Global Perspectives on Sustainable Fashion*. Bloomsbury Publishing. ISBN 978-1350058132.

Huff, D. (1993). *How to Lie with Statistics*. WW Norton & Co. ISBN 0393310728.

ISO. (1991). *Textiles. Stitch Types: Classification and Terminology* (ISO 4915-1991). Genève: ISO.

Jeffrey, M., & Evans, N. (2011). *Costing for the Fashion Industry*. Berg Publishers. ISBN 978-1847882593.

Kilgus, R., Ring, W., & Hornberger, M. (2013). *Clothing Technology*. Verlag Europa-Lehrmittel Nourney. ISBN 978-3808562263.

Laing, R. M., & Webster, J. (1998). *Stitches and Seams. The Textile Institute*. ISBN 978-1870812733.

Lavergne, M. (2015). *Fixing Fashion: Rethinking the Way We Make, Market and Buy Our Clothes*. New Society Publishers. ISBN 978-0865718004.

Lee, J., & Steen, C. (2018). *Technical Sourcebook for Apparel Designers* (3rd ed.). Fairchild Books. ISBN 978-1501328477.

Linda B. Stamper, A. A., & Sharp, S. H. D. (1991). *Evaluating Apparel Quality*. Fairchild Fashion Group. ISBN 978-0870055126.

López Domínguez, M., & Mayayo Bellostas, M. A. (2019). **Moda sostenible: Manual básico de conceptos**. Tierra de Nadie Editores. ISBN 978-8412055209.

Lowe, A. (n.d.). **Fashion Brand Management: Plan, Scale and Market a Successful Fashion Business**. Kogan Page. ISBN 978-1398609008.

Ly, N. G., & Boss, A. G. (1990). **Application of the FAST system to the manufacture of fabrics and garments**. Wool Research Organization of New Zealand, 5, pp. 370-409.

Mbeledogu, E. (2014). **Fashion Design Research**. Laurence King Publishing. ISBN 978-1780671799.

McDonough, W. (2008). **Cradle to Cradle: Remaking the Way We Make Things**. Henry Holt. ISBN 978-0865475878.

Posner, H. (2015). **Marketing Fashion**. Laurence King Publishing. ISBN 978-1780675667.

Taylor, M. A. (2004). **Technology of Textile Properties**. Forbes Publications.

The Textile Institute. (2015). **Garment Manufacturing Technology**. Woodhead Publishing. ISBN 978-1782422327.

Wood, D. (2001). **The Practical Encyclopedia of Sewing**. Lorenz Books. ISBN 978-0754802779.

Web pages and other online sources:

A&E Textiles. (2011). **Selecting Stitches Per Inch**. A&E Technical Bulletin. Retrieved from http://www.amefird.com/wp-content/uploads/2010/01/Selecting-the-right-SPI-2-5-10.pdf

American Association of Textile Chemists and Colorists. (2010). Shanghai Jifa. **AATCC Technical Manual**. Retrieved from http://shanghaijifa.com/UploadFile/201104/AATCC2010%E8%8B%B1%E6%96%87%E7%89%88.pdf

Brown, M. (2023). *Patagonia. Design Stories. Made to Work*. Retrieved from https://www.patagonia.com/stories/made-to-work/story-141715.html

Coats. (2022). *Coats publishes the 2022 Sustainability Report*. Retrieved from https://www.coats.com/en/sustainability/sustainability-overview

Coats. (2018). *When quality control runs amok*. Retrieved from https://www.coats.com/en/coats-in-action/coats-epic-verifi

Cooper, T., Claxton, S., Hill, H., Holbrook, K., Hughes, M., Knox, A., & Oxborrow, L. (2014). Nottingham Trent University. *Wrap. Clothing Longevity Protocol*. Retrieved from https://wrap.org.uk/sites/default/files/2021-03/WRAP-clothing-longevity-protocol.pdf

Cooper, T., Hill, H., Kininmonth, J., Townsend, K., & Hughes, M. (2016). Wrap. *Design for longevity: Guidance on increasing the active life of clothing*. Retrieved from https://wrap.org.uk/resources/report/design-extending-clothing-life#download-file

Cooper, T., Oxborrow, L., Claxton, S., Goworek, H., Hill, H., & McLaren, A. (2016). Nottingham Trent University, Nottingham. *Strategies to improve design and testing for clothing longevity*. Retrieved from https://www.ntu.ac.uk/__data/assets/pdf_file/0039/906897/strategies-improve-design-testing-clothing-longevity.pdf

Fashion Revolution. (2023). *Fashion Transparency* Index 2023. Retrieved from https://issuu.com/fashionrevolution/docs/fashion_transparency_index_2023_ pages

Ghani, S. A. (2011). *Seam Performance: Analysis and Modeling* (PhD diss., University of Manchester). Retrieved from https://www.research.manchester.ac.uk/portal/files/54512390/FULL_TEXT.PDF

ISO. (2004). Textiles — *Determination of the slippage resistance of yarns at a seam in woven fabrics* — Part 1: Fixed seam opening method. ISO 13936-1:2004. Retrieved from https://www.iso.org/standard/36416.html

Kabir, S., Sultana, & Ali. (2016). *Impact of Stitch Type and Stitch Density on Seam Properties*. Journal of Science and Research. Retrieved from https://pdfs.semanticscholar.org/5e30/1434ea134b064b5fc481b3104f82b83ff38e.pdf

Mayedul Islam. (n.d.). Merchandising. Online library for merchandisers. *How to Test Fabric Sewability in Apparel Industry*. Retrieved from https://garments-merchandising.com/how-to-test-fabric-sewability-in-apparel-industry/

Nimonik. (n.d.). Document Center. *List of Standards on Textile Fabrics Including Nonwovens, Felts, Lace, Etc*. Retrieved from https://www.document-center.com/standards/ics/59.080.30

QIMA. (n.d.). *Dimensional Standards to Help Your Textile Products Last*. Retrieved from https://www.qima.com/testing/textile-fabric/dimensional-stability-test

QIMA. (n.d.). *Following the Fiber: Physical Testing For Textiles At Every Step*. Retrieved from https://www.qima.com/testing/textile-fabric/physical-testing-textiles

QIMA. (n.d.). *Secrets of the Big Brand Garments Quality Inspection Procedure*. Retrieved from https://www.qima.com/quality-control-services/garments-quality-inspection-procedure

Ruby Moon. (n.d.). *Durability in Fashion: Why Longevity Should Take Priority*. Retrieved from https://rubymoon.org.uk/blog/2020/07/13/durability-in-fashion-why-longevity-should-take-priority/

Salvador Chamorro, A. (2013). Pecvnia Revista de la Facultad de Ciencias Económicas y Empresariales Universidad de León. Research Gate. *La evolución de las exportaciones de bienes de China: una visión panarómica = Chinese goods exports development: An overview*. Retrieved from https://www.researchgate.net/publication/279207549_La_evolucion_de_las_exportaciones_de_bienes_de_China

TEDx Talks. (2018). *Crecimiento, pero no todo vale* | Ana Plaza | TEDxUDeustoMadrid. Retrieved from https://www.youtube.com/watch?v=b5jxgzqgO3o

TEDx Talks. (2016). *How to Engage with Ethical Fashion* | Clara Vuletich | TEDxSydney. Retrieved from https://www.youtube.com/watch?v=WXOd4qh3JKk

Textile Academy. (2018). *What is fabric sewability?* Retrieved from https://www.onlinetextileacademy.com/what-is-fabric-sewability-sewability-of-fabrics/

Tim Cooper, Lynn Oxborrow, Stella Claxton, Helen Hill, Helen Goworek, Angharad McLaren, Katherine West. (2021). Nottingham Trent University. *Clothing Durability Dozen*. Retrieved from https://www.ntu.ac.uk/__data/assets/pdf_file/0035/1395494/30_04_21_NTU-DURABILITY-DOZEN-TOOLKIT_10-31.pdf

United Nations. (n.d.). *Sustainable Development Goals*. Retrieved from https://www.un.org/sustainabledevelopment/

Velasquez, A. (2018). *Sourcing Journal. Pricey denim isn't always high quality, new study finds*. Retrieved from https://sourcingjournal.com/denim/denim-business/disparities-quality-price-denim-116400/

Wrap. (2017). Youtube Channel. *Introducing durability*. Retrieved from https://www.youtube.com/watch?v=G879BnWGOUY

Ziynet Ondogan, Emine Utkun, Oktay Pamuk, and Esra Zeynep Yıldız. (2010). Research Gate. *Sewability in Apparel Industry*. Retrieved from https://www.researchgate.net/publication/283119506_Sewability_in_Apparel_Industry

ACKNOWLEDGMENTS

The creation of this book would not have been possible without the invaluable contributions of these talented individuals. We deeply thank our esteemed colleagues, industry professionals, and friends for their unwavering support throughout this journey. Your feedback, expert advice, and generosity have significantly enriched the content of this book.

A heartfelt THANK YOU to:

Ahmed Syed;

Ayah Demerdash;

Belén Asensio Navarro;

Ben Tofan;

Carolina Fay;

David Alonso Gómez;

Deepak Maurya;

Gabby BR;

Ila Mirnyy;

Inna Klimova;

Izarra González;

Jane Cruise;

Joshua Rawson Harris;

Júlia Lago Pujol;

Lee Bo-Young;

Li Wenliang;

Lorna Reid-Mullen;

Maite Enciso Cubero;

María Verónica Fourcade;

Matheus Ferrero;

Olga Olmos Gallego;

Robert Cooper;

Samantha Rao;

Sanjay Bhat;

Sarah Dietschi;

Soidée Romero;

Sol Mauro;

Trevor Collins (Hill);

Verónica López Orce;

Vince Fleming;

Vlora Alimi; and

William Sunderland.

ABOUT ABC Seams

An assertive understanding of sewing seams is essential to the **professional success** of designers and product developers. **Clear and precise communication** within your team and with colleagues is crucial to avoid confusion and ensure your design vision translates into reality.

Empowering Communication

We work for you to simplify design communication through a **standardized sewing seam language**. This international *Seams Code System* (SCS) lets you easily **select, name, and reference any seam type**, fostering clear understanding - anytime, anywhere.

Why people use ABC Seams System:

Professionalism and confidence: Our system is a tool that empowers informed decision-making, allowing professionals to work confidently.

Reduced development time: Efficient communication minimizes ambiguity and facilitates quicker development cycles by reducing adjustments and sampling in the development stage.

Boosts Creativity: design unique products that stand out in the market by exploring new constructions, finishes and details.

ABC Seams SERIES

"Strong Seams: The Catalogue to Design Durable Clothing" is the third book of our sewing seam series.

While each book in the series can be used independently, all of them were created to empower fashion professionals with the knowledge and tools to create whatever you want.

101 Sewing Seams
The most used seams by fashion designers

This essential book is a foundational reference tool that showcases the industry's most common seams. It's a must-have resource for anyone seeking a comprehensive understanding of basic seam construction.

Sewing Seams for Tech Packs
A visual guide to produce clothing

This practical guide bridges the gap between design and production by demonstrating how to communicate garment assembly through tech packs effectively. It features detailed explanations of 27 classic styles and provides a solid base for explaining a wide range of designs.

Note: If you found this book helpful, please take a moment to review it on Amazon. Thank you!

ABC Seams®

Digital Seams Sketches in PDF

You can also purchase the PDF illustrations of each seam featured in this book. These downloadable images can be directly added to the assembly sheet of your tech pack, making it easy and quick, and simplifying your job.

For further information, visit our website at
www.abcseams.com/products

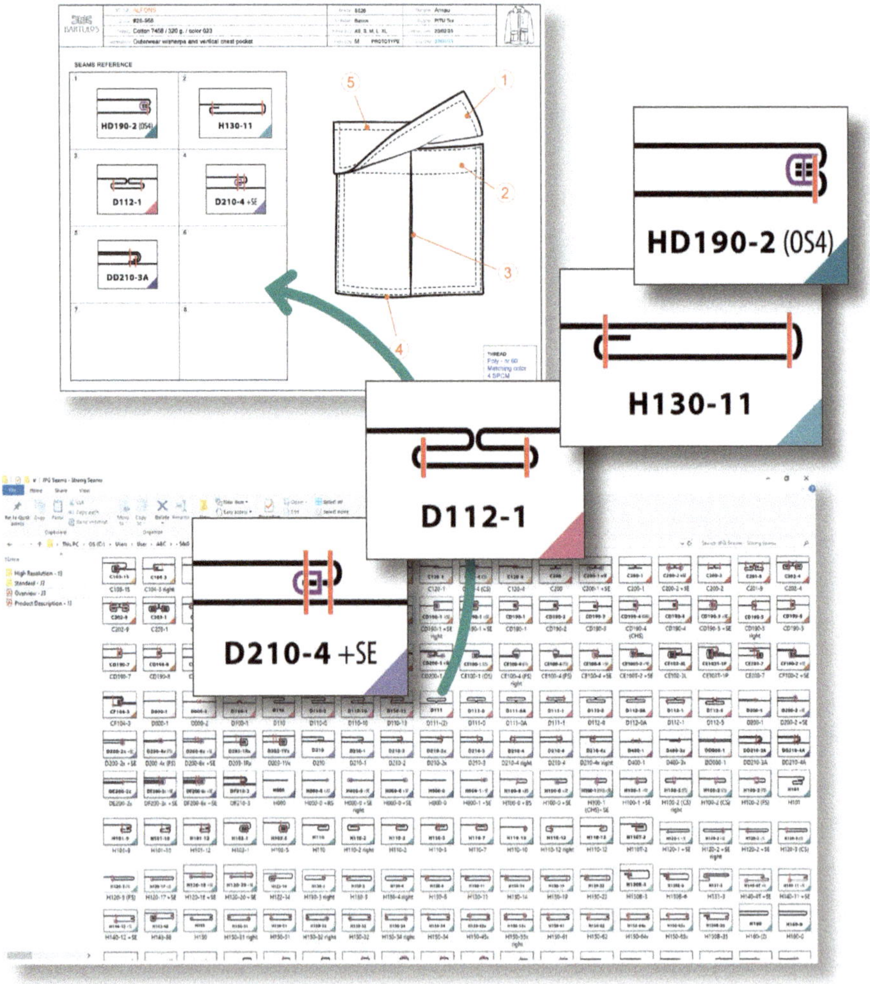

www.ingramcontent.com/pod-product-compliance
Lightning Source LLC
Chambersburg PA
CBHW040221040426
42333CB00049B/3062